CONFESSIONS
OF AN IVY LEAGUE FRAT BOY

CONFES

OF AN IVY

IONS

LEAGUE FRAT BOY

A MEMOIR

ANDREW LOHSE

THOMAS DUNNE BOOKS
ST. MARTIN'S PRESS ≈ NEW YORK

THOMAS DUNNE BOOKS.
An imprint of St. Martin's Press.

CONFESSIONS OF AN IVY LEAGUE FRAT BOY. Copyright © 2014 by Andrew
Lohse. All rights reserved. Printed in the United States of America. For
information, address St. Martin's Press, 175 Fifth Avenue, New York,
N.Y. 10010.

www.thomasdunnebooks.com
www.stmartins.com

Designed by Anna Gorovoy

The Library of Congress Cataloging-in-Publication Data is available upon
request.

ISBN 978-1-250-03367-3 (hardcover)
ISBN 978-1-250-03368-0 (e-book)

St. Martin's Press books may be purchased for educational, business, or
promotional use. For information on bulk purchases, please contact
Macmillan Corporate and Premium Sales Department at 1-800-221-7945,
extension 5442, or write specialmarkets@macmillan.com.

First Edition: August 2014

10 9 8 7 6 5 4 3 2 1

For Ray Peachey, in the debt of whose kindness I write

AUTHOR'S NOTE

This is a work of nonfiction about my experiences at Dartmouth College. However, the names and identifying characteristics of certain individuals have been changed in order to protect their privacy. The names of certain organizations have also been changed. Dialogue has been reconstructed to the best of my recollection.

I shared a dark suspicion that the life we were leading was a lost cause, that we were all actors, kidding ourselves along on a senseless odyssey. It was the tension between these two poles—a restless idealism on one hand and a sense of impending doom on the other—that kept me going.

—HUNTER S. THOMPSON, *THE RUM DIARY*

CONFESSIONS
OF AN IVY LEAGUE FRAT BOY

1

BOOT ON HIS HEAD

Vomit is dripping through my hair. It's warm. Gelatinous. Thick. Somehow this feeling is comforting. Maybe that's because I associate it with other feelings. Acceptance. Validation.

Now the vomit has reached my neck. Squinting down into the trash can I'm bent over—staring into the shadow my head casts from the basement's bright fluorescent lights—I wonder if this is what amniotic fluid felt like in the womb. I try to remember but can't. After all, it doesn't matter, because back then I wasn't even a real person. Kind of like how not long ago I was a whaleshit, a pledge, a nothing. And now I'm a brother.

I'm even a rush chairman. There's a picture of me on one of the frat's composites: ANDREW B. LOHSE, EMINENT RUSH CHAIRMAN. I think it's on the one hanging over the fireplace in the living room, although it could be on the one hanging over the fireplace in the pool room—or maybe it's on the one across from the liquor cabinet, I don't know—people move them around a lot, mostly to snort coke from them, so I'm not sure of the composite's exact location. But in the picture I'm smirking, red cheeks over a pink shirt with a white, starched collar. I'm wearing a three-piece suit. A tie splattered with Ralph Lauren logos. A pocket square the color of money.

Maybe I've taken this all too seriously. Something about our rituals changed me, deeply, and vomit doesn't bother me, or, maybe, it's proof that I survived my hazing. I know that I definitely wasn't always like this; this is something new. I am a Dartmouth man now. This is normal.

The brothers are still chanting, *"Boot on his head, boot on his head,"* even though it seems that Randall, one of my older bros, has fully emptied the contents of his stomach onto my skull—my skull, whose contents seem to be inert, swimming uselessly around in their own fluids. I'm pretty wasted. The chanting dissipates. I lift my head up over the lip of the trash can and scan the brothers arrayed in front of me, an army of preppy statuary, a collection of baby-faced kids from well-off families. Baring perfectly white teeth, they all smile. Again I feel a sense of belonging. We practice secret sacraments that have become expressions of male love, and we will be friends forever.

When I stand up straight, the puke finds the express lane down the center of my back. Suddenly, it has reached my belt, my belt that is embroidered with a repeating whale motif, the belt I got to help myself fit the frat's look, and

I blink, and through heavy-lidded eyes curtained by the typical Wednesday-night binging, I am forced to reassess what is happening.

It's possible that this second review is initiated by the boot's interminable slide into my boxer shorts, the ones my mother gave me for Christmas; getting someone else's vomit in your underwear is the kind of buzz-killing sensation that without fail begs you to reassess your animal behavior, and in this brief moment of illumination the jaw-dropping toxicity of our brotherhood is spread bare, at least for me, and I can't help but wonder how my life became like this. Was it the hazing? Was this just another Ivy League tradition? Why has my emotional responsiveness become a phantom limb?

By the time I reach for my polo shirt—Pulaski, my roommate, is holding it out to me, but between my poor balance and blurry eyes he appears far away, a cartoon on some distant horizon—my moment of doubt has passed and I promise myself to continue evading all morality questions. Until I can't anymore. Hopefully, I'll graduate before these questions run me down, though somehow I know I won't get away unscathed. Eventually I'll be forced to make a decision. Just not tonight.

Pulaski helps me up onto the benches that line the basement walls like coliseum seats. Two other guys take the spotlight, sidling up over the trash can where Randall and I'd just domed, this drinking game—I'd lost. That's why he'd booted on my head. Now everyone is singing in unison. Price hands me a cigarette. Confused, I try to light the wrong end.

One of the brothers boots first, missing the can. He has

lost the dome. His vomit is the color of rotten chicken cutlets and orange sorbet. It pools on the concrete floor. As an English major I wonder if this is a poetic image I should catalog for the future if I ever try to write about my frat, or about how my life got derailed. Transfixed, I stare at the vomit. I hope someone will mop it up. I'm definitely not going to. After all, girls are coming over soon, the sisters of Alpha Phi, and they probably want to party.

This is just meetings. Normal Wednesday. The anchor of our week. Half an hour ago I was doing homework in the library, studying literature; a year ago I was a wide-eyed freshman with romantic expectations about the Ivy League; months before that I was just a normal high school kid with a pretty girlfriend and a garage band; eighteen years before that I was just a couple of cells floating around in my mom's uterus, basically just a little fingernail. Not even a fucking real person.

Someone told me once that the best way to show what you have is to waste it. It was probably one of my older frat brothers who told me this—Ripley or Edwards, two people who always seemed to have a lot of fun wasting things of value. In our case, despite the fucked-up things we do and let be done to us, we don't even believe that we're wasting anything. Because this is just a part of our education. A big part. This, we're told, is a crucial experience that will help us get ahead. If you show you're a team player, valuable connections can be made; someday you might even end up like our frat's most famous alum, this guy the brothers supposedly nicknamed the Ghost back in the good old days. The guy, some argue, who saved the whole Western world. The guy whose signature is on the bills we roll up to snort coke.

But I doubt anyone calls him the Ghost anymore. They probably call him his real name, Hank, or maybe some people still call him Secretary Paulson. I wonder what he went through to become a brother. I wonder if he had any doubts, and, if he did, which mental garbage chute he forced them down. Maybe, though, he never had doubts. Maybe he came out the other side totally normal, then went on to a totally normal investment-banking career, then was appointed to be a totally normal Treasury Secretary who did totally normal things with a totally functional conscience. It's hard to tell how much this shit can change you, right?

Pretty soon I'm not thinking about any of this anymore. Meetings end. I clean myself up with some low-grade paper towels. The Alpha Phis come. I have a crush on one, a dancer, a girl with a nose ring and a cryptic smile. We play pong, but I don't linger long at the table because Price tells me he has some blow, so we go upstairs and bolt the bathroom door and cut up lines on the counter and snort them; I guess I'm always disappearing from the people I'm into and I never give myself a chance. Price and I give each other the secret handshake. For the rest of the night we are invincible.

2
CHILDHOOD DREAM

The thing is, I was no different from any other normal middle-class kid with a miniature American Dream, a dream to break into the old traditions of the Ivy League. Tons of kids are like that. Maybe that means that who I am doesn't matter—but where I came from has always been important to me, so I guess I'm going to have to tell you about it. If you have to know, I worked hard for many years to have the privilege of being vomited on in a frat basement, and I'm not going to let all my effort go to waste.

My parents didn't go to college. My dad was a radio engineer in New York City; for many years he worked relentlessly to give my brother and me a good life. From him I learned about hard work. I learned about what it meant to be an honest person, the kind of guy who did the right thing and never took the cheap or easy way out. Eventually, I'd reconnect with those core values, but it would take me a little while to put them into practice, so I got into a little trouble in the meantime.

My brother and I were taught that if we worked hard and dreamed big, we could go to college. Maybe, if we got really lucky, we could go to Dartmouth. That was where our grandfather went. He was another hero of mine. He told me that if I went to boarding school, a place like Lawrenceville or Exeter, I'd have a better shot at getting into his alma mater, but private school was too expensive—so my brother and I went to public schools. We lived in an average New Jersey suburb right in the middle of the state, a town like so many others with decent schools and a couple of parks and strip malls and developments.

I was the kind of kid who never missed a day of school, who always did his homework as soon as he got off the bus, who tried to succeed in whatever he could—sports, music, grades—and never got in trouble. When I was thirteen, I started working an after-school job busing tables at a pizzeria, and though I usually made less than minimum wage, I was proud of my job. In the summers I worked at a farm stand for the last farmer in town who hadn't sold his land to the McMansion developers. I didn't spend my adolescence partying. On Saturdays I studied at a music school in the city.

Everyone told me that the odds of my going to Dartmouth were against me—our high school rarely sent kids to the Ivy League, and most stuck around at state schools. In some ways I was driven to succeed by the fear that I might be trapped in sterile linoleumed rooms forever, the kind designed to crush your soul in the wide daylight, the kind that resembled the innards of prisons and asylums.

Then my brother got into Dartmouth—and I started to work even harder to follow him there. He rushed a frat. When he came home for breaks, spilling stories about beer pong and suits and ties and secret societies and Wall Street jobs, he seemed different—a little bit smug. At first it bothered me. Then I accepted it. Our grandfather had been in a frat, too, so what right did I have to be so fucking abstemious? I wanted to be a Dartmouth guy, and I was willing to do whatever it took.

THE GOOD OLD BOY NETWORK

Though I'd tried to check all the right boxes—like National Honor Society, president of the Model UN, a varsity letter, good test scores—all the arbitrary bullshit you get hypnotized by the education-industrial complex into thinking you must achieve—my grades weren't perfect.

I applied early and was deferred, which basically means rejected and told to go fuck yourself in admissions purgatory for a few months while some secret committee makes up its mind about you. The Dartmouth acceptance I'd craved my whole life from idolizing my grandfather was almost given a partial-birth abortion, a scenario I found highly dissatisfying as I was, at that point, a Republican.

After my deferral I realized that, probably, no amount of academic improvement could ensure my acceptance. Where merit fails, many turn to nepotism, and that's exactly what I learned to do, no matter how foreign the concept was to my middle-class milieu. I called up my grandfather's best college friend—who'd given a large sum to the school—for help in being "reconsidered."

After minimal pleading on my part, this benefactor said he'd phone someone in admissions, but whispered confidentially through the plastic phone that he couldn't guarantee anything because a "new gal" was in charge "these days." Nothing was more anathema to a good old boy than a *new gal* being in charge, I quickly learned, understanding that connections—preferably of the old, male variety—were the secret law of physics that kept the world spinning right on its axis, something on par with gravity or death and taxes.

Being insinuated into this good old boy network was almost charming, being warned about the new gal as if I were being let in on some colossal secret: *This, son, is how the world works. They'll never teach you that in your public school, eh? I knew your old man's old man—I was in a secret society with the dude, so I'll see what arms I can twist to get your sorry ass through the gate.*

He instructed me to write a letter to the admissions committee about my enthusiasm for Dartmouth. The letter was so earnest and saccharine that if I read it now, I'd probably boot stomach acid onto my genitalia—*boot* is the Dartmouth word for "vomit," and to be candid, I witnessed this type of thing once at an event called Senior Court at ΣAE, when I was a sophomore. Randall lay down on a table in the Beer Die room in the basement, pants off, as a senior chugged beers until he vomited on Randall's dick, while we all cheered, *"Boot on his dick! Boot on his dick!"*

Anyway, Benefactor passed my letter along to President

Wright, the guy who was in charge before Jim Kim. I got in. Four years later, when I wrote my exposé on my frat's hazing, the column that spawned a story in *Rolling Stone,* Benefactor went ballistic. How ungrateful I must have been that he'd lifted his privileged hand for me. Apparently, a family member of mine called the old man to smooth things over, but Benefactor wasn't hearing any of it: he said that he'd called up President Kim himself and had been assured that none of the hazing I'd depicted had ever occurred.

The good old boy network—a web of lies.

TOUCH THE FIRE

I think I changed a lot freshman year. Who didn't?

It would make sense that I did. Dartmouth is a school governed by both fierce traditions and a fierce social hierarchy, and as freshmen we were as naïve as we were vulnerable. Conformity was prized—yet the rules of our new environment sometimes required a suspension of disbelief. *Boot and rally,* we were told: vomit to clear your stomach so you can continue drinking. *Pledge term is what makes you a real person,* we were told: before then we were just neophytes left out of a scintillating, and probably ancient, secret. Even before that, before we came to realize that there was no secret at all except our own misbehavior and fratstar arrogance, we had to be approved as Dartmouth men. We had to undergo the old traditions.

Our initiation into the cult of Dartmouth College began the way it does for every class: we had to run around the homecoming bonfire about 112 times as drunk upperclassmen and alumni screamed, *"Worst class ever,"* at us, grabbed us, told us to *"touch the fire."* This was after being paraded around town, past police barricades, down streets lined with smirking alumni in green blazers; marched up South Main Street like prisoners of war, we could see a giant pyre blazing on the middle of the Green, capped with our class year, '12. A large empty circle was around it, then a ring of riotous upperclassmen. Our throng was injected into the circle. After some speeches, the president and high priests and pharisees of the college looked down from a platform erected in front of Dartmouth Hall to watch. We were told to run. We did.

This was normal. Every class does this—I'm not complaining. We all felt validated at the time, and if it was slightly unsettling, which it was, we morphed our doubts into psychological rationale supporting our new Ivy League membership. Just as with the frat hazing, the weird traditions we had to participate in as freshmen became evidence that we were of a select crowd. Proof that we were above average, elite. We got to run around a fire as drunk upperclassmen yelled obscenities at us. This confirmed that we'd finally arrived.

From there we set out to understand frat life; that was the next big initiation waiting for us. We had to spend freshman year meeting older brothers of the various houses so we could network to win a bid our sophomore fall. Otherwise, we'd be socially irrelevant. We hadn't spent our adolescences overachieving just so we could attain social irrelevance.

A vast majority of Dartmouth undergrads pledge Greek houses—it was considered weird if you didn't, and it raised questions about you that you didn't want raised. It made people suspicious of you. Was there something wrong with you? Had your peers marked you for rejection? Getting a bid at a totally sweet house would be evidence that you'd finally arrived. You know, proof that you were above average, elite.

PETERSON AND PULASKI

I made some friends. Peterson was the earnest boy-genius type. He was a pragmatist who only wore neutral colors, and who was undecided about whether he'd rush at all, but that's why he had Pulaski and me. We were idealists. Pulaski was my other best friend—he started off goofy but ended up more of a fratstar than I'd ever be.

We spent freshman year investigating Greek life. We consumed all of the clichés about the houses—one was known as the rapey frat; another was too bland and wore flannel; we didn't do enough drugs to get into another, plus none of us could grow a beard; Alpha Delta, the original Animal House, seemed to only rush squash players, ruggers, and trust-fund babies; Sig Ep, my brother's frat, was pretty boring; Psi U was full of assholes and members of the sailing team, who made their pledges wear work boots, jeans, and gray sweatshirts every day because, they told them, "You will never be blue-collar again."

Then there was ΣAE.

We gathered rumors about their pledge term; apparently, it was considered pretty middle-of-the-road, not too hard and not too soft. The house had a reputation for being insular and full of preppy, pretentious, hard-drinking corporate whores—kids who'd do anything to get to Wall Street. Some brothers were epic douche bags, though, and maybe that appealed to us. They all wore boat shoes, so we started wearing ours almost every day to fit in. The house wasn't dominated by any one sport, but tended to be more conservative—lots of College Republicans and editors for *The Dartmouth Review.* That was my first hurdle.

I'd briefly written for the *Review* my freshman fall, but left the paper in a way that the ΣAEs who ran it deemed questionable: I went on to write columns for the *Review*'s liberal rival, the *Free Press,* that were critical of the former's knuckle-dragging editorial bent. It was problematic. My departure seemed to raise some altogether valid questions about whether I could ever be counted on to toe the line and not develop my own opinions—outspokenness could be dangerous for a frat. What if I later published columns exposing the frat's hazing and depravity?

YOU'RE ALL GOING TO BE RESPONSIBLE FOR THIS HOUSE'S UNDOING

In light of these challenges I aimed to exploit whatever connections I could find. I was learning, little by little, how these clubby memberships worked.

Edwards, a senior I'd met through my brother, told me that Buzzby intended to *ding* me—the Dartmouth word for "veto" or "blackball"—over the way I'd quit the *Review* and then published columns critical of it for the *Free Press*.

Buzzby doesn't trust you, Edwards said.

Buzzby thinks you're an asshole.

Buzzby thinks you'll sell out the house.

But you wouldn't do that, Lohse, right? You'd never do that?

Of course I'd never do that, I said. After I'd sufficiently denied any possibility of future treachery, Edwards and his roommate, Davis, took Peterson and me out on a rush dinner. Like a bro date. Agreeing to lobby for our cause, they wined and dined us at this hibachi place near the Home Depot in West Lebanon. We tried hard to seem cool.

Edwards, half his face cast in the shadow of a kitschy oriental lamp, red, upholstered banquette glowing behind him, grasped for the soy sauce with one arm while assuring me that he'd be able to lock up enough votes in the frat's deliberations. Delibs, they were called—the private vote immediately following rush where the house would decide which pledges they'd award bids. Then Davis give us the inside straight on the Buzzby problem. Before he told the story, he rolled up the sleeves of his oxford shirt, then crumpled his napkin onto a plate of barely eaten sushi and slid it to one side of the table in a commanding yet genteel gesture. He rotated his baseball cap around on his head. A few strands of black hair fell above his eyes.

Apparently, Clint, this guy who'd later become my big

brother in the house, had shouted down Buzzby in a fight that had almost descended into fisticuffs in the frat's foyer. Davis recounted the exchange.

"He'll sell the house out just like he sold out the *Review*!" Buzzby had screamed.

"He's more of a fucking decent guy than you are, Buzzby!" Clint had screamed back—which was rare for him, Edwards interjected, stabbing at a piece of chicken teriyaki, as Clint was the quiet, intellectual type.

Then Buzzby had got up in his face. "You're fucking insane. You're all going to be responsible for this house's undoing if you let him in. Right, Klinbacker, right? Am I right?"

Apparently Klinbacker was behind him, nodding vigorously like a strung-up doll. Edwards and Davis laughed.

"Typical B-side coalition politics," the former said.

" 'B-side coalition'?" Peterson asked.

"Let's just say . . . the less-*distinguished* brothers of the house."

Davis handed his plate to the waitress. He didn't even bother to look at her. Edwards was saying that Clint's getting so loud and pissed had won over many of the undecided votes because, Edwards pointed out, "Clint is always reasonable."

"Now, just to be clear here," Davis said. "Buzzby may still try to ding you. I just think we have the votes to override his man-*euver*. We're counting on you to be a good pledge, Lohse."

The check came. Davis paid it with the house's card, scribbling a signature that covered half the receipt. The waitress dumped some fortune cookies on the table. All the fortunes were the same: *If the table moves, move with it. Your lucky numbers are 2, 8, 12, 25, 37, 69. "Dian hua": Chinese for "telephone."*

THE BIG DAY

All of a sudden it was the big day. October's second Saturday—rush—was met with the sort of reverence and anxiety reserved on most campuses for commencement. It felt like the most important day of our lives.

Harsh morning light flickered through the window of our inner room. Peterson was one of my dormmates in Wheeler, a nineteenth-century brick dorm across the street from ΣAE; I had a fireplace, and each of my windows was dominated by a view of some beautiful brick building. You couldn't help but feel important waking up there every day. When I climbed out of bed and stumbled into the outer room, Peterson was already sitting there.

"The big day." I rubbed my eyes, hungover from playing pong at ΣAE the night before with Pulaski. We'd been trying to seal up our bids, evidence our enthusiasm for the fraternal way of life, and assuage any doubts that maybe we weren't exactly cut out for brotherhood.

"Are you actually doing work?" I asked.

"Economics waits for no man."

I tried to think of some fratty retort but quickly realized I was trying too hard and instead mumbled something like *Man, homework's stupid,* but I don't even think Peterson heard me. Then I was like, "But, dude, tonight is *rush.*"

"I think we've got this." He smiled cautiously. "Schultz, this bro, brought me up to their secret library last night—they call it the Libes. He showed me some of the old pictures of brothers, black-and-white stuff. Pretty cool." Peterson made a motion of brushing his shoulders off, something he probably saw in a rap-music video once when he was in middle school. For the next few minutes he waxed poetic about the Libes. Built-in bookshelves full of books, he said. Gleaming chandeliers. Leather couches. Big wooden tables. Fraternal artifacts festooned on the walls like taxidermic trophy animals.

HELLO, MY NAME IS

The sun went down. Or, I guess, the earth spun away from it, and it was night, and from my window I looked out at the frat lit up like a desert mirage. The radiator in our room clanked and hissed as I pulled my blazer on over my shoulders, tied my tie. Pulaski, Peterson, and I gathered in our room to prepare for rush like girls doing each other's hair before the big dance.

We each took a shot of Jim Beam, straightened our ties, and walked across the street to ΣAE. Schultz was standing in the vestibule. He greeted Peterson, shook my hand, patted Pulaski on the back. He seemed genuinely friendly.

"You guys need to go check in." He nodded over his shoulder at a table set up in the foyer manned by two

Alpha Phis in dresses and heels and pearls and too much makeup. They guarded a large leatherbound book where all rushees had to write their names, hometowns, and where they could be found later in the night if they received a bid.

I signed my name. The book was massive.

One of the girls looked up at me and said, "This book has the name of every guy who rushed the house."

Nervous, I stared at her pearls. I almost misspelled my own name. She looked down at the book. I wondered if Hank Paulson's name was in there. My brother's name definitely was; he'd rushed the house two years before but only received a callback.

The other girl gave us name tags: HELLO MY NAME IS_____: PLEASE GIVE ME A BID I'LL DO ANYTHING.

We steered toward the living room. It was packed from wood-paneled wall to wood-paneled wall with sophomore boys in their best suits and polished lace-ups, pocket squares sticking out from their breast pockets.

Lots of forced small talk. I moved through the crowd and its polychromatic blur of straight ties and bow ties and banker striped shirts and class pins and brother pins stuck on lapels like polished scabs, nervous smiles bent at the corners, the smell of low-grade processed beef emanating from a mountain of Taco Bell piled on a table on one side of the frat's living room for the rushees to eat—through the din, questions like:

"Where did you prep?"

"What other houses have you visited tonight?"

"Are you ready for pledge term?"

"Have you met Goodrich? You really should meet Goodrich—he's a leader in the house."

I'd met him, I said. Vaguely.

"What house is your second choice? . . . Oh, Tri-Kap—"

"Don't worry, pledge term is a lot of fun."

A few hours in, after running over to Tri-Kap to sign my name in their book to hedge my bets, I returned to ΣAE. It was almost nine. One of the rush chairmen, a junior with short blond hair and a permanent smirk chiseled into his face, climbed onto the check-in table, nearly hitting his head on the foyer's chandelier, and motioned for quiet in the room. A brother standing near the door flicked the lights on and off to get everyone's attention.

"Just to explain how this works for those who don't know," the rush chairman yelled as we all tied off perfunctory conversations. "We are now going to move to the shake-out portion of the evening. *Shaking out* means that you're committing to sinking your bid should the brotherhood decide to award you one."

He paused, smiling. "If you don't intend to shake out at ΣAE, we'd like to ask that you leave now and head to whichever house is your top choice."

The brothers made their way out of the front door. I found Pulaski and pulled him aside, saw that he was beaming.

"I think we're in luck," he said, setting his hand on my shoulder.

"Why do you say that, dude?" We molded ourselves into the line of rushees quickly developing next to the Taco Bell table—now covered in littered wrappers—and past the deep green curtains with their gold ties, into the foyer and out the front door.

"Dude. *Dude,* because I just talked to Ripley one-on-one in the pool room and he seemed to think, seemed to know, actually, that you, me, and Peterson are getting bids."

LOOKING INTO MY OWN FUTURE

Ripley—for reasons I generally can't explain, we looked up to him. Though once a standout tennis player, he now seemed to live life sad-go-lucky from one bong hit to the next. Most often seen wearing pajama pants and tattered Ralph Lauren shirts, he exuded frattiness the same way Peterson exuded meekness—uncontrollably, dripping from his clogged pores like cheap aftershave.

Something about the guy, though, always made me slightly uncomfortable. Maybe it was how he usually seemed insincere, like the way his frattiness was sometimes so overbearing as to be inauthentic, the way he seemed to be trying hard to seem as if he weren't trying hard. He was a mystery. As long as he was backing our rush, though, it was a mystery that I was fine with worrying about later. I'd definitely end up worrying about it a lot, because as the years unwound, as I learned more about Ripley, I'd understand why he seemed inauthentic.

Somebody told me once that he used to be pretty

straightedge before pledge term. I couldn't have accepted it at the time—but watching Ripley whispering to a visibly entranced Pulaski in the pool room, watching him muttering some advice out of the corner of his mouth and then smoothing down the lapels of Pulaski's blazer—I couldn't have accepted that, in a sad way, looking at Ripley was like looking into my own future. Like Ripley, we were all slowly becoming inauthentic and self-defeating, whether we realized it or not.

WE CAME TO SCHOOL TO BREAK THE RULES

As the line of rushees pulled us toward the door, I stopped for a moment to look around one last time: the large Greek letters sealed into the foyer's floor tiles, the chandelier glowing above us, the double doors to the house's pool room propped open with a large rock painted purple and gold with the name DOUGLAS C. NIEDERMAYER on it, and beyond that the composites of brothers past hung proudly on the walls. Lotta history in that room, I figured. I imagined my grandfather and my brother moving through similar scenes at Beta and Sig Ep; I imagined, for a narcissistic, typically Dartmouth moment, my own future sons doing the same. The frat was a place that gave me sharp sensations in my gut—excitement and fear. It was the kind of place where either everything or nothing was possible, but you couldn't tell which.

The front door swung open, creaking on its hinges. Lined down the fraternity's brick walkway, all the way across its lawn, covered in fresh piles of dead leaves, all the way to the sidewalk, every brother of the house stood with his right hand out to shake the right hand of every rushee. Goodrich stood at the end of the yard watching us as we made our way down the line. As I shook each hand, I thanked the brothers for the opportunity to rush—the chance that seemed to be the most important step in one's Dartmouth life. When I shook Edwards's hand, he pulled me in close and whispered, "So fucked, Lohse, so fucked." The bros seemed to say that a lot, something they phrased like a compliment.

On the other end Goodrich commanded us all, the scrum of sophomores, to stand wait. He said he wanted us to see one of the house's special traditions.

The brothers jogged up to the fraternity's Greco-Roman portico and assembled like a choir between the two stone lions anchoring the front step, beneath a massive ΣAE flag hung on its side swaying languorously with the wind. I shivered in my blazer and dug my hands into its pockets as Pulaski and Peterson sidled up next to me. The brothers put their arms around each other. Some closed their eyes. Then they sang.

From Rigsby's Road to Finnegan's Bend, we're gonna get
  drunk tonight!
The faculty's afraid of us, they know we're in the right,
So raise your glass, another glass, as high as high can be,
For as long as sex and liquor lasts, there's gonna be ΣAE!

Oh! I think I need another drink, I think I need another drink,
I know I need another drink, for the glory of ΣAE!

We are the men of ΣAE and we don't give a damn,
We came to school to break the rules and cheat on each exam,
To hell, to hell with Alpha Chi, to hell with Psi U, too;
And if you're not an ΣAE, to hell, to hell with you!

THE RULES WERE THE RULES

Back in Wheeler, two Tri-Kaps delivered my bid, a slip of card stock embossed with a picture of their fraternity and made official by the sloppy signature of the house's president.

Tri-Kap was a pretty normal house. It was my safety. These were pretty normal-looking guys, not pretentious like the ΣAEs, and they seemed genuinely interested in having me as a pledge—too eager, almost. At the time it seemed like a bad sign; we'd expected to be waiting for bids all night. Rumor was that some houses didn't even bother delivering them until two in the morning.

"Can you talk to us out in the hallway?" one of the Tri-Kaps asked.

"Did you shake out at ΣAE?" the other guy asked.

I said, "Yeah, I did."

"We can't kidnap you then," the other guy said, "and I know it's against the rules of rush, but just know that if you want to come to Tri-Kap tonight and sink this bid, you can, even though you shook out elsewhere."

"We'll cover you," the other guy said.

The rules were the rules, though. I was obliged to wait

for the ∑AEs. By shaking out, we'd all tacitly agreed to go along with whatever they'd planned for us. Sometimes, though, I wonder what my life would have been like if I had decided to break the rules that night. Maybe everything later would have been more normal.

The Tri-Kaps turned down the hallway. I watched them stalk away, shuffling their bid cards like some magic trick they were still trying to figure out. I watched them until they disappeared down the stairwell and their footfalls stopped echoing upward through the dorm.

KIWI LEMON

Someone knocked on the door—a knock approximating, I guess, the way law enforcement agents seek unintimidating white-collar criminals from their upscale residences. Game over, the knock seemed to say. You will soon be fitted with a computerized ankle bracelet. Normalcy is a hopeless endeavor. Turn yourself in.

Maybe I was reading too much into the sound of a fist on wood, but it was a knock that changed some things for us. The handle rattled. Our conversation ground to a halt as Clint stepped into the room and his rapping fist became a pointed finger, face frozen into a high-cheekboned scowl.

"Peterson?" Clint pointed.

"Yes?"

"Lohse?"

I stood up.

"Both of you—find blindfolds. Something that will cover your eyes, but nothing ridiculous like a pillowcase. This isn't fucking Gitmo."

He waited in the doorway as we rifled around the inner room. When I emerged, gripping a red-striped Brooks Brothers tie, I made eye contact with Pulaski. His face was tangled in a hopeless wince; his hands fidgeted in his lap. We all accepted the obvious. Pulaski probably hadn't made the cut. We nodded good-bye.

Half jogging, Clint led us down the stairs and out the dormitory door. As we stepped into the night, we noticed another ΣAE standing behind us, a guy who'd been posted up at the door like Secret Service. In his tailored suit jacket, he reached over with one arm and sped the door's arc to a close, not saying anything, just shaking his head and smiling as if to indicate that there was no turning back, no time to linger, that the last door had been pushed closed behind us.

The night was cloudless and the air had a chilling bite; campus smelled like crumbled leaves. Clint led us to a waiting car. More than a few cars were idling near sophomore dorms, and around ours, guys in suits seemed to be dodging through shadows, making their way quickly into and out of buildings, always looking over their shoulders.

When I was close enough to smell the car's exhaust, I thought to myself, like, what a weird, fascinating night—the entire campus seemed rife with a sinister excitement, as if it were a palpable feeling rising out of the root systems of the campus's ancient elms. I climbed into the backseat of the car. The leather was smooth. The driver turned around and frowned at us. Edwards.

In a way I was relieved. I assumed that Peterson and I were getting bids. Then I started to worry. Clint hadn't used the word *bid* nor evidenced a physical bid card. That didn't seem promising.

I forced Peterson into the middle seat as Clint slammed the car door against my shoulder. Another '12 was sitting on the other side. He was blindfolded, clutching a tiki torch.

At first I didn't recognize the guy—he could have been any of the preppy white dudes with boat shoes from rush, guys who'd been introduced to me as my potential future pledge brothers and best friends. For life. Though even then it'd struck me that hazing might not have been a reliable way of ensuring lifelong fellowship, my doubts didn't matter anymore. Whatever would happen to us, we were willing. We were so close. Driven by the social anxiety that keeps the elite universe spinning on its axis, we knew we'd do almost anything for acceptance.

"Tim?" I whispered over Peterson as we buckled our seat belts.

The guy nodded. Then he leaned his head down behind the passenger seat to muffle his voice. "Don't talk. Please don't talk," he whispered.

Clint climbed into the passenger seat. After a clinking of bottles and a rustling of paper bags, we got our first taste of hazing—Kiwi Lemon Mad Dog, a sickeningly sweet twist-cap wine popular among sidewalk bums and hard-core alcoholics. I cautiously spun off the cap. One whiff was enough to make your stomach turn.

Edwards suggested that we *put on our fucking blindfolds*. Classical music came on through the stereo, the first blaring minor third of Beethoven's Fifth Symphony. The car skidded into reverse.

ALL DECISIONS ARE FINAL AND NONNEGOTIABLE

It was difficult to count turns or guess the passage of time, impossible to count the bars of the symphony shaking the car's plastic speakers. Lacking another way to measure what was happening, I kept track of the number of cigarettes smoked in the front of the car. Two flicks of the lighter. Fresh smoke. A little while later—a third flick. Eventually the sound of gravel and dirt under the tires indicated that we were on back roads.

The car stopped. The symphony was replaced by an insistent ping suggesting that maybe the headlights had been left on, maybe the key hadn't been removed from the ignition. Doors opened, doors slammed closed. Someone banged on the back windows. I dropped my empty Mad Dog on the floor.

"Where do you think we are?" Peterson whispered to Tim and me.

"Let's not talk, okay?" Tim whispered back.

I didn't respond.

My door opened. Cold air. A set of hands reached in and pulled me out of my seat by the shoulder of my polo.

"Walk," the voice commanded. I felt gravel, then dirt, under my feet. I was led up what felt like a rough path with my hand on what I assumed to be a brother's shoulder. I tripped on logs and branches.

Up the trail I heard strange mumblings that became louder as we approached them. The brother I followed stopped as the trail leveled out. It occurred to me that I'd never gone hiking in boat shoes before.

Two hands on my shoulder blades pushed me ahead a few paces and spun me around. Again I could make out a light around the edges of my blindfold, not the moon this time, something dimmer. The mumblings stopped. For once even my obsessive internal dialogue ground to a halt.

Then I heard an effete voice.

"Gentlemen. Gentlemen—please remove your blindfolds." It was Davis.

I obliged, stuffing my tie into the back pocket of my jeans as my eyes focused on a group of sophomores encircling a tiki torch thrust into the ground, its small flame lighting the boys' expressionless faces with a flickering orange glow. Davis stood on the other side of the torch looking too serious for his own good, chiseled face hovering over a blue, patterned bow tie and tweed jacket.

We were standing in a forest clearing, some wilderness somewhere. I didn't recognize most of the brothers or sophomores assembled. A few brothers stood behind Davis wearing formal attire—spread-collar shirts fastened with power ties, navy blazers that probably cost a month's rent—and appeared to be serious, concerned, their stoic faces spelling out: *Ritualistic initiations are no trifling matter.*

"Gentlemen, congratulations on your decision to shake out at Sigma Alpha Epsilon. This evening you will be given a series of challenges to assess your worthiness of being accepted into our pledge class. We'll begin with a short quiz on your knowledge of the fraternity," Davis smirked. "Brother Upton, would you please distribute the exam?"

SIGMA ALPHA EPSILON
NEW MEMBER ENTRANCE EXAM

Directions: Answer *ALL* questions below to the best of your ability. Your score will be assessed to determine whether you will be extended an offer to join the brotherhood of Sigma Alpha Epsilon Fraternity, New Hampshire Alpha Chapter. All decisions are final and nonnegotiable.

The bros formed a procession and then disappeared back down the trail. I stared at my paper, dumbfounded, clutching it against a frigid wind that whistled through the clearing. *Who is the Eminent Deputy Archon of Dartmouth's ΣAE chapter? Approximately when was the New Hampshire Alpha Chapter founded at Dartmouth?* Then there were opinion questions. *Which one of your fellow rushees, in your opinion, least deserves a bid tonight? (Please provide a specific name and explain your reasoning.)* Without hesitation I scribbled *Beaufort*, a guy I didn't know well. The seventh and final question, the short-answer portion of the exam, had three parts.

What course of action would you take in each of the following situations? Explain your reasoning briefly. You may utilize the reverse of this sheet if necessary.

A. One of your pledge brothers admits to you that he slipped Rohypnol into a young lady's alcoholic beverage. He proceeds to engage in sexual intercourse with said lady.

B. You notice that one of your pledge brothers is gaining significant weight over the course of pledge term. He begins to have issues with his body image.

C. A pledge brother becomes involved in the trafficking of an illegal substance across state borders. The substance is cocaine. His dealings become increasingly risky. He is thinking of moving on to "harder" drugs.

Looking around the clearing, I saw that most of the pledges were obviously unsure what to answer. Were these things that might happen? Were they just fucking with us?

WE EXCHANGED PARANOID LOOKS

We stumbled back down the trail in the dark—a pledge had knocked our tiki torch over, extinguishing it. Finally we hit a gravel lot full of cars circled in on each other like Conestoga wagons, where we were split up again, and brothers, overseen by Davis, divided us into new subgroups and collected our quizzes. Edwards stood by his car with Tim and Peterson, who were both still blindfolded. Edwards led us down another path. At the end of the second trail, between drags on a cigarette, he handed each of us a bottle of Boone's. Tim and Peterson pulled off their blindfolds.

"You all passed the quiz. Now we have for you an even more important assessment of your fitness to pledge," Edwards said.

I wasn't sure how he could've known that I'd passed—it probably wasn't possible for me to have passed anyway—and I'd just watched Davis collect the quizzes and lead a group down a different trail. Likewise, neither Peterson nor Tim had even been with the quiz group in the clearing. For the first time I suspected that nothing we were being asked to do mattered, though I forced the thought to the back of my mind; it wasn't possible to consider that it all didn't matter, not possible. This all mattered. We were being judged, I reminded myself. I clutched the Boone's. Behind us I watched the intersecting headlights of departing cars as they U-turned and left for the main road.

". . . but we also made a mistake tonight. We gave out too many bids. In fact, we have only two bids to give for the three of you," Edwards said. "So we are going to have to settle this matter using a technique deeply important to the brothers of the house." He paused to stamp out his cigarette on the trail. I could smell wood smoke from somewhere in the distance.

"Drinking. Whoever drinks the Boone's slowest will have to be taken home." He crossed his arms. We hesitated, unsure if he meant that we should start chugging—a skill in which we'd yet to log any formal credit hours. I looked at him quizzically.

"Did I fucking STUTTER?" he yelled.

I tore the cap from the bottle and poured its contents down my throat, coughing on the drink's foul flavor as Peterson and Tim did the same, the former pausing briefly to boot into the brush to the side of the trail. There was no way I'd lose, I told myself, even if it didn't really matter. When I'd drained the bottle, I held it upside down; a single drop slid out and landed on one of my Sperrys.

We exchanged paranoid looks as Tim clocked in just behind me, Peterson not long after him. Despite all this, even though he was one of my best friends—one of my dorm-mates—I didn't feel a single pang of guilt that it seemed that he'd have to be taken home, back to Wheeler, where he'd probably return to his economics homework.

"Hand me the bottles," Edwards said. He pretended to inspect them—to make sure they were completely drained—then threw them one after another into the woods. One by one they thudded dully against a rotted log. He probably meant to dramatically smash them against a rock, I figured. I made a mental note to make that improvement for the future, if I made the cut.

No one said anything about taking Peterson home. We got back into the car and neither Edwards nor Clint told us to reaffix our blindfolds. As we pulled out of the woods, off the dirt roads, through Norwich, Vermont, across the bridge to Dartmouth, I stared out the window like a child drunk with exhaustion on a family vacation, vaguely wishing we'd been told to put our blindfolds back on.

RIPLEY HISSED IN MY EAR

We pulled up to the frat. The floodlights that normally lit the flag hung over the front door weren't on. Shadows from the streetlamps cut the lawn into a euclidean plane of grass and dead leaves, and above this the house loomed larger than usual, as if it were magnified by some camera trick.

I noticed Ripley pacing the front steps, shuttling between two Corinthian columns. He was wearing pajama pants and a red polo, his chin thick with two-day-old stubble, his teeth clamped around a fat cigar. He punched in the door code. The lock clicked open.

"Greetings, whaleshit." He blew smoke through pursed lips, waving us by. The house was dark, too, save for the living room, which was lit only by the glow of the crackling fireplace. Blindfolded boys sat scattered around the room on couches that had been pushed up against the walls to leave a large, empty area in front of the fire, where brothers paced circles and spoke in low voices. Ripley led me to an empty couch. Edwards led Peterson and Tim upstairs, muttering to some bro gripping a fistful of spreadsheets something about how he didn't "fucking care" that he was late.

"You're throwing the whole thing off, Edwards," the guy with the spreadsheets warned. Edwards didn't stick around to flit over the details. I couldn't tell whether their exchange was performed or not.

Ripley hissed in my ear, "Put your blindfold back

on." His breath was sour on my cheek. He grabbed my shoulders. "There are some things you aren't allowed to see."

THINGS WERE NOT GOING WELL

Someone tapped me on the head.

"Is this Lohse?" the guy asked, and I said, "Yeah," but then he went like, "Shut the fuck up, whaleshit, I wasn't talking to you." Out of the edge of my blindfold I saw another form move toward me on one side, blocking out the light of the fireplace.

Then I heard Ripley's voice. "Yeah, brah, that's Lohse. So fucked, don't you think?"

"Exceptionally fucked. Why is he even here tonight? I thought we weren't giving him a bid."

"Must have been a mistake," Ripley said. "Edwards and Davis wouldn't shut up in delibs, so we had to take him." I wondered if he was telling the truth. Maybe he was just trying to psych me out.

"Is he drunk yet?" the other voice asked.

Ripley didn't say anything.

Someone handed me a warm can of beer, then another, then a cup of something grimly sour. I did my best to chug them, but I'm terrible at chugging, and the slower I drank, the quicker the succeeding cups were handed to me, and pretty soon I stopped hearing the scuffling of feet on the hardwood of the living-room floor and the sound of the front door opening and closing as more pledges were brought in, shuffled around, forced to drink more, and then taken away—I assumed that they were taken upstairs as Tim and Peterson had been. I was drunk. I suspected that I must have been sitting on that couch for more than an hour. Maybe it was only half an hour. I don't know.

"Lohse," the same voice said, "take off your blindfold. The interrogation room is ready for you." I removed the tie and unsteadily followed the brother upstairs. He knocked twice on the door to Room 2 and then opened it, elbowed me in, slammed it shut behind me. The room was dark save for one glaring desk lamp on the coffee table facing a metal folding chair. A form sat behind the light but I couldn't identify it until I heard the voice. It was Buzzby.

I understood that whatever was about to happen was most likely going to be unpleasant. As Davis had said, Buzzby would have to find a way of settling his score with me. And as I'd promised Davis, I'd be a good pledge.

My eyes settled enough to trace Buzzby's silhouette on the other side of the lamp. One of his hands hung limply in his lap; his glasses cast a shadow against the wall. A tattered American flag hung over the window behind him. I looked down and saw six cups of beer on the coffee table. An industrial-sized garbage can stood next to the metal chair. I sat down.

"You obviously know by now that I do not want you to become a brother in this house," Buzzby measured out.

"I see." Like, what was I *supposed* to say?

"And I will do everything within my power to make sure that you never wear our letters."

There it was, I realized, the reason I hadn't seen or heard about any bid card.

"Well, but—" I interjected, attempting to begin my well-rehearsed talking points about what an asset I would be to the pledge class, what a dedicated, fratty conformist I could be, but he cut me off. I was feeling too drunk to remember my own talking points anyway.

"I'm not interested in what you think, faggot." That was a word he liked to use.

"Okay," I murmured.

"This house means everything to me. I would bring down the *Review* from the inside if it meant that I could save ΣAE."

Not sure what that meant—or if it would even be a reasonable scenario to imagine—I instinctively replied, "Me, too," stuttering, "I, too, totally feel what you—"

Suddenly I felt as if my thoughts were not just my own. Buzzby could read my mind, I realized. Things were not going well. I must have been smirking.

"Is something *funny* about this, Lohse?" he yelled, kicking the coffee table and splashing one of the beers onto my shoes, the tension in the room either suddenly evaporating or multiplying, I couldn't tell which. I couldn't tell if he thought the whole thing was so self-serious it was funny, too, or if it actually wasn't funny, if I should force myself to be as serious as possible to get through it all. So I opted to be solicitous.

"No. No, sir."

"Is there something funny about how I'm holding your bid card here, between my fingers?"

Finally, the great revelation—the bid card. It seemed as if the interrogation was a joke after all, that I'd been right, that none of the hazing mattered. He held my bid card at last, much more formal looking than the Tri-Kap card. On it was scrawled in curving, pretentious script, ANDREW BUTLER LOHSE, with a watermark of the house's secret letters, ΦA. They must have gotten the paper at some upscale stationery store.

Yeah, it did seem as if none of this even mattered, that we'd all be brothers soon anyway and have a totally epic circle jerk while wearing backward hats and chugging whiskey. You know, like, just doing the normal things that bros do.

Then Buzzby pulled out a matchbox and shook it in the shadow of the interrogation lamp, removing one and striking it against the side of the box.

"You see those beers on the table in front of you?"

Yeah, I did, even though my vision was beginning to tunnel. *Am I a brother now?* I wanted to ask. Instead— "Should I drink one?"

This caused him to chuckle. He shook his head slowly, the shadow of his face stretching and slimming on the wall as he moved his neck. "You can drink all six. Drink them in the time it takes your bid card to burn. Or you can leave and go sink your bid at Tri-Kap. But didn't you think you were too cool for Tri-Kap? Didn't you think that? Like a total asshole?"

BIG SECRETS WE JUST DIDN'T KNOW ABOUT YET

My circumstances had suddenly taken on a new dimension of seriousness. I was finally exposed to what, in Dartmouth life, is called the quick six—the chugging of six cups of beer in rapid succession, a feat intended to be performed in thirty seconds tops, though respect was only accorded to those who could do it in under fifteen.

"Word, bro," I mumbled, rising to my feet as I imagined my walk of shame to Tri-Kap after I inevitably failed this quick-six challenge. Without any warning Buzzby lit the card on fire and I watched as he held it between his thumb and his forefinger and then I looked up at the frayed American flag and reached for the beers and at some point tried to vomit in the trash can but missed and vomited all over my polo, but then the card stopped burning and crumbled into a pile of ashes on the coffee table and I believed, fully believed in that moment, that all of the hazing was a serious test that I'd failed. I'll admit it—I started to get choked up. Like, I'd come so far, did everything I was supposed to do to make it into the supposedly elite crowd, and then blew it.

Buzzby just shook his head.

"I'm sorry," I blurted, staring dumbfounded at the last cup, which I couldn't drink quickly enough. "I'll do anything." I was almost begging. I was definitely begging, and the tone of my plea might have been misinterpreted.

"Get out. Just leave."

I turned to the door, but before I could open it, he went

like, "Lohse, you piece of shit, turn around." When I did, he was holding another bid card scrawled with my name. He choked on his laughter. Then the door behind me cracked open and I saw Goodrich standing there with his arms crossed, smirking.

He gave me a bro hug and said congratulations and placed a cigar in my hand and led me down the hall to Room 4, where all the other pledges were, and the room was loud, filmy with smoke, pledges and brothers congregating on the sofas ripping massive bong hits. I'd been the last to go through the interrogation room. I climbed through the window onto the frat's balcony—it's called Pebble Beach, though no one seems to know why—where the rest of the pledges and brothers commingled, trading hazing experiences like cheap war stories. Baker Tower hovered over the scene. Its grandiose clockfaces, the two we could see, were out of phase, as unreliable as my internal clock.

I fumbled around on the unlit balcony, moving toward familiar voices in the dark. On the other side I heard Pulaski drunkenly blabbering to the other new pledges about the hazing the guys in his car underwent—all I caught was something about wading into Occom Pond, something about bottles of Mad Dog—"too many bottles, to be exact," he was saying. When he saw me, he stopped the conversation and slapped me on the back in a way that suggested he was a generation older. It was if he'd been confident of getting into the house all along.

"We were all worried about you," he said, biting down on a cigar.

"Where's Peterson?" I asked. "Did he make it through?"

I knew it was a redundant question. We'd all made it. All the hazing was a setup and there didn't seem to be any big secrets anyway—besides, of course, the hazing itself. These themes would continue. Funny how, despite gaining experience on the matter, we'd all still remain uncertain to varying degrees about the ghost of being depledged if we didn't do what we were told, the ghost of whether it was all serious or not. Whether there were big secrets. Big secrets that we just didn't know about yet.

"Peterson had to drink a little bit more than little Peterson's stomach could handle. Some of the seniors have him on a couch in Room 2 now."

Though it probably didn't matter at all, I felt bad about leaving Peterson in the dust when it had come to chugging the Boone's earlier in the night. I knew I had to go make sure he was still alive and not in need of a stomach pumping.

In Room 2 I found him facedown on one of the couches, writhing like he was going to boot. Passed out on the other couch was the upperclassman Upton, who was supposed to be watching him. Throat sputtering, Peterson wretched blindly—a watery, yellow river of vomit redolent of egg yolk, splashing across the cushion. I held his head over the trash can where I'd booted, too, not so long before. His eyes were glazed, and he seemed incapable of language, and I realized that I'd never seen him that drunk before. He wasn't the kind of guy who'd ever drink himself unconscious. It was just another warning sign we chose to ignore. We were pledges now.

I HOPE YOU'RE HAPPY

Since two of the main points of being a frat bro are party-ing and hooking up with girls, as many as possible, not much time is left over for serious monogamous relationships. Frats are where romance goes to die—who's surprised? Death by a thousand beers, a thousand blurry sets of wet lips, a thou-sand sandpaper-quality handjobs. Drink, wake up next to some girl you met the night before, one of your bros roasts you over your story at meetings, bros give you beers, you chug, you boot, you repeat until unsatisfied.

Similarly, things fell apart with Blair and me, this girl I'd been dating since freshman year. I was pretty much in love with her, in a deeper way than I have time to explain right now, but—we were fading out. She pledged Tri-Delt and our houses weren't friendly, and after that we didn't have any mutual social territory anymore. Also, as pledges we weren't allowed to go to any other houses without a brother, and we had to remain in his eyesight the whole time.

Not to mention that hazing erects walls between peo-ple, an us-and-them dichotomy. That's the whole point of it—to bring you into a collective identity. Even the people you love fall into the "them" category, and they are never in on the secret, even if the secret is that there is no secret except the appearance of one. Those people you love are probably sad about what they see happening to you, but they don't have the leverage to tell you not to keep participating.

No one can tell you, "You're better than that," partly

because they don't know everything you're being told to do, partly because all your older bros are telling you every day that the things you are being told to do are the things that make you better than the people who aren't told to do them. They say that's what makes you better than the people who are telling you *not* to do them. It's tortured logic.

Blair was probably sad on my behalf. The morning after bid night she said she had a gift for me. I invited her over to Wheeler. She handed me a small, white envelope with pristine lettering reading CONGRATULATIONS. I HOPE YOU'RE HAPPY. Inside was a yellow ΣAE bottle-opener key chain.

FURTHER INSTRUCTIONS

We returned to the house to find a different vibe from the night before. It was the second and last night of rush, and everyone was wearing suits again and all were pretending to be friendly to one another. We patronized most of the callback guys and random second-night rushees who turned up desperately trying to get bids after being left behind on the first night. Pledge term had hardly started and we were already thinking in the us-and-them dichotomy.

As we filed toward the front door, having been excused for the night after voting to bring one more sophomore boy into our midst, Davis and Goodrich stopped us.

"Don't be openin' that door yet," Davis yelled. "We

have some words for you." We paused expectantly for a monologue that didn't come. Goodrich crossed his arms. All he said was "Do your homework tonight, pledges. And wait for further instructions."

Our instructions arrived via blitz mail the next morning. We were to assemble, in full formal attire, on the thirteenth hole of the golf course at exactly seven that night. We were each to have a backpack stocked with a large uncooked vegetable, a lubricated condom, a pair of women's underwear, a notebook, and a pen.

YOU'RE SO FUCKED

I've never once played golf in my life, so fuck if I knew where the thirteenth hole was—but luckily some of the more privileged guys knew the golf course as if it belonged to them. During the afternoon those guys plotted our outing while other pledges made trips to the supermarket to stock up on produce.

The first group returned with cucumbers and zucchini. Word spread that phallic vegetables might be playing too literally into whatever the brotherhood had planned for us, so subsequent groups made a point of acquiring what were, in Tim's words, "non-assable" vegetables: cabbage, onions, broccoli. The assability of various types of produce became our first intellectual debate.

Eating dinner together in the dining hall, we speculated nervously about assable produce and lubricated condoms. I met more of the guys I didn't know well—Beaufort, Price, Douglas, Gibbons, and, of course, Wallace, who was already trying to appoint himself our leader. Then we made our funeral march to the thirteenth hole. There didn't seem to be anything happening there when we arrived, so for maybe half an hour we stood that way, circled against the woods on two sides, a steep hill and a sloping hill on the other sides, standing in a rough oval facing outward on the hole's green.

Soon it was completely dark. Clearly, the brothers had picked this green because it was in a geographically protected area; whatever was going to happen, the scene was far enough removed from Route 10 that it would be sufficiently secret. We watched a lamp, followed by a procession of dark figures, float across the hill toward us. Goodrich's voice echoed over the greens and sand traps. *"Up here, pledges!"*

We made our way up the hill.

"Not so close!" The brothers—only seniors—stood on the high ground, peering down on our nervous formation.

"This night is very important to our house," Goodrich began. "My first advice, as always, is 'Don't fuck this up.' You will be given very specific instructions that you will be expected to follow. Any failure to do so and we'll have to cut you from the class."

He paused.

"First, Bradford will be collecting all of your cell phones and wallets. Tonight, like other nights, you will not need identification or a means of communicating with the outside world. Is that understood? We'll return those things to you later."

We nodded. Bradford, who also held the lantern, dragged a garbage bag down the hill toward us. One by one we threw our phones and wallets into the bag. It was a powerful conceit—losing our identities in a plastic garbage bag. It would make more sense later when it became literal, when we'd be hanging our faces over trash cans and slinging them full of bile together.

Though I didn't know Bradford well, I knew his reputation for being sketchy; he kind of looked like Bill O'Reilly, too. Once he'd collected all the phones and wallets, each senior offered a monologue on what ΣAE meant to him, how it had changed him, what advice he would give the pledges. Together their speeches presented a glorious portrait of the frat. It would make us men. It would get us laid. It would get us jobs. It would define our lives. It was everything.

"Good luck tonight, pledges," Goodrich concluded. "Give us sixty counts to get back to our cars. Make your way back to the house. Open the back door of the house at exactly eight oh five—not a minute earlier or later—and then assemble in the pool room and await further instructions."

They floated off again across the course, following the lamp.

After Wallace counted to sixty, we began our run up the hill, under pale moonlight, air crisp with rot—my ankles slipping as we jogged up another green, over its crest, through sand traps, and toward the street, toward the hushed group of brothers extinguishing their lamps and climbing into their cars. Though there wasn't much time to organize, we formed an incoherent phalanx of brass-buttoned, navy blazers and boat shoes down Route 10. We ran.

Peterson looked at me querulously as our dress shoes beat a polyrhythm on the road's shoulder. "It was seven fifty-five when we tossed our phones in that bag," he panted. "That doesn't give us a whole lot of time to make it back."

"No, it doesn't."

"I think it's designed that way," Wilson offered from behind us. Peterson winced.

The brothers' cars sidled up next to our jogging column. As they sped past, out the windows the dudes were screaming, *"You're so fucked!"*—the words echoing down the road back to the college. When the cars were gone it was quiet again.

DON'T TRY TO BE THE HERO

It was just past eight when we made it to the house, splitting off from North College Street and dejectedly jogging past the woodpile to the back door. Cold sweat collected around my ears. Guys were panting, the breast pockets of their blazers rising and falling.

There is a church on North College Street, behind the house. Its parking lot is at the base of the hill the frat was built on, and our Dumpster was down there—topography was not on the Lord's side, and in this rare instance the frat held the higher ground.

Over the years, people from the church would continually complain that a foul odor haunted them on Sunday mornings, the frat smell to which they weren't desensitized as we were, the clotted pools of beer, vomit, and urine that dripped from a crack in the Dumpster's base—I imagined all these nice old people in Sunday clothes strolling through the puddles. I looked back over at the back door. Douglas was saying something, trying to organize the pledges.

"We need to get the time right," he was hissing. "Remember, *we can't fuck this up.*"

Since our phones had been confiscated at the thirteenth hole, we used, or tried to use, the two visible clockfaces of Baker Tower to figure out the exact moment to open the door and march inside. The sides were still out of phase. A last-second debate about minutiae played out between Blackstone and Douglas over when, exactly, to open the door. The pledges huddled together as we tried to work as a team to make the decision. Most agreed it was stupid—"Better to be early than late," Pulaski offered while adjusting his sweaty collar—and it ultimately didn't matter anyway since Blackstone vetoed Douglas's caution and threw open the door with one authoritative, take-charge-bro gesture, shepherding the others inside.

The frat was empty, as if it were in mourning or something. We stomped up the back steps. Faint light emanated from a constelled spiral of small candles set on the staircase's railing, flickering upward through the center of the frat like a galaxy seen in cross section. In the pool room we discovered a trio of basement-grade garbage cans arrayed in strategic locations.

Spreading into an oval around the pool table, we waited for some sign as to what would happen next. No instructions had been left for us. Dead flowers crept up from forgotten vases on either side of the mantel. Darts jutted from the wall around the dartboard. We were surrounded by the fraternity's composites on the walls, hundreds of miniature rectangular pictures of smirking white boys with undeveloped facial hair and aristocratic chins; someone was always leering at you.

Overhead lights flickered on, then off, then dimmed. Fists pounded on the doors. Then silence. Something hard was thrown at the other side of one door, and the knob suddenly thrust inward before slowly latching back into place. More banging. Two '11s burst in and passed Mad Dogs—one Strawberry Kiwi and one mysteriously named Orange Jubilee—to the first pledges at the far end of our oval, who, without hesitation, spun off the caps and drank until the brothers grabbed back their half-empty bottles.

"Are you going to be the hero tonight, Tom?" one brother asked. Tom, one of the pledge class's rugby players, stoic in a black suit and garish tie, just stared back. Were we supposed to talk? Blackstone flattened the lapels of his plaid blazer, watching, curious.

"Take a gulp and pass the bottles. Don't try to be the hero and drink the whole thing, whaleshit. Make sure everyone has their fair share."

"You succeed or fail together," the other brother said, scowling. They walked out and slammed the door. This continued for at least the next hour. It was almost like every brother had to have a cameo. So we ended up drinking a lot.

Ripley appeared in pajamas, cradling an armful more of Mad Dogs, his gut hanging out over the drawstring of his pants. I'd gradually been relocating closer to the door to try to grab the bottles as they came in—I had to seem like a team player. Ripley handed me a bottle and set the rest down on the pool table, walked out, slammed the door. I chugged it. Wiping my lips, I knew something was wrong.

I paused to let a column of bright green vomit rip into one of the cans as Douglas tapped me on the shoulder and pointed to his mouth and nodded vigorously, so I rolled to the side and made room for him to boot, too, and then this continued until we all felt pretty dazed. Then for a while the bottles stopped appearing. We stood there in the dark whispering to each other like mannequins.

WHO THE FUCK LIKES SCOTCH?

The overhead lights flickered, then dimmed to a warm, low light. Edwards sauntered in. He was wearing a three-piece suit, clutching a tumbler filled to the lip with Scotch, smirking.

After a poetic monologue on the pleasures of whiskey drunkenness, he circled the room with his eyes and approximated the smile of a seasoned salesman.

"Now, who likes Scotch?" He held the glass up to his cheek and swirled the amber liquid. No pledges spoke. We all looked away—at our feet, at the composites on the wall, into the fireplace's empty hearth. Eye contact became impossible. Eye contact probably meant drinking more, which probably meant booting again.

"Who the fuck likes Scotch?"

Pause. Silence.

"Don't make me *fucking* ask *again*!"

Compelled by a self-destructive tendency that blossomed at Dartmouth, I raised my hand, earning warning glances from the other pledges, not the least of whom was Douglas.

"I'm convinced by your persuasive language," I said, surprised at my recklessness.

Edwards's eyes homed in on me. "I'm sure you'll love this Scotch."

He circled around the pool table, face screwed up in a wince, and handed me the nearly overflowing cup. I wasn't sure if we were still friends, or if, because I was now a pledge, we were enemies. Did he haze us because he hated us? Did he haze us because he liked us? Was he indifferent? I was so confused I could barely tell, but somehow I'd known that the right answer was just to say, "Yes, hand it to me. I am a yes-man."

I booted again. Edwards laughed. We'd all vomited so much that the room had begun to reek of a festering total-ity of all the cafeteria food we'd consumed that day, or at least of undigested pizza. Nausea shimmered over me. I closed my eyes, got the spins, leaned up against the liquor cabinet to steady my legs.

ANTIHAZING CONTRACT

When I opened my eyes, the doors swung open again. Two figures in black robes entered. I wasn't sure if I was still zoning out until I saw the ΦA's embroidered on the front of the robes and then the figures threw off their hoods and I saw that they were Davis and Carver.

"You've done well so far, pledges," Davis said.

"We are your pledge trainers," Carver said. "And we are here to educate you."

"We have some rules to share with you. I am going to recite them quickly without any pause, so compare notes with your pledge brothers after we leave if you must."

"First three are—" Carver began.

Davis cut him off. "What happens in the house stays in the house. Trust the brothers, each other, and yourself. And do not, for any reason, blitz the brotherhood."

Then Carver went through the litany of door codes, making sure to tell us that we weren't permitted to use the front door.

"If a brother asks you what time it is in the Libes, it is always 'ten till two.' In the basement it is always 'five till one.'"

"If one of us asks you what day it is, you must always say, 'It is the greatest day of my life because I am one day closer to being a brother of Sigma Alpha Epsilon.'"

"Here are more papers." Davis threw stacks of printouts down on the pool table. "Memorize the Pledge Trainer Salute. You'll have to holler it at us as loud and fast as possible wherever you see us besides in class or the library. Memorize

'The True Gentleman' as quickly as possible. You will be tested on that. Soon. One of those sheets outlines what you must carry at all times as the contents of your pledge pack . . ."

I looked at the paper as Davis ranted commands. Cigarettes, dip, gum, pong balls, pong paddles, dice, gummy bears, a picture of your mother, beef jerky, condoms, a sex toy, a porno mag, chalk, something purple, something gold. It would all be expensive to assemble, especially because Carver added that brothers could ask for whatever they wanted from our pledge pack at any time. We'd have to run all over town restocking the bag.

"Also, every Friday you must wear formal attire from sunup to sundown. You are not allowed to wear a hat while wearing the formal attire, either," Davis added, while Carver passed around membership cards for us to sign.

One of the cards was an antihazing contract from the college—by signing it, we indicated that we understood the school's hazing policy and would be obligated to report hazing if it went on during our *new member education period*. I stared at the words. Something about them didn't seem to make sense, but there wasn't any time to wonder at what I'd missed. Davis began ranting again, something about *beer privileges*. Sloppily, I signed my name on the card.

NO!

Schultz appeared and led us up to the Libes.

There he passed out copies of *The Phoenix,* the official

handbook of the fraternity's national organization, and told us to sit down on the carpet and begin studying. I gripped the book with shaky hands, examining its binding, then flipping through the first few chapters while pledges were removed from the room one by one and then brought back a little while later.

> Welcome to the first step in what will be a truly remarkable journey in your life. You are embarking on an experience that I think you'll find is one of the best decisions you'll ever make. . . . Thus we are grateful indeed to those young men at the University of Alabama who gathered together in March 1856 to give new meaning to their affection and respect for each other. Little could they have dreamed of the immense, and indeed positive, influence their fraternity would have on generations of men. . . . The mission of Sigma Alpha Epsilon is to promote the highest standards of friendship, scholarship, and service.

At some point while the pledges were gone we'd hear a chorus of *"No!"* reverberate from somewhere down the hall. I sat on the floor, legs crossed, trying to process the words inside the book, so drunk I could barely read. Then Davis said, "Lohse, you're up," and led me down the hall to Room 8.

WHAT HAPPENS IN THE HOUSE
STAYS IN THE HOUSE

He pulled the door closed behind me. I'd never been in 8 before.

This double was on the third floor, an inner room with bunk beds, an outer room with a desk and a couch and a windshield-size TV and a dormer window and a regular window with a black metal ladder down to Pebble. But I couldn't see much of that at the time. It was dark.

As my eyes adjusted, I saw that I was surrounded on almost every side by sweaty, shirtless bodies, their shadows flickering against the walls by the light of three small candles lined on a tall table in the middle of a room. My nose was sloshed with a locker-room putrescence, a smell like jockstraps or tube socks. It was grim. Between that smell and my eyesight's being consumed by candlelight and half-nude male bodies, I was overwhelmed.

The brothers to the front and side of me were arrayed in two tiers as if standing on risers, like a church choir or a Reign of Terror court. The room was crowded. It seemed to perspire as one collective organism, the air dense and hot, stale and junglelike, and I seemed to know that it was always supposed to be like this, the moment. I got a creepy candlelight déjà vu.

Goodrich stood behind the table. I shuffled toward him and looked up and first saw three shot glasses arranged with the candles, then Goodrich's pecs, then his expressionless blue eyes—I tried to look away.

"There are three things you have to remember," he said.

I nodded, unsure if I was supposed to speak. The other brothers stared me down. I didn't want to look up and recognize them, because I didn't want to remember later who was there or that this strange thing was happening. No one spoke except Goodrich.

"Number one. Always trust the brotherhood."

"Always trust the brotherhood," I repeated.

"Good. Take a shot." I reached for the first glass. My hand shook. Cheap gin. It was warm. My throat burned—my lips puckered and I almost dropped the shot glass trying to set it back down on the table. Innumerable eyes trained on me, wreaking a havoc of anxiety on me from my peripheral vision.

"Number two. Always trust your pledge brothers."

I repeated Goodrich's injunction and drank the second shot, this time gagging more than I did on the first. I couldn't tell if it was salt water, spit, urine, or some mix of all three. By this time I was already drunk and tired and my stomach was beginning to send urgent messages to my brain. Sadly, these messages went missing between depressed nerve endings somewhere in my spinal cord, and the warning diffused, beaten into submission by my desire not to disappoint the bros. Onward, my willpower demanded. Always trust the brotherhood. You heard the dude.

"Number three. What happens in the house stays in the house."

"What happens in the house stays in the house," I muttered, reaching for the third shot. Before I could touch it, Goodrich grabbed my wrist and I accidentally stared into his eyes, then quickly averted my glance. He released his grip. For some reason I looked down, expecting to see a mark, but there was no mark.

Then it was time for the twist.

"Now, whaleshit, what were the three things I just told you to remember?"

The three things that were, fuck, like, impossible to recall in order, even though I'd learned them only seconds before.

Goodrich stared me down over the flickering candle. He had eyes like a mad Puritan minister. The brothers on the risers leaned toward me in unison, staring. They were expecting something, I realized. I had to say something. How was I supposed to remember? Who can even remember these things?

"Always trust—the house—" I stammered.

"*No!*"

Just like everyone else before me, I'd fucked it up. The instructions were so easy, but I'd fucked them up. I felt devastated. Davis opened the door, frowning, and led me back through the dim hallway to the Libes, forced a copy of *The Phoenix* back into my hands.

"Sit back down on the floor and study, whaleshit," he said. "You clearly have progress to make." His head swiveled around the room as he barked, *"Beaufort! You're next."*

One by one the remainder of the pledges were shuttled to 8 and back to the Libes. I flipped through chapters on the fraternity's founding and tried to memorize as much information as I could: *1856, Noble Leslie DeVotie, University of Alabama, the goddess Minerva, 1856, Noble Leslie DeVotie,*

"The True Gentleman is the man whose conduct proceeds from goodwill and an acute sense of propriety . . ."

Then, bored, I started to make alternate words for the frat's creed.

"The True Gentleman is the man whose conduct proceeds from goodwill and an acute sense of irony . . ."

ALL WE GOT WAS THE FUCKING FRAT T-SHIRT

Davis returned to the room with the last pledge, who had, predictably, failed the task in 8. The guy looked as if he could crack at any moment—he was red-faced, misty-eyed, and utterly wasted, like a kid who'd just been beaten stupid behind the slide on the playground.

After all the cigars and congratulations, all the affirmative welcomes to the elite crowd, we were being ground down. We were just a bunch of drunk kindergartners trying to fit in, trying to learn how to tie our own shoes and memorize the alphabet, but it was hard when our brains were so sedate, when the lighting was never good enough to not feel as if you were being played against some secret you'd never understand.

"We're done with 'em, Schultz," Davis muttered.

A few pledges lifted their heads.

"Heads down!" Schultz screamed. His voice frayed. Then the two spoke in whispers and Davis left in a hurry and I realized that my feet had fallen asleep on the purple carpeting.

"Your pledge trainers aren't very happy with your performance, but I've convinced Davis to let you guys move on to the next round. These are your pledge jerseys." Schultz pointed at a stack of purple T-shirts emblazoned with golden lettering and shining gold piping on the sleeves, neatly folded on a wooden table in the center of the room. "If you guys can get through the next few rounds, you'll wear these shirts every Wednesday from sunup through pledge meetings. Sleep in them on Tuesday nights if you must. There might be random checks."

Despite our despondent mood, we were twisted back to another strange feeling of accomplishment—we'd get to wear the frat's letters every Wednesday. We'd also get to wear them *tonight*. Unaware of what events lay ahead for us, getting to wear the T-shirt seemed like one of the coolest things in our lives because it was a tangible sign of belonging. Belonging to what, and whether it was right or wrong, seemed pretty irrelevant.

I pulled off my blazer and button-down and tossed my rep tie into a pile of clothes under one of the room's large mahogany tables. I pulled the fresh jersey over my head. Few things at Dartmouth could compare to that feeling—we thought we were, like, donning epaulets or something. Other generations had wars, struggles, religions, customs inscribed with ancestral energy. All we got was the fucking frat T-shirt. For some reason it meant a lot to us.

"You probably want to take off your suit pants and khakis and put on the gym shorts and old shoes Goodrich instructed you to bring," Schultz said. Then he led us down the staircase and out the back door, where we'd entered earlier. Following his plodding footsteps, we made our way along the rear of the house until we reached the door to the back room of the basement—a single, plain metal door with no handle. Beyond the door was what the brotherhood called the Beer Die room, though its old-school drinking-game namesake was rarely ever played anymore.

Never trust a room named after something that doesn't happen in it anymore, especially when you have to enter it from the outside; I knew there was a door to it from the inside of the basement, so why couldn't we use that?

Not to mention that Beer Die had no windows. It was built into the slope leading up to the house, sealed crypt-like under the concrete floor of the patio. It had one handleless door to the lower back patio and an inner door to Varsity, one of the two main basement rooms along with JV. Beer Die was so well buried into the hill, so well insulated by earth, that it was almost soundproof to the outside world. Kind of like a panic room, but one that you panicked in instead of entering because you were panicking.

I'VE GOT A BEER FOR WHOMEVER

Schultz knocked three times. The door swung open. By this point, even in this nascent stage of pledge term, the whole "knock three times and the door mysteriously opens" trope was no longer all that impressive. Schultz whispered, "Good luck."

Inside the small, rectangular room hundreds of cups of beer littered almost every available surface. The room smelled musty—I guessed that it hadn't been used, at least not in a full-scale hazing operation, since the previous pledge term; the single, low bench built onto the wall, circling the room, was conspicuously dusty, as were the arms of the wooden throne constructed in the center of one side's wall, the throne where Edwards sat, drumming his fingers, legs crossed, still wearing his three-piece suit.

Spray-painted phrases and pledge names stuck to the walls like the Day-Glo graffiti of some prep school dystopia where everyone had a condescending nickname. To one side of the throne MASON DICKSON ΦA was gouged into the paneling with shallow cuts from a small blade. A tally was next to the name. Screwed into the wall across from the throne and over the bench on the other side of the room were two metal house numbers, 5 and 7. Like the nicknames, those signifiers were lost on me. In one corner of the room sat a wooden coffin—less elaborate than the one in JV, just a plain rectangle—with ΦA painted onto it. ΦA was scrawled everywhere in the basement.

We sat down on the benches.

Edwards looked us over.

"This will be your introduction to pledge meetings." He sounded bored. Idly cracking his knuckles, he informed us of the various rules and regulations governing pledge meetings, our future Wednesday nights. We'd be occupied from nine o'clock onward every Wednesday. The Beer Die room would become as important to us as Baker Library, he said. We'd learn a lot here, things we'd be tested on, things we'd be punished for getting wrong, things that would define our time at Dartmouth.

He tore through the litany so furiously, as the pledge

trainers had earlier in the night with the first set of rules, that it was nearly impossible to remember them all.

Raise your elbows in a "flipper" to answer a question.

The numbers 5 and 7 are now to be called Bizz and Buzz, respectively.

Beers are to be poured by the pledges before meetings, the exact number requested by the trainers, and filled to slightly above the lines—"pledge beers," not "brother beers" (a distinction with which we'd become familiar).

You may not "pull your own trigger" to vomit; you must ask a pledge brother to stick his fingers down your throat if you want to puke.

Boot in the trash cans unless otherwise directed.

Every pledge needs ten empty cups to leave the room, but in future nights the number will grow.

You succeed and fail as a group.

Don't say Phi Alpha; say PA or Five Apples.

No leaving the room at any point for any reason.

Pee in the trash cans if you have to pee.

Got it, whaleshit?

"Now drink."

So we started drinking.

Edwards instructed us on how, in pledge meetings as in brother meetings, guys were to "give" each other beers and tell embarrassing stories about them: the time they fucked a girl when she was on her period but they were too drunk to notice, the time they got so high they passed out on the grass in front of the library; juvenile shit like that. You'd say, "I've got a beer for" whomever, tell the story, he'd chug it.

You could also give a "friendship beer"—maybe two

pledges had hooked up with the same girl. Maybe they'd aided each other in cheating on an exam. Maybe they'd plagiarized an internship cover letter together. They could commemorate this new watershed moment in their friendship by each hoisting a beer, facing each other, arm linked in arm like a pretzel, and chugging.

Then Edwards explained the concept of doming.

BECAUSE IT'S FUN?

"You've all probably heard the term, I assume," he said. We nodded. "It is, after all, a Dartmouth tradition. One of the drinking traditions that sets us apart from our peer institutions." He paused. "Can one whaleshit who knows about doming explain to the other whaleshit who don't know?"

Douglas raised a flipper. Edwards nodded at him.

"It's a competitive drinking game where two people stand over a trash can chugging beers until they boot. First person to boot loses," Douglas deadpanned. We'd all mostly learned this information during freshman year; the word *dome* had slipped into our vocabularies and we'd sometimes used it nervously, believing we understood what it meant. No one, however, can grasp the true meaning of a dome unless he's experienced one himself.

"Close, but not exact. Let's get another volunteer." Edwards's eyes slid down the benches, stopping on Pulaski. "You. You goofy-looking motherfucker."

Pulaski and Douglas stood up and walked over to one of the trash cans. It already smelled like a cesspool.

"There are two types of domes," Edwards said. "Either it's two people doming each other, or one person doming himself. When it's two people doming each other, the beers are timed—five, ten, or fifteen seconds apiece. When it's one guy doming himself, it's one beer per chorus of one of our drinking songs. Either way there's singing. To set the mood. Sometimes, a rule is enforced that the winner gets to boot on the loser's head. Brothers can call for this by chanting, 'Boot on his head, boot on his head!' A dome begins for a single guy if he's given four or more beers at a time and doesn't drink them quickly enough.

"Now, does anyone know *why* we dome?"

Wallace raised a flipper. "Because it's fun?"

Not exactly, I thought to myself.

"Partially." Edwards nodded. "But usually to settle a score. When it's two guys. Say they fucked the same girl. They might dome over it. When it's one guy, it's usually because he did something retarded. Say, the time when someone got drunk and jumped off Pebble during sophomore summer. You better believe that at the following meetings he had to dome over it—that kind of dome begins by a group of people chanting, 'Which begs the question, whooo is _____!' Then the brothers start singing, the guy starts doming, et cetera, et cetera, until he boots.

"Let's practice. Doming is one of the most important parts of meetings." Edwards slid his watch off his wrist, said we were going to start easy with fifteen-second beers, and started timing. We didn't know any songs, so we didn't sing. Neither Douglas nor Pulaski lasted long. Pulaski booted after only four beers.

"Embarrassing." Edwards chuckled. "Very embarrassing."

We went back to telling stories about each other and giving each other beers.

I held a tall stack of empty plastic cups in my hand and, through shaky tunnel vision, sought out a final beer or two to complete my pledge responsibilities. I'd already booted twice; once, my dinner, the consumption of which seemed like a distant memory, and then later a mucilaginous half-liquid that I'd dry-heaved in the corner of the room by the coffin.

At the end of all this we elected our pledge class president, a position infelicitously known as PCP. Some pledge named Sullivan won. No one seemed to know who he was or how he'd ended up in our pledge class, but his chugging was pretty elite. In reality that was all the pledge class president had to do: inaugurate pledge meetings every week by chugging five beers. Beyond that the position was apolitical.

Pulaski was elected pledge class chronicler, the other position up for a vote. Kind of like secretary. His job would be to write and present a thematic top-ten list of stories and inside jokes every week at meetings.

SWIM, WHALESHIT, SWIM

A bro walked in from Varsity and motioned at Edwards. "Are they done?"

We went silent. Edwards surveyed the wreckage beneath his throne, the scrum of stumbling sophomores in purple jerseys, the hundreds of empty cups, the filthy smell wafting up from the trash cans.

Noticing this final note of ambience, the brother breathed deeply. "Smells like ass in here, bro." He winced. He nodded back toward Varsity. "Almost as bad as it smells out there." I wondered how any other room in the frat could possibly smell as feculent as the one we were already in.

"Is the next phase ready?" Edwards giggled.

"Yeah, dude. Have them strip down." The bro turned back to Varsity. Silence gripped us.

"You heard him, whaleshit. Strip on down. Keep your old boxers on, but no gym shorts, and please, for the love of God, no brand-new pledge jerseys."

Then Edwards instructed us on how to "waddle," because, apparently, that's how whaleshit were supposed to exit pledge meetings every week.

We put our hands on our heads and squatted low to the floor and waddled out of the Beer Die room into the darkened Varsity room, which *did* smell worse. The whole basement basically smelled like sewage by this point. As a strobe light pulsed, brothers chanted, *"Whaleshit! Whaleshit!"* Varsity suddenly became a very different place from the basement room where Pulaski and Peterson and I had played innocent games of pong all freshman year while trying to meet brothers. It would be impossible to remember it the way we had; shocking events have a way of imbuing spaces with subconscious power.

A brother's hands on my shoulders guided me to a spot

on the sticky cement floor; in front of me I could see, through the light's intermittent flashes, a blue plastic kiddie pool in the room's center—that seemed to be where the smell was coming from.

Davis's voice boomed above us, calling pledges' names one by one: Douglas, Torrentino, Nelson, Wallace. At first there was some confusion over what we were supposed to do when our name was called. We were too wasted to imagine. Surely we weren't supposed to climb into the reeking plastic pool in front of us. That'd be too messed up to imagine. But the game became clear with the aid of those brothers' hands reaching out of the shadow circle around us, guiding the first few pledges, one at a time, into the reeking kiddie pool.

"*Blackstone!*" Davis called out. He recited a short blurb about Blackstone as he sloshed helplessly in the sludge, ending with "I now present to you, whaleshit _____," the blank being Blackstone's new name, his pledge name, something clever and cast with a brotherly significance. So it was with each pledge. He was guided into the pool as brothers roared, as Davis read his blurb.

Then it was my turn. "*Andrew Butler Lohse!*"

Forcing all doubts outward from my mind, I waddled toward the kiddie pool. The concrete floor was cold and slick beneath me as I reached out to climb over the pool's edge. I'd later learn the tradition of its ingredients—the same stuff, we were told, was in it when we swam in it: food products, beer, vomit and urine, even shit and semen. I either saw or heard about what was put in the mix for the next two years, when I became a brother.

Of course, we didn't know then and could never prove

its contents as pledges. The secrecy of the frat works through compartmentalization of knowledge, and we couldn't scoop up a sludge sample to bring to the biology lab—we just knew the scent, the feeling of the mixture sticking to our skins, and knew that disobeying was probably pointless. You can't beg out of your fratty baptism. What would everyone think of you? Were you not a team player? Didn't you uphold the old traditions?

Images blurred together. The smell of the pool made me gag; I felt violently sick as the mire enveloped my legs and elbows and then torso. Some brothers yelled, *"Drink the pool!"* Others yelled, *"Swim, whaleshit, swim!"* Davis shouted my blurb over the din:

"For the pledge known for his preppy critter pants, cardigan sweaters, and bitchy social climbing, much like Regina George from the movie Mean Girls, *I now present to you, WHALESHIT REGINA!"*

This was all traumatic, and whether it was from all the booze or from feeling humiliated, I blacked out. My perception clicked off like a busted video camera. Last thought—it's always the middle-class kid who gets called a social climber.

WAS I SUFFERING FROM STOCKHOLM SYNDROME?

It's possible that I just didn't want to remember what it felt like after that pivotal first moment—maybe my brain intentionally shut down to repress the memories before they even had a chance to form. I don't remember climbing back out of the pool, and I don't remember sitting back in the circle with my legs crossed waiting for the others to swim, and I don't remember waddling back to the stairs. Apparently, all those things happened.

When I blacked in, I was stepping out of one of the upstairs showers, naked. A brother handed me a towel. I felt the cold tiles beneath my feet, then the damp carpeting in the upstairs hallway. As pledges stepped out of the showers, we were told to don our stolen women's underwear. I found mine, a yellow-and-baby-blue thong I'd stolen from the Wheeler laundry room, in my pledge pack; I'd later forget that I was wearing it underneath my formal attire. Descending the stairs, I noticed that all the lights had been clicked on and the house was full of life again, sickly jubilant, and we walked in a line down into the foyer, shaking hands with a gauntlet of cheering brothers. Congratulations, they said. You did it, they said. We just ordered you guys a shitload of pizza, they said. We're proud of you, they said.

Suddenly they were our best friends again and everything was cool again, and then we had a pizza party until I left for Hitchcock to see Blair. I wanted to tell her what had just happened, share my tense mixture of gratification and humiliation. Was I suffering from Stockholm syndrome? I wondered. I'd sunk my bid. The sinking feeling persisted.

AT LEAST WE HAVE THE HOUSE

"Where are you going?" Peterson asked.

He watched me stumble past a stack of empty pizza boxes piled next to the fireplace. I threw my backpack over my shoulder. I squinted, forcing my eyes to focus on him. Behind him brothers were talking and laughing about the kiddie pool as if it hadn't left them feeling the slightest bit uncomfortable, as if it had just been routine—like watching TV on a Sunday afternoon or going to the movies or having dinner with your parents. Most of the pledges still seemed confused. They ate their slices in silence.

"I'm gonna go see Blair," I slurred back. "Are you gonna stay here?"

"I don't know." He seemed dangerously sober.

"Well, whatever."

I found Davis in the foyer and made sure my obligations were complete.

"I give you my blessing, Regina," he said. "Say hello to your girlfriend for me." He smirked. I noticed a few other brothers laughing about some secret knowledge, something I must've forgotten. The stolen thong—I was too blacked out to remember it—but it was one of the numerous and inexplicable faux pas committed that night that ultimately caused Blair to summarily kick me out, maybe because she was trying to study for an exam, or maybe because I peed on the floor in her bathroom, but either way she called Pulaski, of all people, to come pick me up,

Pulaski, who was just as wasted as I was, eyes bloodshot, lips mumbling something about *the undying ideal of brotherhood* and how he *finally understood*. Blair pushed me out the door without a second look. I mean, I guess I couldn't blame her.

"Some charming girlfriend you've got, dude," he slurred as we passed by Sanborn, the lone light on the third floor still glowing like a beacon leading us through a mined harbor. I shivered. The night had gotten colder—fall had taken its turn toward desolation, bringing us, and everything happening in our lives, with it. We kicked through a pile of decaying leaves on the walk up to Wheeler.

Pulaski stopped. He put his hands on my shoulders and looked at me sternly. His breath smelled like smoke. "At least we have the house now."

PHI ALPHA, WHALESHIT

When I woke up the next afternoon, I could already feel the vomit caught in my gut, begging to disembark. There was no way to defuse it. Suddenly, it popped—pink chunks, liquid that looked like pond water. After I was done embracing the toilet, I stepped into the outer room and found Peterson crouched over his desk.

"Dude, we have to talk," he goes.

"Yeah?"

"Dude."

"Dude, what?"

Quietly he began to rant, voice thin and meticulous, about how he'd ended up far too sober for the kiddie pool since guys like me and Blackstone and Douglas had drunk more than our fair share of the Mad Dog, all those disgusting bottles of Orange Jubilee and Strawberry Kiwi and Kiwi Lemon, and how he saw the whole series of events clearly, how he'd just blitzed Goodrich to say that he was dropping out of the pledge class. The dude was ashen, hands shaking and all. I halfheartedly tried to convince him to stay.

"It's social suicide to quit now," I argued as I gargled mouthwash, spat it out into the trash can, lowered my useless body onto the futon. "It's social suicide enough to not rush in the first place. We have to pledge, man. No way around it." I sprawled out, facedown, willing the pounding in my head to cease long enough to make sense of what had happened the night before. Minor details bubbled to the surface—the slick basement floor, the smell of the kiddie pool, all the vomiting in Beer Die, the purple T-shirts, Blair's fury. It had been an all-night odyssey.

Peterson sat bolt upright at his desk, staring at me with melancholy eyes. Like an animal who'd been transplanted from his native habitat, he knew, viscerally, that he wasn't the kind of guy who belonged in a frat like this one.

"I already sent the blitz, dude. I'm done. I can't do anything like that ever again."

"Maybe it will get easier," I suggested unconvincingly, not even believing it myself, but Peterson snorted derisively. The guy was trapped. No pledge brother could in good conscience let him drop out. It would raise questions about the hazing, questions that we'd all have preferred not to raise. Questions we were trying to ignore personally.

Within the hour a group of brothers appeared at our door to cajole him to stay in the pledge class. Together they played good cop, played the "we are your best friends" ploy. One of them eyed me on the futon. I pretended to be asleep but did a bad job. Through swollen eyelid slits I watched the guy adjust his backward hat.

"Heard about your little tryst last night, how your girlfriend threw you out," he said. The bros laughed.

"Phi Alpha, whaleshit," another said.

Then they convinced Peterson not to drop out.

BOOTED BLOOD. YOU SAW ME

We came to know one of the older bros well—Rector. Edwards and Davis had described him to me as "the most disliked brother in the house," and there were reasons no one liked him.

Maybe many of the pledges feared him because of how he'd made this pledge Torrentino scrub the basement Tank Room clean with a toothbrush once, right at the beginning of pledge term. The guy dropped out of the pledge class not long after that. No one heard from him for a while. None of us could imagine the consequences of quitting after what we had seen; we knew too much. I wondered what had actually gone through Torrentino's mind, what had gotten him to quit.

Rector was also responsible for overseeing one of the more mundane daily pledge activities: the sign-in sheet, an attendance sheet to be signed by each pledge every day and then countersigned by two brothers to prove that each of us had been to the house at least once. The trick about the sign-in sheet was that we had to find it before anyone could, well, sign in, and the hiding places became more elaborate as pledge term developed. We were told that being at the house every day would help us develop a sense of ownership over it. It was a way to get us to fully grasp the privileges we were earning—our connection to the house was for life, we were promised. As brothers, then as alumni, it would be our spiritual home, our temple at the alma mater.

At first the sheet was easily discovered behind living-room curtains or taped to bathroom-stall doors. Then Rector began hiding it in ceiling tiles, in between the slats of old radiators, behind black-and-white photographs of frat brothers past, inside the basement fireplace. The sheet had to be discovered and filled in daily by midnight. If we hadn't found it by eleven-thirty, pledges could gather to chug beers for clues.

Rector also took the loss of pledge books seriously.

He was clearly on the hunt for any wayward pledgewear or artifacts, especially, God forbid, our notebooks, which held sensitive house secrets ranging from hazing to door codes, lest the information fall into the wrong hands. Pulaski made one of our pledge class's first blunders on this point.

One October day not long after sink night, we received a blitz from Rector instructing us to assemble in Varsity at three o'clock. A special ceremony would take place during our mandatory basement cleanup. Since it was a Thursday, many pledges blitzed the pledge trainers complaining about having class, having work to do, meetings with profs, you know, the excuses that were supposed to be secondary to pledge term.

This warm, clear afternoon, with basement windows propped open to rays of sunlight electrifying the dust in the stale air, was the kind of day when you'd much rather have been outside reading than mopping up someone else's spilt beer, congealed vomit, and puddled urine ten feet underground. Some guys paced around clutching mops, waiting for others to shovel all the cups and cans into the garbage so they could get to work cleaning the grimy floor; some dragged the full bags of cups and cans up the steps and out the back door to the Dumpster, leaving behind thin lines of mottled liquid that dripped from unseen holes in the plastic; some scrubbed the bars and benches with oil soap.

At three we dropped our cleaning implements and gathered in a circle around a pong table where Rector had earlier poured ten cups of liquids in varying colors, from the gold of what we assumed to be stale Keystone to the clear of what we assumed to be water.

"Greetings, whaleshit." He spread his palms like a preacher. "This will be brief. We are only gathered here today to make an example of Whaleshit It. Whaleshit It lost his pledge book last night."

Rector revealed a black composition notebook from behind his back. A couple of guys cringed. Rector adjusted his glasses. Pulaski, who'd been baptized Whaleshit It because the brothers had uncharitably asserted that his appearance took after that of the infamous serial-killer clown of Stephen King's *It,* didn't blink.

Rector continued, "Whaleshit It then had the . . . gall, the gumption . . . to blitz out, to *drunkenly* blitz out, to the brotherhood asking for his book's safe return.

"Remember, you are *not* permitted to e-mail the brotherhood. You are *not* brothers. You are *whaleshit*. And what does whaleshit do?"

"Whaleshit sinks to the bottom of the ocean," we mumbled in chorus.

"Glad we've cleared that up. Do yourself a favor and don't forget it."

Pulaski snapped off his plastic cleaning gloves and stepped forward from the circle. He clasped his hands in front of him and arched his eyebrows comically, acknowledging his mistake as Rector read his blitz aloud, with all its misspellings, and gave special punctuation to its conclusion, *"I demand me book back!!!"* We tried to avoid laughing. It was still early in pledge term and the rules still seemed funny because we didn't believe that we'd actually ever find ourselves in pain by breaking them. Optimistically, we figured that sink night had been the worst of it.

Rector nodded toward the cups. "As punishment, Whaleshit It will perform a quick ten for us. Take this as a warning to never, ever leave your pledge materials unattended." He folded his laptop shut and placed it on the other pong table, far removed from the line of cups and the freshly relined garbage can he had dragged toward the center of the room for Pulaski to boot in.

"Excuse me? Rector?" Douglas raised a flipper.

"What is it, Whaleshit Angelica?"

"Should we sing the doming song?" We barely knew it, but it seemed like an appropriate thing to do. Of course, we assumed the cups were just beer and water, assumed, as if it were not wrong to do so, that Pulaski would dispatch the challenge with minimal suffering. This was all in the name of chugging practice, I figured.

"Yes. Please sing."

"*FROMMMM Rigsby's Road to Finnegan's—*" We belted out the words, but somewhere near the end of the first verse, so I guess not that far into the song, we realized from Pulaski's rapidly changing facial expressions as he downed the cups that something was gravely wrong—from that and from the hue his boot took on as he wretched into the trash can. Clearly, the cups were not all stale beer. Some were beer, some were beer laced with hot sauce, and the clear two I'd thought were water were both straight vinegar.

As Pulaski's pain became apparent, the song deteriorated and no one could stand to watch anymore. I even saw Wallace cringe and look away as the rhythm was lost, and most of the pledges despondently mumbled through the final verse. We realized that a line had been crossed. We realized that things were not going to be as easy as we thought they'd be. When the spectacle was over and Pulaski, gagging, had thrown down the last empty cup, we all went back to our cleanups as if nothing had happened.

I caught up with Pulaski a little while later as he emptied his mop bucket into the toilet in the Boot Room. "You all right, bro?"

"I think I booted blood. You saw me." He winced, then smiled stoically down into the mop bucket. "Booted blood."

Underneath his gaze the filthy, seatless toilet glimmered in the gauzy sunlight streaming through the Boot Room's broken, ground-level window. The room was like a mausoleum cracked open with autumn glow. Spiderwebs and graffiti, dried vomit from months ago. It was all kind of sad and beautiful.

BASEMENT APPRECIATION NIGHT

Without going too far into gory detail, let's just say that after sink night, Blair and I didn't see each other much. Maybe this was because I peed on the floor in her bathroom. There were probably other reasons, too.

Some Friday. This hazing event called Basement Appreciation Night, where we all had to stay in the basement all night, sleep on the benches or the pong tables if we wanted to sleep. Brothers stood by the back door from the Beer Die and the stairs to make sure none of us snuck away.

There was no reason to sneak off anyway, as Davis told us at the beginning of the night when we'd all congregated in Varsity and he'd explained to us that we were quartered until sunup.

I raised a flipper and asked why.

"Why would you *want* to leave?" he boomed. "You've got everything you need here—beer and brotherhood."

"What about pussy?" someone yelled from the back of the group.

"We never said that girls couldn't visit you."

Some guys snickered.

Like Blair would come hang out with me here, during a hazing event no less. Where would any of us hook up anyway?

Davis had already thought that one through. "Whaleshit, that's why God made the Tank Room, the Boot Room, and the Cave," a crawl space under the stairs. "All of those locations offer you privacy. Just don't forget to tell all about your hookup at next week's meetings."

He leapt off the benches and strutted toward the stairs. "Revel in the basement," he yelled over his shoulder. "Own your space."

Strangely enough, girls did come. Brothers did hook up in the Tank Room. This surprised me. My phone lit up in the middle of a pong game with Pulaski, Wilson, and Blackstone. Blair. She was breaking our post-floor-urination estrangement.

Her text was something like "Want to come over and watch a movie tonight?"

"Guys, hold on." I waved to the other team and showed Pulaski the text.

"Don't pause the game just 'cause we're winning, Lohse." Blackstone rolled his eyes.

Wilson, who was always in everyone else's business, walked around to our side of the table. "What are you guys looking at?" He tried to grab my phone from me. "Blair?"

"Yeah," I said.

"Quite a conundrum," Pulaski said. "On the one hand, you can't leave the basement until sunrise. On the other hand, you have to go see Blair and fix shit and potentially have makeup sex."

It was the usual pledge-term catch-22. We continued the game, debating the merits of my staying or going.

"I think you should go," Wilson argued. We volleyed.

I hit the ball back across the table and Blackstone lobbed it high, with a little slice, and it sank in one of our cups. Pulaski downed half and passed the rest to me.

"You can't go, man. It's Basement Appreciation Night," Blackstone said. "Does pledge term really mean that little to you?"

Pulaski concurred, nodding gravely.

I paused the game to seek out Peterson's counsel. I found him sipping a can of beer on the benches in Varsity, staring into his phone.

"Don't risk going," he said.

I texted Blair something like "Sorry, have to stay here until sunup. Tomorrow? Sorry." She didn't respond.

Seven games of pong—fourteen beers—later, I was having second thoughts.

"I'm sneaking out," I told Pulaski as we smoked cigarettes in the corner of the Beer Die. "I'm just gonna do it."

Schultz, who'd been guarding the back Beer Die room door, overheard our conversation. His eyes shot wide.

Shit.

"You're going to do *what*?" he wailed, walking toward us past the throne, his boat shoes crunching on empty cups.

"You didn't hear that," I said.

"You can't leave, Lohse. There are rules. I don't want to have to tell Davis and Carver about this."

"It's a Blair thing. You know how it is."

Schultz did know how it was. I'd asked him for advice a few times on how to handle my disintegrating relationship with her, and he'd even talked to her once on my behalf. He leaned against the throne and stroked his beard. He was thinking. Through the door in Varsity I could hear the pledges screaming through one of the songs we had recently learned:

> *In the Beta House we sit, with our fingers dipped in shit,*
> *And our balls are playing checkers on the floor.*
> *When the ΣAEs walk past, we stick our fingers up our ass,*
> *I don't wanna be a Beta anymore.*

> *I'm an asshole, I'm an asshole, I'm an asshole till I die.*
> *But I'd rather be an asshole than a Beta Theta Pi!*

> *'Cause I'm Phi Alpha born and I'm Phi Alpha bred,*
> *And when I die, I'll be Phi Alpha dead!*
> *So rah rah Phi Alpha Alpha, rah rah Phi Alpha Alpha,*
> *Rah rah Phi Alpha Alpha S-A-E!*

> *Got a Phi Alpha girl in my Phi Alpha bed*
> *And when she goes down, I get Phi Alpha head!*
> *So rah rah Phi Alpha Alpha, rah rah Phi Alpha Alpha,*
> *Rah rah Phi Alpha Alpha S-A-E!*

Beta being my grandfather's frat, I wondered if he'd ever sung a fecal-matter-themed song about our house back in the day. Schultz lifted his hand from his chin and turned toward us.

"Here's what's going to happen. Pulaski, go back to Varsity. You didn't see this. Lohse, I'm going to let you walk out that door to go talk to her, but be back in an hour and I won't tell Davis or Carver, okay?"

EQUATIONS ABOUT ARBITRAGE

Some afternoon. Sitting in the room with Peterson. Outside the window over my desk the sky was one thick band of pale blue, and across the street the shingles on the frat's roof glowed like gold ingots. The day was windy; we'd shut the window, leaving us to choke in stale air as we both tried to read assignments. I kept interrupting to complain about everything happening with Blair.

"Best thing you can do," Peterson said, "is find someone else and move on."

"Not sure if that's possible, but who knows."

"I guess I understand." He looked back down at his econ textbook. I wanted to ask—*Do you?*

I flung the novel I was reading onto the floor, giving up. I could barely focus on the minimal academic work I was supposed to be completing, which, beyond anything else shitty occurring, was depressing in itself because I was an English major who planned to go to grad school, get a PhD, and hopefully become a literature professor if I couldn't make it as a writer. Pledge term was hollowing me out. How could I become a professor if I couldn't read one single fucking book?

Like most pledges, I'd crafted my entire sophomore fall class schedule around frat life. I was taking only one course for my major—Victorian Lit—and two layups, through which I could sleepwalk without doing any heavy lifting.

"Get your mind off it." Peterson flipped glossy pages, line graphs of gross domestic product, equations about arbitrage. "Hook up with someone else. It's not that hard. We have the house to help us. Even I've been pulling it off." He paused to chuckle to himself before reverting his eyes to a boldfaced section about fractional reserve banking.

THE CATFISH IS A SLUT

Music 9: Music and Technology. Staring at a clock hung high on the lecture hall's wall. The minute hand clicked by insufferably.

It was a Thursday afternoon and I was viciously hungover, head pounding, one eye barely open, body bruised from some fall I couldn't remember. Having forgotten to brush my teeth—I'd been nearly half an hour late to class—my mouth still tasted like Keystone. In my seat I clutched a giant catfish stuffed animal I'd been given as pledgewear at meetings the night before. The catfish was given every week to the pledge with the grimmest hookup story. Post-breakup, that was often me.

It was part of the rebound remedy my pledge brothers had prescribed: get a grip, lower your sexual standards, find some perspective. This remedy seemed plausible up until the last part, considering that *perspective* and *pledging* were antonymous *p*-words. Probably no number of afternoons waking up in strange beds could change anything.

Music 9 was a massive lecture course with a median grade of A, a gut class, and it made me feel vaguely guilty as a once-serious musician to be sleeping through it to salvage my GPA. I was already worried about getting into grad school—but that thought had to wait. I was sitting next to Chad, one of the older bros. When the professor had just about finished his lecture, once he'd pressed a button on the dais and watched detachedly as the projector screen rose into the ceiling, I stood up to leave.

"See you later, Chad," I muttered.

"Later, whaleshit." The way he said it—he made it sound fucking wholesome, as if he were talking to Lassie or something.

The prof saw me trying to slink away up the aisle, saw the giant, whiskered fish under my arm, its fins trailing down to the carpeting. He called out, "Excuse me?" I somehow knew he was talking to me—he didn't have to say my name, if he even knew it. I doubted he did.

I stopped walking. Stared straight at the wall ahead of me. Counted to three. Turned around. The lecture hall paused as the prof asked, his British accent dripping with earnest incredulity, "Why *are* you carrying that *bloody* catfish around?"

I sighed. I looked back at Chad, who beamed like a proud father, clasping his hands at his waist where his polo met his jeans, nodding at the fish. He didn't have to tell me what to do. The rules of my pledgewear had been made explicit the night before. I'd been taught a certain recitation.

"'The catfish is a slut, the catfish will sleep with anyone, would you like to sleep with the catfish?'" I recited as loud as I could without yelling. Contagious laughter, everyone except the prof and me. Stupid pledge, everyone else was thinking. By this point in the fall, for both fraternity and sorority pledges, stunts like these were commonplace. I half smirked, half frowned at Chad, adjusted my backpack, threw the giant catfish over my shoulder, and walked up the aisle as the prof stood dumbfounded behind the lectern.

"Excuse me?" he called out after me. I made for the exit. "*Excuse* me?"

CONFLICTED VIEWS

Another afternoon pretending to do homework.

Lounging on the futon, hanging out with Peterson, idly flipping through one of those yawn-inducing Brontë novels. We started talking about academics. We tried to imagine what our lives after Dartmouth would be like. It was easier for him than for me.

"I think I'm going to go into investment banking," he said. "And stick with econ, drop my biology double major." I eyed him over the top of my book. Finance had become a recurring theme for most of us in ΣAE; banking was glorified. From the older bros we learned about the contours that the average ΣAE bro's post-Dartmouth life took on— consulting, finance, Wall Street, or corporate law, each path in its own way serving the same master—and since twenty-five of the twenty-seven guys in our pledge class were economics majors, everyone was working to subsume the language and terminology of finance. Peterson was a quick study; I was a conscientious objector.

I stared at him from across the room; even having to hear about mergers and acquisitions for the seventh time might be more interesting than anything having to do with Jane Eyre and Mr. Rochester, I considered. "Following the money?"

"Yeah and no," he said. "It's not just the money."

"Come on, you're a genius, man. Banking is crooked. You could do anything you want—you could use your brilliance for the betterment of mankind in a lot of ways."

". . . and, of course, a high salary would give me a great deal of freedom in life."

"Or slavery, dude." I closed my book for good and geared up for a potentially all-day debate about the nature of capitalism. "Depending on how much you value freedom, or how you look at it." But then, before we could sophomorically hash out our views on the social contract, both of our e-mail accounts simultaneously pinged.

"Oh, no," Peterson groaned. "It's from Davis."

"Subject line?"

"Just the word *TONIGHT,* all caps."

"It's Wednesday, after all . . ." I yawned, trying not to get too rattled. Whatever it was going to be, I figured it couldn't be *that* bad.

"Don't bother getting up," Peterson replied, shaking his head and sighing. "All it says is that we don't have to worry about pouring beers before nine tonight. I wonder—" His face lit up. "I wonder if this means we won't have to drink?"

"Unlikely, Broseph, quite unlikely." I got up anyway

CONFESSIONS OF AN IVY LEAGUE FRAT BOY 91

and threw the book in my backpack, slid my computer off the desk, grabbed a fistful of papers and folders. "Gotta run. Just realized I'm late. Catch you later."

Peterson just stared at the wall, deep in thought.

Surreptitiously I tried to slide into Victorian Lit, but the professor was already tits-deep into her usual subdued yet long-winded monologue about Heathcliff, and the door was in the front of the classroom right by the lectern. The prof didn't stop talking, though, just glared in my general direction as I walked in. I felt eyes linger on my pledge jersey, purple and gold under my flannel jacket. Pretending to scan the room for a good seat, I automatically shuffled toward a vacant spot in the back row, nearly tripping on my unlaced boat shoes, which smelled terrible. I realized that in my haste I'd slipped on my "basement" boat shoes—the ones I'd worn to sink night—and not my clean, respectable "class" boat shoes.

I flipped open my Mac as the prof droned, "You see, in this scene, if you turn to page 287 of the novel, in this scene Catherine is clearly expressing her conflicted views about . . ."

Well, nothing new in the Facebook newsfeed. I clicked on BlitzMail. At least twenty black dots were lined down the left side of my screen, all about PIMPs and RACs. PIMPs were errands we had to run for the brothers; RACs, redeem-a-chugs, were basically the same thing except a little bit more time-consuming. More important, RACs were points we'd collect over pledge term to redeem against cups we'd have to drink on Hell Night—the culmination of our hazing, a night no brother would tell us anything about.

Like the end of history in some apocalyptic religion, Hell Night hovered at the conclusion of our semester like a fiery revelation of judgment. We'd either finally become brothers or, supposedly, have to redo pledge term in the winter. We believed that threat even though it clearly sounded ridiculous.

I scrolled through the blitzes.

Chad was PIMPing pledges out for two spicy chicken sandwiches, an iced tea, a ripe banana, and a can of Coke; Goodrich was offering one RAC for a pledge to play squash with him at three—but the pledge would only get the RAC if he won; Bradford was offering a RAC for pledges to come rearrange the woodpile.

Class ended. Went to get food at Collis. Ran into Blair at the salad bar, pretended not to see her, noticed that she looked good in leather boots and a Polo oxford, ate lunch, went home, fell asleep on the futon, dreamed about my parents, wondered if they still loved each other, wondered if Blair still loved me, slept through my subsequent class, watched the rest of the day evaporate, ate a dinner I assumed I'd have to regurgitate during pledge meetings, wondered if my life was normal, assumed none of our lives were normal, wondered if there was something wrong about this, reminded myself that we were totally sweet frat pledges at Dartmouth. Then Peterson and I left for the house at 8:50.

YOU HAVE LOST BEER PRIVILEGES

The columns and bricks and white trim around the campus buildings all took on a foreboding slant with the leaves fallen from the trees, each dorm and library like the citadel of some dead civilization. I guess that was the idea with the Ivy League after all—the schools were built like that, insinuated into traditions to which they had no actual connection, incoherently suggestive of the same rot that had crumbled Rome or something like that. I dug my fingers into the pockets of my flannel, found a hole I could fit my finger through. Wondered if that was the breach through which my self-respect had been escaping.

Peterson was talking about something. I realized that I'd been nodding the whole time but not actually listening. We stepped up to the house's yard—hedge funds, I realized, that was what he was talking about. Hedge funds.

"Mhm," I said as we made our way around the yard, past the woodpile, up to the back door's portico. "Yes, hedge funds."

Though we'd been best friends throughout freshman year, I began to realize that our paths were divergent. ΣAE was becoming all we had in common, but even that didn't appear substantial enough to maintain our relationship—I felt myself beginning to change. The first crack was things getting fucked up with Blair. The second crack was the hazing. The two things, though, felt related.

This isn't to say that I was anywhere close to exercising my conscience yet, but after a year at a school where everyone was constantly telling you how much better than everyone else in the world you were by nature of your attendance there, I was beginning to relocate my internal skepticism. Or maybe the propaganda was wearing off. Peterson punched in the door code, still waxing poetic about leveraged buyouts. Next to his face on one of the portico's white columns was a poorly proportioned black spray-painted penis. Things like that used to bother Peterson. He'd stopped noticing them. Once, I'd even offered Rector that I'd get a group of pledges to paint over the giant dick, but he never responded. Secretly, I think, bros liked it, in the sense that they imagined the house to be a temple of masculinity; phallic symbols fit.

"So there's a few differences here," he was saying. "There's private equity, there's hedge funds, there's M and A—"

I nodded. I tossed my flannel on one of the leather couches in the living room. We walked down the basement stairs. My boat shoe stuck to the last step and my foot slid out. Obliviously, Peterson continued talking as he passed into Varsity, as I hung back to peel my shoe from the grime.

"J. P. Morgan seems to be the most prestigious banking job, but there are all sorts of different directions you can take after that—"

"Uh-huh, yeah, cool." We walked past the pong tables in Varsity, stepping around puddles.

"Anyway, so, yeah, private equity seems to be one of the ultimate goals, you know, managing a large private sum of money and buying out different companies and changing the management structures to focus on profit and productivity—"

He went silent once we set foot in Beer Die, though, as if someone had ripped the wire out of his internal speaker. No beers were on the table. No evidence of what we'd be told to do. We took seats on the benches. I sat next to Blackstone and slipped him the grip; he smirked, fixing his sheening side part. Whereas in previous hazing sessions most of the pledges had been worried by the presence and egregious amount of beer, most guys seemed to now be even more worried by its absence.

"Any idea on the surprise tonight?" Blackstone asked.

"None whatsoever."

Carver walked in and sat in the throne. He was the quiet pledge trainer. This time, too, he didn't say anything. Just gazed down at all of us as we listened to an ominous rolling sound making its way through Varsity toward Beer Die, a rough plastic-and-metallic noise, something that didn't seem right, a sound that we could all sense had been sliced from its proper context. The door swung open. Davis dragged in a mop bucket. He didn't bother sitting down.

He looked pissed. Really pissed.

"Greetings, whaleshit," he blurted, red-faced, lifting his baseball cap up on his forehead and wiping his brow. "If you haven't heard the rumors going around the house this week, you're lucky. But I'm about to tell you now. The brotherhood is not happy at all with how this pledge term has been progressing. You have shown no discipline whatsoever—I have brothers blitzing me, informing me that, among other things, *you all* have been quite *lu-gu-bri-ous*. Delivery of PIMPs has been slow. Also, three of you were spotted wearing baseball caps with your formal wear this past Friday. That's not to continue." He stared down at the mop bucket. It was lined with a garbage bag and appeared to be full of water.

"Even worse," he continued, "some pledges have big mouths when it comes to what went down on sink night. Girlfriends and hookup sluts have been hearing about our traditions, and that is simply unacceptable. Whenever you are asked about pledge term, even if by a *dean,* for Christ's sake, you must say only, 'It's a good time.' Don't think that word doesn't get back to the two of us." He gestured at Carver, who nodded solemnly.

Eyes swiveled on me.

"One more thing," Davis growled. "You wouldn't call your country a *cunt,* so why do some of you find it acceptable to call your fraternity a *frat*? Act with some fucking class, whaleshit."

"We're going to instill some discipline in you tonight," Carver said blankly. "You have lost beer privileges for pledge meetings. You'll be drinking something a little bit stronger." He handed Douglas a sleeve of cups. "Pass two to each of your pledge brothers, whaleshit."

"What a suck-up," I whispered to Peterson.

"Come on, we're all in this together."

"Funny coming from you," I said, "the guy who tried to drop out after sink night."

Peterson glared back. At that point I was just barely beginning to see our roles reverse. Like if you were looking through a telescope at an eclipse or something, waiting for it to start because you knew it would, but you weren't sure if it had yet.

"Fill your cups, whaleshit," Carver said. Sullenly, we formed a line. As I approached the bucket and ducked down to dip one of my cups into its liquid, I got a strong whiff of vinegar. It wasn't vodka or Everclear. It was clear vinegar. We were going to chug vinegar.

"Now, I'm not sure how to do this fairly," Davis said. "Maybe two whaleshit at a time? Each chugging one cup? So everyone else gets to watch? And then we go round again for the second cup."

The universal expression in the room was a grimace. Stoically, we all watched the pledges ahead of us in the line, two by two, cycle through chugging the vinegar. Then it was my turn. I had to chug off against Blackstone. We linked arms like in a friendship beer. I felt my stomach turn inside out before the cup even touched my lips. I threw my head back and swallowed the vinegar—gagging, feeling something go out of my body and then come back as I stumbled toward one of the trash cans in the room and heaved, eyesight speckled with strange shapes, choking out boot that burned even worse on the way up. Then I took my seat on the benches. We cycled through for the second cup.

TRUE GENTLEMAN ONE

It was getting repetitive—all the instructions to show up wearing formal attire only to have to remove it, strip down, do something gross, do something unexpected. I wasn't surprised this night. It was a Tuesday, maybe a Thursday. What's the difference? I only remember because I had to call out of my rehearsal for Barbary Coast, the college's jazz ensemble, making up some unconvincing excuse about having the flu.

"Fever of one hundred and three," I claimed to my director. "Chills and nausea and complete body fatigue." It was funny because those words were all descriptive of the way most of the hazing made me feel—and in forgoing important parts of life for this hazing, I felt something worse: hollowness.

So anyway, yeah, we all had to strip down in the Libes again. Guys disappeared one by one. Then it was my turn.

Davis and Carter stood on either side of me, steadying my confused body as I waddled down the basement stairs toward a strobe light pulsing in JV. One moment all I could see was darkness. Then for a flash the room would light up—pong tables pushed against the wall, slats of wood paneling, a speaker hung in the corner. Couldn't make out much else. Beneath me the steps were slick with cold water. Beads of condensation wicked through my boxers, and when my bare feet slipped and my ass slid down a step or two, the pledge trainers had to right me by grabbing my shoulders. It was a slow decline into the dark, a real "abandon all hope, ye who enter here" kind of thing.

"Damnit, Regina," Davis hissed. "Waddle like a fucking pledge, would you?" At the bottom of the steps he gave me a little push. "Go on now. Go on. Waddle to the pool."

Not this, I thought. Not this again.

There it was—the kiddie pool, laid in front of a group of brothers. As I waddled toward it, I looked up for a moment and saw only two recognizable faces in the semicircle of brothers, Bradford and Rector. Between the flashes the other faces were shadowed, half-seen, abstruse.

"Climb into the pool, whaleshit." Rector's voice.

I couldn't tell what was in the plastic tub in front of me, but, using the pulsing light as my guide, I could in flashes see that it didn't look that grim. It didn't smell, either, which was a promising sign, though it did appear to be the same kiddie pool from sink night. Same cute little fish designs meant to appeal to toddlers. Same ridged, indented bottom.

Seeing it sober, I was reminded of a backyard kiddie pool I had as a kid—it had the exact same design. My parents used to fill it with lukewarm hose water, and my brother and I would swim around on summer days until we got bored, or until clouds obscured the sun, or until we realized that the water had dirtied with blades of grass and soil molding to thin mud. We spent a lot of time outside as kids. We didn't really go in the basement.

I forced the comforting memory from my mind. *Trust the brotherhood,* I told myself, though still making allowances for feeling violated by having a childhood memory, for the second time, desecrated.

I climbed over the side of the pool and landed on a sea of ice. The chunks and cubes pressed into my chest and their cold stung. Gasping, I arched my back, exhaled, tried to catch my breath, tried to find a position where I could lift my testicles off the ice lest they immediately contract gangrene and float away on the pool's miniature tide.

"Whaleshit, have you memorized 'The True Gentleman' yet?" one of the brothers boomed. Bradford.

Biting my lip against the cold, I tried to look up and find a face to politely address. "Yes, I think so—"

"Don't fucking speak!" another voice screeched. It sounded like Ripley's. *"Do NOT look up!"*

"Have you memorized it or not?"

"I—I have," I stammered.

"Good," Bradford said.

I stared down into the ice. Light from the strobe reflected from the cubes and hung in my retinas in sharp periodic flashes. My nostalgic thoughts couldn't be tuned out—my backyard as a kid, the garden hose, the lilac bush, the wooden picket fence, chipped paint flaking off the house, the water in the pool like dirty glass, our parents watching us. They were young and happy. Maybe we'd been their American Dream.

Pledging a frat, you almost forget that you've ever had parents; you almost forget there's once been another system of authority in your life. What would they think if they knew what I was going through to become a brother? All the report cards, all the music lessons, rides to lacrosse practice, the sacrifices they made, my dad's long hours, his endless commute—that this was what it had come down to, moments like this in kiddie pools, that that was some extra price of upward social mobility? Was this anyone's American Dream, anyone's undying old tradition?

"Can you begin it for us?" Rector asked.

"Put your head under!" The screeching voice was clearly Ripley's.

"Yeah, how about that," Rector agreed. "Put your fucking head under, whaleshit."

I took a deep breath and thrust my skull under the waterline. For a split second it felt okay. Everything was quiet underwater. When the cold began to sting too intensely, pins and needles and visions of the North Pole, I came up for air.

"Now, can you please begin 'The True Gentleman' for us?"

"Yes," I whispered.

"Well?"

I took a deep breath. "'The True Gentleman is the man whose conduct proceeds from goodwill and an acute sense of propriety and, and, whose self-control is equal'"—I accidentally lowered my back and a sharp chunk of ice singed my balls—"'is equal—to all—emergencies,'" I whispered, breathless.

"No!" the brothers screamed together.

"No stuttering!"

"Get the fuck out of the pool," Bradford muttered once the yelling had choked off. I lifted my balls off the ice and sidled over the edge of the pool amphibiously, letting loose a splash of water that rushed over the edge of the plastic and cascaded away in front of me. I slipped trying to regain my waddle pose and instinctively stood up—looked up and saw Davis standing with his arms flat across his black robe.

"Did I *tell* you to stand up?" he asked. "Fucking *waddle* right, whaleshit."

I waddled up the stairs, step by step, shivering, dick so shriveled it was nearly inverted into some vague protuberance my hands could barely identify.

"Keep your hands on your head like you're supposed to," Davis spat. He jostled my shoulder. "What are you doing . . . touching yourself?"

"No, I'm just making sure I didn't get frostbite on my—"

"Do not speak unless spoken to!"

The yelling was getting old. For the first time I ignored the trainers and felt justified in doing so, maybe even a little excited. Small acts of meaningless rebellion that could amount to little—I was starting to experiment with them. In the foyer I stood up straight, stretched my legs, rubbed my pecs to get the blood flowing again.

"I'm fucking freezing," I muttered.

"As you should be."

"Whatever, guys, seriously." It was the best rebellion I could manage, though a weak counterattack against everything they'd done to me and told me to do to myself so far.

"Go in the pool room." They walked away to get the next guy from the Libes. I cautiously opened the door.

The fireplace was lit, roaring heat, and Edwards, smiling, turned from throwing logs into it. "We're done educating you tonight." He threw me a towel.

REVOLUTIONARY WAR

Another Wednesday. For pledge meetings Davis and Carver said we should wear old clothes. The kind we wouldn't mind not seeing for a while, if ever again.

Peterson and I showed up in Beer Die. The floor was covered with a massive blue tarp, the kind of tarp you'd use to cover your roof if the shingles blew off in a hurricane. Except this tarp seemed destined to collect something instead of repel it.

"Dear God, no," Peterson muttered. He shuffled to a free spot on the bench, tarp crinkling under his Adidas.

Davis sauntered in. "Good evening, whaleshit!" Our heads swiveled to one side as we watched him make his way to the throne, thumbing a thick cigar, decked out in a pink-striped polo, crisp khakis, Sperrys, and a Stinson hat. He was upbeat, almost gregarious. Behind him trailed Carver, then a group of '11s lugging gallons of milk. Davis hopped up onto the throne. He eyed the jugs, then ran his eyes over the pledges arrayed on the benches, then nodded back to the jugs. The '11s slammed them down one by one on the table in the middle of the room that usually held hundreds of beers. There was one for every pledge.

"Woops." Davis giggled, covering his open mouth and

barely containing his smile. "Looks like we just gave away the *surprise*."

Peterson turned toward me. He was quivering. I kid you not—straight up quivering. But he seemed to be quivering for my sake, too. "The Milk Chug," he whispered in my ear.

Quickly, I petitioned Davis for soy milk, citing my fictional case of lactose intolerance. Surprisingly, he granted my request. Even more surprisingly, they actually had soy milk to begin with. They were often thoughtful and detail-oriented about their hazing.

"I assume you know the rules of this game," Davis intoned. "You will have twenty minutes to chug your gallons. Of course, I *also* assume that you *also* probably know that doing so is physically impossible without, shall we say, clearing your stomach a few times."

We grunted in acknowledgment.

"Carver and I will be offering RACs for every time you boot on one of your fellow pledges." Davis waved a pad of paper on which he'd ostensibly be keeping score.

I caught Pulaski's eye across the room. He smiled back deviously.

"We'll also be playing a little game called Revolutionary War. Quite frankly, the game is self-explanatory. Five pledges line up facing five other pledges. When I yell 'Fire!' one line of soldiers boots on the other. Vice versa when Carver yells 'Fire!' But if so much as a spot of regurgitation lands on one of us"—Davis gestured at his expensive clothes—"I'll rescind all the RACs you've earned tonight."

He looked at his watch. Then he screamed, *"GO!"*

We ripped the caps off our jugs. Peterson, Price, and I climbed onto the bench to get out of the line of fire. I started pouring the soy milk down my throat.

"Do you think you'll boot less with that stuff?" Price yelled in my face. He wiped dribbling milk from his lips. He was one of the frattier, more aggressive pledges—that spring he'd be kicked off the rugby team for, in the words of his coach, coming to morning practice "smelling like a fucking brewery."

I spouted a froth of boot before I could answer Price's question, but there didn't seem to be a correlation between the soy milk and the amount of vomit anyway. Only the consistency was different; it wasn't as thick as the traditional milk vomit. For the sake of comparison, from my vantage point I saw Pulaski, soaked with someone else's milky chunks, maniacally booting on Wilson, who stood in the opposing line, and noticed that their vomit seemed to be more gelatinous. Pulaski's curls were dripping with it.

When the twenty minutes had expired and we were all covered with each other's boot, Davis tossed one of the pledges a large garbage bag.

"Put all your clothes in there. Wilson, there are shovels in the houseman's closet. Go bury the bag in the backyard."

Price raised a flipper.

"Yes, whaleshit?"

"Um . . . like, why?"

The trainers laughed.

RECURRING DREAM

After everyone had left, Pulaski and I sat on the benches and smoked the cigarettes from our pledge packs. I don't know why we stayed in the room—it smelled like festering milk vomit—but maybe we stayed because everyone else had left. I was getting sick of them. Even Pulaski's earlier enthusiasm had deflated. Neither of us had anything left to say.

At some point we just nodded to each other and I left and walked back to Wheeler and took a long shower. Shampooed my hair a few times. Then I lay down on the futon. I guess I was going to do some homework, but, instead, I fell asleep and had a very particular dream, one of those dreams that takes real memories and juxtaposes them with fantasies that don't make sense.

It's the summer after freshman year. Everything's still perfect, everything's intact, and I'm in Nantucket with Blair, at one of her friends' houses, this other Tri-Delt, Zoe; maybe it's July. We're eating dinner on the porch. Everything I can see is lush. Green hedges. Lightning bugs. There's a pong table on the porch, too, on which Zoe has painted an argyle pattern, and beyond that there's a view of the water: a dock with a boat. We are all drinking gin. Blair smiles at me and we excuse ourselves and slip upstairs and I gaze out of one dormer window at the inground pool's aquamarine glow below us as we fuck on the edge of a wrought-iron bed. I look down and see a pink-and-green-patterned comforter beneath her body,

bikini tan lines on her skin—lines that seem to offer a geo-
metric proof that the good life is spread before me. The
whole dream is silent.

ONLY THROUGH YOUR GRACE AND GUIDANCE

Summer was long gone, though—it had faded like washed-
out salmon-pink shorts, and the Nantucket dream lingered
as a memory displaced by interceding events. The trees lining campus streets had lost their leaves; ΣAE's lawn had
browned under the fall's first frost. A barren seasonal depres-
sion settled over the campus, and with it came the feeling
that pledge term had somehow become normal, something
we didn't think about too much, something we just did because we had no other choice or had forgotten that a short
time earlier our lives had different, more forgiving dimensions.

I was at the house one afternoon. Maybe I was looking
for one of my grandfather's Paul Stuart ties I'd lost in the
last few weeks of constantly being told to strip down, or
maybe I was sitting around the Libes with Tim and Beaufort and Wallace pretending to do homework while just
trading drinking and fucking stories—I don't remember—
regardless, I stumbled into Davis in the upstairs bathroom.
He was washing his hands, and from an odd angle behind
him as I walked into the bathroom, I could see him staring
into his own eyes with piercing curiosity. Was he starting
to crack, too? What did it feel like to do these things to us?

I launched into the Pledge Trainer Salute—which I'd finally mastered—and, catching him off guard, caused him to recoil in abject fright as I screamed, *"Hail, great pledge trainer, sir, I bow down before you and wish you would go away for your presence is a constant reminder of how truly* low *I am and only through your grace and guidance can I come to deserve the name* whaleshit, *which you have humbly bestowed on—"*

"Enough, Lohse." He waved a hand at me and then dried it on his khakis, wincing in annoyance.

"—me and hopefully someday I will be worthy of—"

"Did you hear me, whaleshit? Christ Almighty, do I have a pounding headache. Would you shut the fuck up?"

"Sorry, Davis. Following orders."

He squinted at me, remembering something. "What are you doing tonight?"

"I don't know. Probably just hanging out. *It's a good time,*" I said from the urinal. I guess it hadn't actually been a good time so far, but what happens in the house stays in the house and Stockholm syndrome eventually clicks into place and what begins as "grim hazing" fluidly transforms into "a good time" when you're commanded to describe it that way. Eventually I even started to believe it myself, the further into the game I got. I wondered how much Davis believed it.

"There's going to be an event tonight. Small event, private. Come to Nine at exactly nine. Bring Beaufort." He smiled broadly while adjusting the collar on his polo. Then he walked out the door.

"Should I tell the other pledges?" I yelled after him, flushing the urinal with my elbow and wincing at the moist grime that had slimed onto my sweater sleeve.

"Absolutely not!" The door had already swung closed behind him.

SUPER SHOTS

At nine Beaufort and I knocked on the Room 9 door. Inside we heard muffled voices, inscrutable music playing. Maybe it was "Paparazzi," that Lady Gaga song—I heavily associate that song with what happened that night. Beaufort ran a hand through his hair, nonchalantly brushing it to one side, clarifying his side part, looking over at me with eyebrows raised expectantly, good-natured, maybe a little worried, but who could blame him. By then we were used to having our expectations toyed with.

Beaufort and I hadn't been friends before pledge term, and though we certainly weren't anything like best friends yet, we'd become closer than we'd expected to over the school year. He'd be one of the guys who'd appear to get through it all unscathed.

The corridor outside 8 and 9 was dark save for the word EXIT glowing red above the 8 door, its light reflecting from the glass of the composites hung down the hallway. This high in the house nothing smelled like piss and everything seemed to be in its right place—the third floor had an air of formality and exclusivity. I pounded on the door again. The music stopped, leaving only hushed voices suspended in stale air.

"Who is it?" Edwards called from inside the room.

"Lohse."

"And Beaufort." We smirked and gave each other the grip, the secret handshake, as a form of preemptive congratulations at being invited to hang out in 9.

"Who's that? Those don't sound like pledge names to me."

"Regina and Vincent Van Bro," I called back.

Edwards unbolted the door and motioned us inside. "At least you remember something from sink night."

"Not much, but it's something." I tried to seem earnest about it but wished I could've forgotten everything from that night anyway.

"It's a good time," Beaufort added. Then he saw Davis, paused, took a sharp breath as if he were about to launch into the salute—

"Naw, please." Davis sighed, leaning back in his desk chair and sliding his hands over his Dartmouth Indian T. The Indian mascot had become a relic of the past—it was no longer politically correct—and thus had become a symbol of conservative angst and rebellion at the college. It made sense for Davis to wear it. The T-shirt looked crisp, as if he'd ironed it, something he'd do.

"I'm off duty tonight, fellas." He crossed his arms, smirking. Edwards bolted the door behind us. I looked around. Ripley and three girls were there, too, watching us intently, watching us the way zoo animals watch tourists.

Nine was the most sought-after address in the house. It was the anchor of what the brotherhood called "the Ivory Tower" of Rooms 8 and 9, so named for its secluded location on the third floor of the house; 9 especially had supposedly elite connotations—it was the two-room double populated every year by two of the frat's top officers, and in this regard its history bordered on the sacred. Its walls displayed sentimental artifacts and bequests: a vintage squash racket hanging next to a hand-painted, wall-size mural of the Polo Ralph Lauren logo; a purple-and-gold ΣAE flag signed with all the names and years of summer presidents past; an antique J. Press sign with some ironic tagline about "goddamn preppies"—a bequest, we were told, dating back to the glorious Nixon years.

But the primary thing I noticed about the scene was the coffee table. On it was a still life of vices, the centerpiece being something special.

Cocaine.

It was piled on a framed photograph of New Hampshire's famous Old Man of the Mountain, the old man's stone face obscured by a pile of glittering powder, its whiteness fading into the deeper whiteness of clouds stuck in the sky.

Constellated around the frame were a bottle of Patrón, a whippitizer, and a massive bong. Davis was already sniffling. Edwards, who seemed too excited to sit down for long, was charmingly animated, a demonic glint in his eyes. Ripley was unshaven and looking particularly apathetic in baggy pajama pants and a pledge jersey no doubt purloined from one of the sophomores, leaning back in a swivel chair next to the three attractive upperclasswomen perched nonchalantly on the room's love seat.

Edwards watched the two of us stand awkwardly near the door—watched our eyes dart from the coke to the girls and back to the coke.

"You didn't know it was Edwards's birthday?" Davis asked. "You look like you've never seen *co-caine* before."

As I tried, and failed, to mimic the girls' insouciance, Edwards stood and offered Beaufort and me seats on the larger sofa. When we'd sat down, and the others were all safely making small talk and not noticing us, Beaufort whispered in my ear, "I've never done this before, man."

"Me neither," I replied softly, so that the older brothers wouldn't hear. Davis acquainted us with the ladies present; "I'd be remiss if I didn't," he said. Rachel, Liz, and Caroline, he informed us. I shook the latter's hand over the pile of blow. That was how we met; not super-romantically, and not a story we'd ever tell people when they asked, when we later started dating.

"So, like, super shots," Edwards goes. "In honor of my birthday, the rules are as follows: we go around in a circle, one line each, one bong hit each, one shot of Patrón each, one whippit each. Continue until we don't know what's happening."

Everyone looked a little scared.

As pledges, Beaufort and I didn't seem to have a choice in the matter, though no explicit commands were given to ingest the substances at hand. We took our cues from Davis and Edward; luckily, we had them to guide us. Was it hazing? The vibe of the gathering seemed to carry a note of prestige rather than dehumanization—a sense of elite induction into a privileged inner social circle within the fraternity's privileged inner social circle.

By this point, why would our older brothers even have to be explicit? We would probably have done anything they'd told us to do anyway.

"Allow me to put on the official playlist." Davis turned to his computer and restarted the music. Out bled the opening strains of Eric Clapton's "Cocaine."

"Ah," Davis sighed. He stepped into the inner bedroom and, a moment later, reappeared wearing a resplendent, but soiled, white dinner jacket.

"Whaleshit," he said to us, "this is the preeminent cocaine bequest, passed down in the house for nearly two decades." He unbuttoned the jacket and showed us the lines of names and class years with little ΦΑ's next to them climbing the inside of the blazer—up the lapels and into the collar, down the other side and around the breast pocket like linguistic ants.

Bequests are sacramental objects passed down from brother to brother over the generations. Real important stuff. Stuff like dirty clothes and drug paraphernalia.

"There are blue-collar drugs and white-collar drugs, whaleshit. Cocaine is the best white-collar drug there is. Remember that." Davis nodded down at the inside of the jacket. "See this?" He was pointing at a name; the hand-writing was flawless.

Skip Pendleton '09 ΦΑ.

"Skip gave this to me for a reason. On bid night, when everyone was out on Pebble smoking cigars, he brought me up to the Libes. I snorted my first line from 'The True Gentleman.'" Davis's eyes assumed the misty hue of nostalgia. "That was where it all began."

Not that there was much time to dwell over fraternal annals, though. Super shots started. Edwards handed Beaufort the rolled-up hundred. "Do the honors?"

"It's your birthday, Edwards," the pledge replied. Everyone was so polite. Up until that point I'd thought of cocaine as the drug of choice in dark alleys and crack mansions—who knew that some rich kid would give you a white jacket just for snorting the stuff? Didn't seem like a bad deal. That night I learned to associate drugs with secret house traditions, privilege, and attractive women, like three gleaming lines of blow cut before us, three arrows directing us to where the good life was hidden.

DAZED IN A YELLOW POLO

Coming out from under a whippit's cold gas, Clapton still blasting—*She don't lie, she don't lie, she don't lie, cocaine*—I eyed Caroline from across the druggy tableau. She was perched stoically on the edge of the love seat, waiting for Ripley to hand her the razor, pouring a trio of Patrón shots. Not in some party-girl way, though—diligently, handling the bottle with a childlike precision.

I felt naturally attracted to her. A poetic tension existed between her cherubic mien and the grace with which she wielded the coke razor, and though it sounds strange to say—as I watched her reverently cut the blow into thick, even rails—she had something wholesome about her.

I thought this over as I snorted the coke, hit the bong, drank the shots, leaned back into the couch as the whippits pulsed in my head, as my eyes focused and unfocused on the huge black Polo logo painted on the wall over Caroline's head. It had seemed to gain some sort of symbolic importance.

I figured I'd try to get to know her. I caught her looking at me curiously as I blew a cloud of smoke into the room and laughed about something Ripley said or didn't say. My nose hurt. My throat felt numb. Was it supposed to be like this, my body tight and metallic and focused? I didn't want to ask. For some reason someone handed me sunglasses. I put them on. Someone took a picture of Beaufort and me. In the picture I'm dazed in a yellow polo, he's got his arm around me, he's smiling past the camera, and to a casual observer the image might seem like the beginning of a great friendship.

THE WHITE MONKEY ON MY BACK

Ripley liked inside jokes.

After pledge meetings were through at ten every Wednesday, the pledges had to waddle out into Varsity and sit on the sticky, gross floor as the brothers performed their meetings rituals, though we weren't allowed to participate and weren't allowed to even look up unless someone was doming, so all we ever saw was people throwing up. The Wednesday after super shots, during brothers' meetings, Ripley awarded me a new piece of pledgewear, a life-size, white gorilla stuffed animal.

He'd won the thing with Jack at some state fair in Middle America the summer before they pledged. They'd named it Gabilaur after some girls, Gabi and Lauren, they'd met at the fair. The story was so cute and innocent and out of character, something I couldn't have imagined them doing, because I could only imagine them as bros.

Anyway, Ripley dragged Gabilaur into Varsity and got up on the benches and said, "This week I am awarding Gabilaur to Lohse. He's to carry it around with him all day and night and protect it any cost from being stolen. Let's just say it's the eight-hundred-pound white gorilla in the room, the problem that everyone in the house knows about but won't acknowledge."

He winked at me. No one got the joke except Davis and Edwards and Beaufort, even though everyone pretended to, fake laughter spilling out between teeth like regurgitated beer foam. I had to drag that gorilla everywhere for a week—my prize for super shots. I'd find out later that that night had also been the first time Ripley had ever done blow, which surprised me, so I guess his assigning me Gabilaur had some kind of emotional significance. Like, I guess it was something over which we were supposed to bond as brothers.

If anyone asked me about Gabilaur, even a professor, I was instructed to explain that I had a white monkey on my back, a white monkey who convinced me to do things I probably didn't want to do.

TRUE GENTLEMAN TWO

Pledges who hadn't passed the earlier "True Gentleman" challenge in the pool of ice—most of us—were graciously granted another opportunity to recite the creed. I was terrified of that opportunity. It had to be worse, I figured.

We were called one by one into the Libes one night. The lights were off. As I walked into the room and one of the trainers pushed the door closed behind me, I noticed a group of shadowy forms standing in the U-shape the mahogany tables made around the golden frat letters in the carpeting.

"Come here, whaleshit," one bro beckoned.

More haunted-house shit, I figured. Like, just give me the booze to chug and let's get this over with.

"Closer," another one said. I buttoned and unbuttoned my blazer and took another pace toward them.

"Closer." They were only a pace and a half away. I realized they were trying to trick me into stepping on the letters so they could fail me. That's another rule. Don't step on the fucking letters.

My eyes adjusted to the darkness. I peered at the brothers. They were wearing the house's ritual robes. Bradford, Rector, Jack, Ripley—the usual suspects.

"We're giving you another chance," Rector said. "Recite 'The True Gentleman' in the time it times this match to burn."

Without warning he slid a matchbox out from the sleeve of his robe and struck a match. There didn't seem to be any tricks or surprises. Staring into the burning head of the match, I fired off the recitation:

"'The True Gentleman is the man whose conduct proceeds from goodwill and an acute sense of propriety, and whose self-control is equal to all emergencies; who does not make the poor man conscious of his poverty, the obscure man of his obscurity, or any man of his inferiority or deformity; who is himself humbled if necessity compels him to humble another; who does not flatter wealth, cringe before power, or boast of his own possessions or achievements; who speaks with frankness but always with sincerity and sympathy; whose deed follows his word; who thinks of the rights and feelings of others, rather than—'"

Almost to the end, I coughed and lost my concentration. Before I could even try to regain my flow, the bros screamed, *"No!"* as loud as they could. I turned and walked out of the room. Game over. Davis caught me on the third-floor landing.

"Looks like you'll be enjoying True Gentleman Three with us, pal."

"When's that going to be?"

"Later tonight."

"Davis, I told you that I have a rehearsal tonight. I'm already going to be late as it is. Our concert is coming up."

He rubbed his fists on his eyes in the mock gesture of an infant bawling. "Excuses, excuses, excuses. Go for an hour. Come back. I'm sure your director will understand that you have more important things going on in your life right now." Then he thought for a second. "And it's not like you have a choice anyway."

TRUE GENTLEMAN THREE

I rushed back to the house an hour later, but when I jogged up to the Libes, I found no sign of the pledges or pledge trainers there. On the second-floor landing I ran into Jack.

He was trying to restrain the frat's obese Labrador, Fitz, from eating a pile of stale nacho chips, cheese sauce, and uneaten pizza that littered the carpeting in front of the bathroom door.

"Fat, stupid dog," he was muttering. "Ugly piece of shit."

"Hey . . . Jack?"

He looked up at me, surprised. "Did you pass TG2?"

Fitz slipped out of his grasp and dug his snout into a plastic clamshell smeared with marinara and cold french fries.

"No, wait, you definitely didn't."

"Yeah, but—"

"Aren't you supposed to be in the Cave, whaleshit? What the hell are you doing up here? The pledges just did a little digging in the backyard, and then Davis and Carver locked them in the Cave."

Digging? Then I remembered what had been buried in the backyard.

"That's what I was going to ask. Where am I supposed to go? I texted Davis but he didn't respond."

"The Cave, like I just said. Go now."

The Cave was a crawl space under the basement stairs with a dwarf-size, padlocked wooden door; move the coffin and there it was. I'd thought its only real purpose was storage, as the place where pledges who had the recycling cleanup would store bundles of old cardboard beer boxes until recycling day, or the place where brothers would hide stolen traffic cones, or of course the place where some pledges had gotten blow jobs during Basement Appreciation Night, but I didn't realize the cave functioned as a hazing space; its cramped dimensions and lack of windows seemed great for that.

I jogged down both flights of stairs to the basement and ran straight into Carver. Over his shoulder Davis was locking the padlock on the Cave door. The song "Mahna Mahna" from *The Muppet Show* looped over the basement speakers—sickly annoying scatting over repetitive chord changes and a cloying jazz beat.

"Whaleshit!" Carver eyed me contemptuously. He held up his hand. "Davis, wait."

"Lohse," Davis said, turning up from the door. "You're lucky there aren't any more clothes from milk meetings for you to wear. Get in the Cave. Your pledge brothers will explain the task at hand." He opened the door and stuck in his head. "Make room for one more!"

I crouched into the crawl space. Unsurprisingly, it smelled fucking rancid—the vomit-stained clothes must have acquired some exotic strains of bacteria while buried in the backyard, or maybe some sort of feculent multicellular organism had begun to evolve in the garbage bag. I unbuttoned my collar, loosened my tie. Inside the Cave were the eight other pledges who'd all failed both TG1 and TG2. They were all wearing the clothes dug up from the backyard—each kid swathed in multiple boot-stained shirts and gym shorts. Utter foulness, in my face, the miasma of rotten milk seeping into my lungs and my brain and probably blackening my soul a little bit more. Gibbons sat in one corner clutching a roll of toilet paper. Douglas cupped the flame of a small candle next to him.

"Better late than never," Price growled, shifting to give

me space to crouch. Davis closed the door behind us. The padlock clicked into place.

"What are we supposed to be doing?" I asked, holding my breath. I found a tiny spot to fold myself into but accidentally bumped into Douglas. The flame flickered behind his cupped hand.

"Relax," Douglas hissed. "Gibbons needs this light to see."

"We have to write out 'The True Gentleman,'" Blackstone offered "One letter or one punctuation mark per toilet-paper square."

"Get it wrong and we have to start again. No one leaves until we get it right," Douglas added.

"Sucks to suck," Price said.

Everyone turned to him. *"Shut the fuck up!"*

An hour ticked by interminably. I couldn't feel my feet anymore. The smell in the cave continuously made me gag. When he was done, Gibbons passed the roll around for other pledges to check. "Mahna Mahna" still looped through the speakers. A pledge banged on the Cave door. I heard the padlock click open.

Davis's head appeared in the door's crack. "Well?"

"Check it," Gibbons said.

I peered out the door. Davis read the roll square by square. Then he tore it up and threw the pieces onto the floor. My heart sank. In the other corner of the cave Pulaski gasped.

"Good job, whaleshit," Davis said.

"You're not going to check the whole thing?" someone asked.

"Hell no. I don't care if you guys got it right or not. That's not the point."

TAKE A BEER AND MAKE IT DISAPPEAR

Our pledge class posed for a picture in Varsity one night. We linked arms behind two pushed-together pong tables on which 550 cups of beer had meticulously been arranged. Behind us was the basement's boarded-up, spray-painted fireplace.

We'd agreed that it was important to capture the moment; after we started drinking the beers and booting, we'd be too drunk for a good picture. Plus, no one was allowed to take any pictures while hazing was taking place. That would've been a huge liability.

I had to wear a red women's peacoat for the picture. It was my pledgewear from the Wednesday before. It was so tight that my arms had ripped through the sleeves so much that I had to tear them off, something I felt kind of bad about since the jacket had probably belonged to some nice, drunk girl who'd lost it at the house during some party. After the picture we started chugging. Davis always had good sayings about hazing us and about how we could be good pledges. He'd always say, "Take a beer and make it disappear."

Even though the first event of the night, we'd been

told, was called Brothers' Meetings, I was surprised when I actually saw brothers descend to the basement, don pledge jerseys, and join us. They were excited. Already nostalgic for their days as hazing victims, they joined us in quick sixing, boat racing, and doming to Davis's and Carver's orders. We displayed all of the drinking techniques we'd been learning over the term. Frankly, we'd made a lot of progress. We made a lot of beers disappear. Even Peterson could chug like a pro.

WHEEL OF MISFORTUNE

After we'd crushed all 550 cups, Davis told us that we were going to "play a little game." He walked into JV and returned with a Frisbee haphazardly attached to the end of a stick. Affixed to the Frisbee were little numbered slips of paper.

The brothers smirked.

"This," he proclaimed, "is the Wheel of Misfortune." He climbed up on the benches and removed a crumpled piece of paper from his pocket. "Round and round it goes, which misfortune it lands on, you'll soon know." He looked at his paper. "Let's start with Whaleshit Rafiki and Whaleshit Zulu."

Two African American pledges, Larry and Nelson, stepped up to Davis and spun the Frisbee. Nelson's spin landed on number fourteen.

"Oh, *no,*" the brothers yelled, "not number *fourteen*!"

Larry's spin landed on eight.

"Oh, *no*," the brothers yelled, "not number *eight!*"

Davis ripped the little slips of paper off the wheel and pretended to look at their backs while also furtively checking his own paper.

"What a coincidence!" he called out. "You two whaleshit will be sharing a Wheel of Misfortune. For your challenge, Larry will be dressing up as a predatory lion and Nelson as safari prey. You will be performing and videotaping a hunting scene on the college Green in full costume, and then presenting your video on Skit Night."

A few pledges later Peterson whispered to Pulaski and me, "Dude, I think this is already preassigned. I don't think the spins matter."

"No, really?" Pulaski said.

Then Peterson was summoned up to spin.

"Whaleshit Lingonberry!" Davis called out. Peterson's pledge name had come from the "small fruit" lineage of brothers, a tradition of exotic berry pledges who were supposedly named on account of their small testicles.

"Spin the Wheel of Misfortune!"

His spin landed on number two.

"Oh, *no*," the bros yelled again, "dreaded number *two!*"

"Lingonberry, for your Wheel of Misfortune, you will be waxing all of Schultz's chest and back hair in a full performance for the brotherhood."

Peterson cringed and returned to the scrum of pledges.

I got called up. I was assigned to make a documentary

on the inhabitants of the Ivory Tower, to be presented at Skit Night.

Pulaski was to make a documentary on the inhabitants of the Ghetto, predominantly Rooms 1 and 2.

One of the Hispanic pledges had to get a push mower and mow the Green in a sombrero. Filmed, of course.

One of the Jewish pledges had to be Ripley's Jewish mother for a week, including waking him up daily, forcing him to shower, and monitoring his homework completion. All nearly impossible tasks.

One of the rich pledges had to cater breakfast for the brothers every morning for the coming week. The list went on. We were given a week to prepare our projects. Skit Night was, apparently, a big deal.

"These movies better be fucking funny," Jack advised Pulaski and me as we shuffled out the back door later that night. It was windy outside. The trees had gone completely skeletal. The next day we rented video equipment from the library; I'd blow off a Victorian Lit paper to focus on getting footage. Studying, writing solid papers, doing all my readings, and attending every class in a wakeful state of mind—those were all luxuries I couldn't afford anymore. Compared to pledge term, work didn't matter. So I basically just didn't do it anymore. Who had any time or sobriety?

WE GET ACCUSED SOMETIMES OF LEADING THESE DOUBLE LIVES

"The idea you want to aim for," Edwards told me when I met with him in 9 to plan my documentary, "is the eliteness of the Ivory Tower and how Rector is not a part of it." He giggled. "Think anti–Rector propaganda."

I wondered if it was a good idea to needle Rector by making him the punch line of my film—he always seemed a little unhinged, a little unpredictable, and dangerously self-righteous.

Yeah, maybe I shouldn't needle him, I thought.

Then I thought, well, an assignment is an assignment. I'd do exactly what Edwards told me to do since he was Davis's best friend and Davis was, to the pledges, the supreme arbiter of ΣAE's identity. By extension, that included our burgeoning identities, too, our fratty sense of justice and amorality.

Rector also lived on the third floor, but in a windowless closet of a single wedged between the Libes and 8 that was outside of the area designated the Ivory Tower. He generally kept to himself. Davis and Edwards and the two other brothers who lived in 8 would stop at nothing to exclude him from whatever they were doing—mostly because he was an asshole, so no one felt bad for him. He was especially cruel to the pledges; I considered the film a chance to get even with him for making my best friend chug until, so Pulaski had claimed, he vomited blood.

Shooting footage, I spent nights stalking Davis and Edwards and the other Tower members around the house. Then, the afternoon of Skit Night, hours before we were supposed to present our projects, Pulaski and I rushed to the library to finally edit our films—his documentary about the Ghetto had mostly entailed getting stoned with Ripley.

Staring at an iMac in the library's media center, Final Cut open, I felt a burst of anxiety. There wasn't much time left. I had no clue how I'd splice together all of my footage. Pulaski and I were taking this way more seriously than our homework.

I took a deep breath and plugged in the video camera.

Made a title page. That was easy. Then I began with a shot of Rector knocking on the Ivory Tower door, the door to the 8 and 9 hallway, and Edwards on the other side yelling, *"What's the password!"*

Decent shot. Would definitely meet Edwards's injunction about the slant of the project, the whole Rector-being-an-outsider thing.

Was this a bad idea? I wondered again.

No time to think. Too late. *Make it funny.*

Then I cut to an interview with Davis about what the Ivory Tower meant to him. Like an effete diva, he refused to get out of bed for the taping. I sat on a chair across from his bunk.

"I feel like," he was saying, "the biggest things that separate Tower members from the outsiders, as one may choose to phrase them, is really more of a mind-set, and a spirit, and a, um, psyche, than it is a room address. Because there are days when I wake up and I am, frankly, an outsider to the community." He rustled his head on the pillow. He was still wearing a baseball cap. "There are days when I wake up and I'm not in step with the goals of what this community values and what we hold dear—"

Then I cut to a grainy shot of Davis stoned on one of the Room 9 couches, giggling. Some random person out of the shot asked him, "What are you high off of, just weed?"

"No," he giggled. Then he said, "Yeah."

Community values—what we hold dear. Perfect.

Then I cut to a shot of Rector sitting in his cramped room. He'd painted the walls orange when he'd moved in because, he'd claimed, the color caused extreme sexual arousal in women.

"The Ivory Tower is my home," he said, smiling stupidly.

Pushing onward, I cut to an interview I'd taped with Pulaski. In the shot he was sitting on the throne in the Beer Die room. Over his head in green spray paint were the words THE ACCUSED.

"The Ivory Tower means a lot to me," video Pulaski was saying. I nudged real Pulaski at the computer cubicle next to me.

"Check it out, man, I'm putting your interview in the film."

He slid his rolling chair over toward me. "No face time is bad face time," he said. I unpaused Final Cut. Video Pulaski was saying, "It represents the sort of selectivity, the exclusivity, the sort of two-tiered system that we like to see at Ivy League institutions. We like to have separation between those who are *included*"—he gestured to one side—"and those who are *excluded*"—he gestured to the other.

"Put it in." He rolled back to his iMac.

I moved some of my footage around and then cut to a brief clip of Rector from the orange room again, saying, "I'm serving the entire community of the Ivory Tower."

I dragged some text to the bottom: *Rector: Servant of the Ivory Tower by His Own Admission.* Then I cut to my interview with Harrison Beardsley, resident of Room 8, the house's "eminent alumni coordinator." *Eminent Alumni Coordinator Harrison Beardsley Discusses Security Measures to Keep Rector Out.*

"So, the Tower itself," Beardsley was saying, "is kind of blocked off to outsiders, to intruders, as I like to call them. Notice how we have a door, you know, that remains mostly closed throughout the, you know, the day and nighttime here in our house. And we, I mean, we interact with outsiders, but they have to come to us. You never see the Ivory Tower members going down to the second floor and hanging out there."

To get that point across, I cut to a short clip of Ripley hanging out in 9, disheveled, wearing only a Ralph Lauren T and boxer briefs, nodding at the bong.

"Can I have another hit? How we doin' here?" he grunted.

"I hear Ripley's voice," real Pulaski said from his cubicle. "You probably want to put on headphones, dude. I've got some good footage of Ripley, too. All we did was get stoned and eat pizza. Check it out."

I rolled over to Pulaski's cubicle. My eyes were graced with a clip of Ripley sucking a monstrous hit from the Room 2 bong and then pulling his pants down to show the camera his anus.

"Sweet Jesus, Pulaski, you can't be editing this footage in the library. That's Ripley's anus."

Pulaski looked over his shoulder. "No one's gonna see, don't worry. And I obviously don't have Final Cut on my computer, so where else am I gonna do this?"

"Somewhere that's, like, not the library."

"We're coming down on the final hour before showtime. I have no choice, dude."

"What happens in the house . . ."

I rolled back to my cubicle, glanced at the clock, furiously dragged random scenes into my reel.

Then it was back to a cut from my interview with Davis: "One of the things that really bothers me about my place in the community is that we get accused sometimes of leading these double lives, or leading these secret lives of luxury." So I cut to a scene of a restaurant in Lebanon, New Hampshire, we'd gone to a few days before—a pricey dinner for all the Ivory Tower residents, plus me, the embed, paid for by the house.

Then back to Rector to close the whole thing out: "I chose this specific room on the outskirts of the Ivory Tower because I feel like the life inside the gated community is too decadent and, uh, a little too rich for my style. I prefer the austerity of a brightly colored, sunshiny room, where I don't have the outside world peering in through my window to bother me." The room didn't have a window anyway. Just a Coors Light mirror on the ceiling over his mattress.

Pulaski and I ran out of time. We sprinted over to the house and presented our hastily edited documentaries. Rector didn't like mine.

CHEESEBURGER IN PARADISE

One classic recurring hazing event was the Feat of Strength, a competitive eating challenge. Performing in small groups, every pledge had to complete a feat; the challenges became more demanding as the term progressed.

Peterson had completed his early in the term with the first group. Their challenge had been the easiest: canned peaches. Since not much vomit was involved—just four pledges and a stack of school-cafeteria-grade canned peaches that had to disappear in twenty minutes—the performance wasn't given for the entire brotherhood, but mostly for just a group of young alumni who'd come up to party over the big weekend.

"Outside of the Dartmouth bubble," one the alums said gleefully, smiling wide, teeth gleaming iridescently white, "you never get to see people do gross shit. So I'm really enjoying this."

"Yeah, me, too," another alum giggled, still in his suit from work.

I'd stuck my head in the room to see what was up and discovered Peterson, for some sick reason, laughing earnestly and genuinely enjoying eating the never-ending cans of fruit. Syrup smeared over his lips, he dug his hands directly into the cans and shoveled handfuls of peaches into his mouth. He was warming up to frat life.

I didn't know what my feat of strength would be. All I knew was that it would be harder than Peterson's, probably slightly crazier—and when I got a blitz from Davis reading,

"Eight o'clock, no excuses for tardiness, be prepared to perform for the entire brotherhood," or something along those lines, fear overtook me. The message was addressed to seven other pledges as well. It was going to be a "double feature," Davis wrote.

I punched in the back-door code—the year ΣAE was founded, 1856—and sprinted up the back steps. Loud voices in the living room. All the couches had been moved again so that they faced one wall. In front of them was a large wooden table on which were stacked maybe a dozen plastic takeout containers of double cheeseburgers and fries, along with a line of soda cups in front of them. All the food was slick with a Red Sea of hot sauce.

"You are fucking *late,* whaleshit!" Davis yelled over the voices of the brothers gathering on the couches to watch.

"Hail, great pledge trainer, sir, I bow down—"

"Take your place, whaleshit. And quick. The clock is about to start." Davis looked at his watch. "Brothers, I now present to you the final Feat of Strength: the infamous double-burger, special-double feature. Time starts now. Music?"

Chad spun some knobs and pressed a few buttons on the living-room stereo, and the Jimmy Buffett song "Cheeseburger in Paradise" blasted out of the room's speakers. The song looped straight through for twenty minutes while I stuffed my face until the hot sauce inflamed my lips so much I couldn't feel anything I was eating. Reached for one of the drink cups. Watching me, the brothers laughed.

I bit the straw and took a big sip and realized that the cups weren't soda; they were vinegar, and I choked, and then the vomiting began, the upward rise of my boot colliding with the next burger I was forcing into my throat, and then everything began to taste the same.

HE WAS HUNGRY

Pledge term was winding down. That meant a few things. Primarily, it meant that our hazing got gradually worse until it was supposed to peak on Hell Night—more PIMPs, more RACs, more chugging, more yelling and theatrics. It also meant formal season.

Two sorority formals fell on the same night that fall, a night that, coincidentally, was a Wednesday. To further the coincidence, Davis was invited to one of them and Carver was invited to the other—a pledge term scheduling conflict of epic proportions. So, for one night only, Buzzby and Ripley were appointed guest pledge trainers. Pretty much a bad idea.

Between the two formals, only a handful of pledges were left for meetings anyway—nine or ten out of our group of twenty-seven. Buzzby and Ripley were given free rein to haze them in whatever way they deemed fit.

Luckily, Jackie Campbell invited me to AΞΔ's formal. I walked over to the sorority with the other pledges who'd been invited, and the whole time Douglas talked about how excited he would be to finally be a real bro come winter.

"Think about all the rights and privileges," he said, hands stuck in his blazer pockets. "Rights and privileges," he repeated as we walked past the Sphinx. "Rights—and—*privileges.*"

"Think about hazing next year's pledges," Gibbons pointed out.

"Just think about all the possibilities . . ."

ΑΞΔ had rented some bed-and-breakfast for the formal. Cash bar, an undercover cop arresting obviously drunk kids, buffet, dance floor, the usual things we'd come to expect. My table was populated solely by ΣAEs I didn't like—Gibbons, Douglas, Carver, and Bradford—and their dates.

"Carver, why won't you *dance?*" some pale girl in a frilly dress kept asking him. "Why *won't* you?"

"Not drunk enough," Carver grunted.

When the spectacle was over, the bus dropped us off back at ΑΞΔ. Girls put their heels back on. I walked back to ΣAE alone, and though I'm not completely certain as to the exact logistics of what happened next, it went something like this:

I walked down the basement stairs into JV.

Peterson, standing by himself near the coffin, looked glum. "Lohse, you were so lucky to get invited to ΑΞΔ's formal."

"That *is* something you would say."

Peterson sighed. "You don't even understand."

Pulaski walked over toward us. He was drunk, slumped

over, dragging a case of beer behind him the same way cavemen drag their clubs. His face, though, was animated—eyes manic, lips spread wide. He handed me two dented cans of beer and said, "Little Peterson didn't like pledge meetings tonight."

I always got the sense that something gross or extreme had just occurred if Peterson was downtrodden and Pulaski was acting weirdly excited.

I cracked open the two cans, feeling the cold metal of the pop top under my thumbnail. "Well, how was it?" I put the cans down on an adjacent pong table and loosened my tie.

Peterson stuttered, "The vo—vo—"

Pulaski grinned stupidly. "The *vomelette*."

"What the fuck?" I said.

Peterson: "Buzzby and Ripley are batshit crazy. Crazy. Just, like, insane."

Me: "Story. At now."

Pulaski: "I booted into a pan and then Ripley cracked eggs over it and added cheese and cooked it."

"And then . . . ?" I barely believed it. I assumed they were just trying to mess with me. But, I knew, Peterson's traumatized eyes couldn't be faked.

Pulaski: "We ate it."

Peterson: "Actually, Pulaski ate most of it."

Pulaski: "I was hungry."

Me: "What the fuck?"

Then they described what else they'd each had to do—something called ass beers. One pledge lying on the ground, one pledge squatting over his face with no pants on, in the sixty-nine position, I guess. Someone would pour a beer down the upper pledge's bare ass crack and the lower pledge would drink it as it cascaded down the former's anus.

I wasn't sure whether to be more creeped out that a group of my pledge brothers had performed these acts or that Pulaski had seemed to enjoy them. During pledging, I realized, sanity was entirely relative. Beyond all the alcohol-poisoning-level drunkenness was a whole other level of absurdity, with one of my friends drinking a beer poured down some other dude's ass crack, and my best friend explaining his digestion of vomit as a function of his appetite.

PRICE SAID NONCHALANTLY

When Peterson and I walked into Beer Die as usual, some other Wednesday at nine, 255 beers poured, all that, nothing was going on. We sat down on the benches with the other pledges. They were confused. I assumed that some vile surprise was waiting, some big reveal. How could things have gotten worse, though? What bodily fluids were left?

Blackstone would know—he always seemed to know more than you did, so I got up and walked over toward his corner of the benches. He was sitting with Wilson near Beer Die's coffin. I always thought it was kind of creepy, too, that the frat didn't have one but two coffins proudly displayed in the basement. Or maybe it wasn't. Maybe it made sense. The frat was a place where a lot of good things came to die.

"Thoughts, predictions, prophecies?" I asked.

Blackstone brushed a shock of hair behind his ear, ran a finger over one of his patrician cheekbones. "Not sure." Baffled, he made a face as if trying to augur the weather or something. "On one hand, the beers are poured. On the other, Davis and Carver are MIA."

Just as he said that, Davis walked into the room, looking pained, face contorted like a plastic mask. "Pledge meetings are canceled. Go home."

Everyone: "?"

"Do I have to shout at you?" He sighed. "Go home. I mean, I guess if you want to play pong you can with these two hundred and fifty beers or whatever, they don't have to be wasted, but other than that, go the fuck home. Except . . ." He read off some names. Mine wasn't one of them.

"The pledges I just named come up to Nine with me. We have to talk." He walked out. The pledges followed him.

"Dude, that was weird," Peterson said.

I grabbed as many cups of beers as I could carry. I nodded at Price and Pulaski. "Pong?"

Them: "Yup."

We commandeered a table in JV. As we racked up the game, lining seven cups of beer per side into shrub formations, Price said nonchalantly, "Yo, you know we were supposed to have something called diaper meetings tonight?"

"What?" I asked.

"Something about booting into diapers and then wearing them. I don't know, ask the '11s." Price rolled a pong ball on the table, bored, then lit a cigarette. Someone turned on the basement speakers. Music.

INVESTIGATION

Not sure how long we played, but I guess we drank a lot.

Nights ran together. My Dartmouth career seems to me like one long Wednesday night when the sun never rose—when you spend the better part of your formative years underground, everything begins to feel like one endless night.

At some point, all the brothers and pledges were summoned to the living room. Goodrich had bad news.

We were having a meeting, a serious meeting, not one where we booted everywhere. I stood near the fireplace and watched the thoughtful looks on the faces of the older brothers sitting on the couches. Everyone looked so sincerely contemplative.

". . . because," Goodrich was saying, "Judicial Affairs is investigating us for hazing violations."

"Come again?" someone called out.

"We're being investigated. For hazing."

Everyone started talking at once. Voices overrode each other and no one was forceful enough to quiet them. That was normally Davis's job, but he was too distraught to speak.

After the din had died down, the brothers instinctually

organized themselves into a strategy discussion, as if we were all prepping together for a corporate consulting interview. Goodrich related that the pledges that Davis had named earlier were being called in for interrogation interviews the following morning with the Administrator, who specialized in disciplinary hearings.

"They clearly know a fair amount about the scheduling of our hazing events if they know enough to call in pledges for a nine A.M. meeting on a Thursday," one brother pointed out.

"True." Goodrich nodded. "They have substantial information, clearly."

"The pledges should look good for this shit," another added. "Like, khakis, shirt, tie, blazer, that kind of shit. Formal wear. Gotta look upright and respectable."

"Let's do that." Goodrich seemed to be taking mental notes.

"Brothers should be sent to wake them up, too. To make sure no one is late," the same guy added.

"Got it." Goodrich was a take-charge CEO. If a major corporation is ever under his control, I can guarantee its shareholders that it will be run efficiently. That's my solid-gold guarantee. However, there will probably be a lot of dissembling, just FYI, because that's exactly what we were doing—organizing an elaborate system of lies to fool the Administrator, like a bank trying to throw off meddling regulators.

"Do we know what specific allegations are being made against us?" another asked.

Goodrich took a deep breath. "Not completely sure, but

apparently it has something to do with milk meetings," he sighed.

Snickers echoed off the room's wood-paneled walls. Milk meetings were fairly average in terms of the degree to which they had violated the college's hazing policies, so apparently they didn't know *all* that much. Vinegar and vomelettes were worse as far as I was concerned—not to mention the kiddie pool.

"The main argument needs to be that the 'Milk Chug'"—the brother speaking even made finger quotes— "was a completely 'optional bonding experience' that certain pledges elected to undertake of their own 'volition.'" Come to think of it, that guy would later go to law school.

"Exactly."

"That should be our main argument."

"Good idea, bro."

"Yeah, that should do it."

"Done and done."

It was fascinating to watch how the brotherhood parsed its reaction to being under serious investigation. The house faced an existential threat. That night I realized that the frat brothers were far more clever than the administration, not to mention many, many steps ahead—a realization that would stick with me years later.

The pledges lied admirably in their interviews. The investigation was dropped. As one bro later told *Rolling Stone,* "We win."

HELL NIGHT

Hell Night was supposed to be our final night of hazing, the culmination of our reeducation, our grand finale of alcohol and degradation and bodily fluids—our worst nightmare made real—but, because of the investigation, it was dry. No booze. Basically just yelling, psychological mind games, recitation of "The True Gentleman," and one station in 8 where Xavier, the house's token muscular dude, made us do push-ups and squats.

The night began with each pledge receiving a personalized blitz from one of the pledge trainers with specifically timed instructions. Mine said I had to put on formal attire and go to Baker Library and find, in the grandiose, wood-paneled Tower Room, an old book called, like, *The Adventures of Sir Roger Waverley* or something like that, where on page 57 I'd learn what to do next. All the secrecy made you feel important, as if you were on some kind of quest. This kind of shit appeals to nineteen-year-old boys.

As I walked through the Tower Room in khakis and a blazer and tie and pocket square, gliding past the long library tables, girls stared up at me from books laid out under green reading lamps, books that might once have held secret, important initiation instructions.

Finding *The Adventures of Sir Roger Waverley,* I flipped through its musty pages to 57. A note said to go to the Robert Frost statue. Jogging out of the library, I made my way down North College Street and up the trail behind Dragon, a secret-society clubhouse, to where Frost—a guy who had, supposedly, been kicked out of Dartmouth for hazing—sat bronzed and frozen in time at the top of a ridge overlooking the school's amphitheater, the BEMA.

Larry and two other pledges arrived at exactly the same time. Coming up through the autumnal gloom of the trail behind us was Schultz, mysterious in a black overcoat. He drilled us on "The True Gentleman." Then he led us back to the house, where Hell Night anticlimaxed. Nothing was all that intense besides the Room 2 "Would you rather . . . ?" station, where a bro grilled us on a series of choices ending in "Would you rather kiss one of your pledge bros or lick cheese off Ripley's balls?"

Larry said he'd rather kiss a dude. He kissed me on the lips before I could dodge him. Another guy, trying to be clever, said he'd rather lick the cheese off Ripley's balls. As soon as these words escaped his mouth, the door to the inner room flung open and Ripley jumped out, completely naked, phallus in hand, revealing that his testicles were, in fact, covered with Easy Cheese. But it was just shock and awe—thankfully nobody had to lick Ripley's balls.

When Hell Night was over, the brothers took us to Fort Lou's, an all-night diner. When we got back to the house, we played pong until six. I woke up the next afternoon to Pulaski rustling me out of my bed.

"We're brothers now," he was saying. "We're brothers."

Term ended. Snow piled up on ΣAE's lawn. One afternoon in Wheeler I sat at my desk, the radiator hissing and clanking, and looked out the window at the brothers' cars leaving one by one for Christmas break. Eventually the lot was empty. I wish I could have said that I felt accomplished about my supposedly elite social acceptance, but I was just happy pledge term was over, and I even started to wonder if maybe I'd made a mistake. I started to wonder if maybe I'd miscalculated Dartmouth or Dartmouth had miscalculated me. It was hard to tell the difference.

5

ALL ROADS LEAD TO ΣAE

Our hazing was over. Now, we agreed, it was time to enjoy the privileges we'd earned. We could use the front door. We didn't have to do gross shit—if we didn't want to, though we occasionally still wanted to. We had full rights on the basement, the pong scene, and the entire house itself. We could wear the letters. In less than a year, we could even haze the next class of pledges.

After this initial feeling of excitement, my life reverted to a winter-long emotional hangover, reduced back to the glowing, color-coded squares in my MacBook's iCalendar—classes, X-hours, lunch dates, pong dates, deadlines, professors' office hours, frat meetings, course requirements, short-term goals, long-term goals, potential internships, gainful employment opportunities, prerequisites for my major, etc.

Then, of course, house politics.

The first rush-chair election had happened at the end of pledge term; only '12s were eligible. Wallace and I had lost to Tuckerman. Gibbons was an also-ran. Tuckerman's off-term plan worked out so that he'd be on campus in the winter and off campus in the spring, so when politicking season for the second election rolled around, most people knew that the second rush chair would have to have the opposite semester schedule—off in the winter, on in the spring.

Problem was, I was supposed to go on a foreign study to Rome in the spring. Art history—don't ask me why. I'd skated through my only art history course with a C+ and had loathed sitting in the sweaty lecture hall staring at endless slides of cave drawings and Christian sculptures. I mostly wanted to go because of this beautiful art history major who'd lived across the hall from me in Benefactor freshman year. She was going. I wasn't at all sure about now privileging frat politics over cultural education, but I stuck with the decision anyway.

I scheduled lunches with key brothers to make my campaign pitch that the house meant so much to me, that bringing in a *totally solid, utterly A-side rush class, bro,* was so essential to my life that I'd forgo Rome for it. Aggressively leveraging retail politics, I worked the brothers one by one. I hired a team of savvy consultants, mostly just Pulaski and Price, who, between chain-smoking and losing games of pong, helped me twist arms and broker deals. I kept a tally of prospective votes by brother and faction, calculated the odds of voter turnout, and hypothesized my advantage against Wallace, who was off campus. Running for office in a petty and highly political house, one with significantly more College Dems and College Republicans than it had athletes, was a full-time job.

Election day came, the brotherhood packed the Libes, I gave my speech, walked down the hall to 9, waited for the results, and returned to find that since Wallace and I had split the vote exactly fifty-fifty, the brotherhood had decided to take both of us.

More important, I got one of the real prizes a lot of us were after: my picture would go on the 2011 composite with the words EMINENT RUSH CHAIRMAN printed underneath it. Composites were important to us. Someday, some future brothers might snort a line of coke off my face and wonder about me, what I was like, what I'd wanted from life, what I thought I saw in the house or what the house had seen in me.

I SUGGESTED

My first job as rush chairman was to organize the house's Super Bowl party, a mixer of brothers and freshman dudes. The hardest part was pretending that I cared about football.

Then there were endless pong tournaments, endless late nights in the basement taking shots of cheap tequila with annoying freshman boys as I tried to convince them, whether I cared or not, to shake out at ΣAE.

The house is quickly moving from B-side to A-side, I suggested.

We have all the best parties with the hottest girls, I stretched.

I promise the house will get you a banking job, I assured them.

We're getting half the heavyweight rowers and squash team to shake out, I speculated.

Maybe next year the house will pay for us all to spring-break in Cancún, I hypothesized.

Wallace, Tuckerman, and I focused on putting up numbers: maximizing our shake-outs at rush for the subsequent fall. Together we made a PowerPoint presentation of the potential rushees, copping their pictures from Facebook and adding snarky impressions of whether they were A-side, whether they were fratty enough, what they would bring to the house, whether they potentially suffered from a mild case of Down syndrome. As freshmen, I realized, we must have all been profiled like that, too.

SO FRESH AND NOVEL

Since super shots, I'd only done coke intermittently. Every now and then—if a bro happened to have some and happened to invite me. It wasn't much of a big thing to me, I guess, but to some dudes it was just another old-fashioned frat *tradition*.

Then one of the older guys started distributing baggies he got through his secret society to any guy who wanted them, anyone who had sixty dollars to spare. Secret societies are just like more exclusive frats made up of other frat and sorority members, sports team captains, and "campus leaders." But they have weird rituals—you have to get their tattoo—and mysterious names like Dragon, Sphinx, Abaris, Cobra, and Phrygian. Most of their clubhouses lie in secret corners of the campus, and every winter and spring they select a new group of initiates from the junior class; every year at commencement, members carry the carved wooden cane of their society.

As we came to understand these multiple other levels of social advancement above just passing pledge term—from elections to getting tapped to, possibly, elections within the societies for which you'd been tapped—we started to obsessively speculate over which older brothers were in which society, whether certain positions in the house came with a guaranteed tap, what the secret society hazing was like.

But, at first, it just made you feel cool to have one of your older bros take your sixty dollars and give you a baggie of blow, nonchalantly mentioning that he got it from his "Monday-night club." In the beginning I saved my bag for special occasions—big parties, formals, Fridays. But then I found myself taking a little plastic vial of Brooks Brothers collar stays, emptying it out, and filling the thing with coke. We'd pause pong games to do key bombs or lock ourselves in the bathroom and rail lines off the counter, dip our cigarettes into the bag while we walked across campus from Alpha Delta to Theta Delt to Sig Ep to Tri-Kap.

There were nights when we'd blow lines in 9 and take over the basement until sunrise, blasting bad classic rock and smoking menthols as if the world were ending. We'd pause games to run up to the Libes and blow lines off "The True Gentleman." Once, for some reason I can't remember, we blew lines off the hood of someone's car. It all seemed so fresh and novel, as if no one had ever done it before, but they had, and there was nothing new about us. We couldn't accept that we were just one more set of guys to believe in our own importance and the house's importance, one more set of dudes stumbling through the labyrinth of adolescence into a supposedly real world we believed to be defined by our own false privilege.

WET GARBAGE AND FLOWERING TREES

Price, Beaufort, and I were walking back to the house from frat row one night after coming up dry in our search for an adequately stimulating party. Collectively, we were in a nasty mood. It was probably three in the morning. Frat row smelled like wet garbage and flowering trees.

"For a while I've been thinking," Price was saying, "that hanging out not on coke isn't fun at all. Now I'm starting to think that hanging out on coke isn't fun either."

I said, "Yeah, it always ends weird."

"I guess you're right," Beaufort said, staring down at the sidewalk underneath his boat shoes as we passed behind the library. "Either way is weird." We got back to the house. Lacking anything meaningful to do, we turned the basement music back on and played pong until we couldn't remember what was happening, even though nothing was happening.

At least it was spring. Campus thawed out; daffodils suddenly appeared one morning. I was an officer, already in my second term of full-fledged, dues-paying brotherhood, and had started dating Caroline, the gorgeous senior I'd met at super shots. Most of the fall seemed like a distant, repressed memory, something we only talked about in self-congratulatory terms, as if we'd enjoyed it. In forgetting pledge term's uncomfortable realities, we'd rewritten in nostalgic tones the story of how we came to be brothers—we laughed off the bad, underscored the bonhomie, and forgot the rest. Things sped up until they were moving so fast no one could control them.

APRIL FOOL'S

Some Wednesday, another round of meetings, the last in March. Underground in the basement as usual, I drifted among fake friends, yelling all the chants and songs we'd learned, telling grim anecdotes and oral histories of fellatio and corporate internships.

By the time chugging dues were over, I felt so drunk I could've been underwater. We linked up in JV, hands clasped in a circle for our ending ritual as Schultz recited the Greek that was supposed to be our creed.

Then ritual ended.

Bros formed a bucket brigade to distribute beer cases

around the basement, passing them two by two out of the kitchen's industrial fridge. I walked over toward Beaufort, who was making small talk with Goodrich—what I immediately perceived to be house politics, though I didn't think much of it at the time.

My phone read March 31, though that calendar day was almost through, and in the planet's transit around the sun we more accurately found ourselves nearing the night's imperceptible pivot into morning that occurs in the minutes around midnight.

I felt uneasy but didn't know why.

Maybe it was Beaufort's demeanor talking to Goodrich, my suspicion that he didn't want me to hear what he was saying. I don't know. But he and I slipped out of the house and crossed the street to Wheeler. Caroline, who was away for the weekend, had left her blow in my room—stashing it in what we all called the drug box, an ornately carved wooden box I'd bought in Bangkok. As bad luck would have it, by the time we flipped open the drug box's hinges, it was already the first of the next month.

THE MAN IN THE MIRROR

Exactly six years prior my grandfather had passed away in a turbulent sleep early in the morning of April Fool's Day. It was like the man to slip from his body on a day like that, without telling any of the family members who'd kept a vigil around his bed. He left without any profound advice; his last words I remember, from days before, as he stared straight ahead at the perfectly white wall, were "It appears that no one has anything of any value to say to anyone at any time." I didn't understand what he meant.

Unbeknownst to Beaufort as he was cutting up the blow on the glass top of a picture of the deceased as a handsome young man at Dartmouth during the war years—side view of his side part, it's winter, and he's holding a bud on a dead bush with one leather-gloved hand, wearing an impeccably tailored suit and overcoat—my grandfather had carried his apoplectic energy into the beyond. But the man wasn't gone yet, I could tell you that. He was still around. And he was pissed about something.

"Let's talk house politics." I leaned back on the futon. The room was a fucking mess. As usual, the TV was stuck frozen on the N64 menu page of *Super Smash Bros.* Dirty oxford shirts were crumpled in a heap under the coffee table, wrinkled in on themselves. The refrigerator door wouldn't close and I could smell the gamy putrescence of a rotting turkey sandwich if I leaned too far in that direction. Michael Jackson blasted from my Mac: *I'm starting with the man in the mirror.*

"I'm running for Social. I think I have a pretty good shot," I said. "I can count on your support, right?"

"Of course, brah." Beaufort fixed his hair's ostensibly effortless coif. He was well liked in the house. I don't think he had any enemies. Any sophomores wanting to run for anything, they'd need his support. This was about as far as the discussion got. Tweaked, feeling the coke's numbing, metallic drip down the back of my throat, I walked with him back to the house.

MINIMAL BABY POWDER

Something felt off—the brothers in the basement looked tense, their sweaty faces taut in frowns, their eyes stung with cigarette fumes. Price sat by himself smoking Marlboros on the benches, yelling, "Sink more cups, faggots," at the nearest pong game as everyone tried to ignore him. Kegs ran dry early, their fuel coming up as foam. There was a problem with the lights. Despite these setbacks the night progressed like a typical Wednesday: endless pong and directionless bacchanalia until Beaufort passed out somewhere upstairs.

I suspected that part of his popularity derived from his always hanging out yet seldom being drunk enough to say or do ridiculous things; he had the admirable quality of shutting himself down when he reached a certain point of intoxication, finding a comfortable spot to sleep on a brother's couch, then waking early enough the next morning to reflect fraternally, "Bro, I was so wasted last night." Maybe that's just speculation—it doesn't make a difference now—but he was coy and consolidated social capital slowly and deliberately, as is the Dartmouth way.

His departure left me, for a period, the last man standing from the binge. So I decided to take a seat. After Price had stumbled upstairs, I sat on the benches in Varsity and watched an intense pong game, Wallace and Randall versus two seniors. I wandered between the kitchen and the boot room, wondering if I should pull my trigger to clear my stomach, boot and rally, then deciding not to, deciding that there was always time to sober up later.

Despite my sentimentality for remembering dates, it never occurred to me that I'd snorted drugs off a picture of my grandfather on his death day, that such an act probably had a lot of karmic gravity, that coincident with that oversight a slow and painful process of personal dissolution had begun.

As if on cue, Pulaski appeared in the basement and graciously joined me in continuing a path of post-meetings merriment. We resolved to snort the rest of the blow in the pool room. No one was around and no one came in to bother us, and he was still drunk from meetings and clapped me on the back as I pulled tight the drapes and then shook the contents of the baggie onto a composite.

"You're a lucky man," he said, then dipped a finger in the powder and rubbed it on his gums. "Good stuff." He smiled.

I stared down at my dim reflection on the glass next to the coke. "Why?"

"I don't know, minimal baby powder? No powdered household cleaners mixed in? I don't know these things."

I must've given him a weird look. "Lucky?"

"Yeah, lucky."

"I guess I can't complain."

He pulled his head back and squinted at me sternly.

"Don't blow it." He licked his finger and dipped it in the pile again, pulling up more than he had before.

I handed him the rolled-up bill. I can remember the taste vividly, the vague gasoline scent, the nasal drip, the feeling of supreme confidence, the psychotic belief that you were at the center of some incredible unfolding drama of which everyone else was ignorant. The smell of coke always came with the smell of money.

Everyone knows it's a hard habit to break. You get too many cold sweats. Your blood flow slows, you gain weight. You enjoy the coke because you know there will come a time when you'll have to stop. You just know it's not tonight.

ABANDON ALL HOPE, YE WHO URINATE HERE

One night around that time didn't end well. Some Kappa Omegas showed up in the basement around four for a few casual games of pong, but our kegs had run dry, and since some involved brothers were coked out, mostly just me and Pulaski, we opted to use a powdered-pink-lemonade-and-vodka punch, speckled with dead flies, that had been sitting in a dirty recycling bin for at least a few days. The whole game devolved when Randall peed in the punch, then a bet was made and not honored, an ΣAE suggested we should dome, first cup being pee, which Pulaski guzzled—my pee—and an altercation broke out when some was offered to one of the Kappa Omegas, during which the fist of a small-time donor's son seemed to have made contact with my face. All in all, a bad scene, and not the kind of thing you can amicably resolve before breakfast.

Not long after this I was summoned to the basement of Parkhurst, the Administrator's office—same person who'd attempted to investigate us for hazing violations a few months earlier.

"Please, Mr. Lohse, have a seat."

I stood in the doorway running my hands over my torso to make sure my button-down was tucked into my jeans— despite late-night debauchery I at least attempted to appear respectable when dealing with the high priests and pharisees of Dartmouth College.

The Administrator looked up at me icily from an open manila folder on his desk, reading glasses perched precariously on the end of his nose. Whether the file was mine or the Kappa Omega's, I couldn't tell. I'd never been summoned to Parkhurst before. I'd never even been inside save for a formal tour or meetings with my academic dean— which, sadly, were rare occurrences. Increasingly rare after I pledged ΣAE. Like maybe I didn't even know who my dean was.

I slumped down in the chair facing his desk. His office sat in the front corner of the building's basement, and through a ground-level window over his head I could see feet passing on the sidewalk outside—thin, feminine legs ending in Tory Burch flats, the occasional pair of khakis, pale pink critter shorts, boat shoes.

"Well, Mr. Lohse. Hello. I'm sure that you are aware that the college, and the Committee on Standards, has a strict, zero-tolerance policy toward fighting. The minimum penalty for such an offense, should a student be found responsible—now, mind you, we don't use the word *guilty*—is suspension; the maximum is expulsion. That policy is, of course, enumerated in your student handbook."

"I am aware of that, yes." I nodded from where I sat, seemingly watching the rest of my tenure in the Ivy League hang from a great height by only a single thread of some kind of expensive fabric.

"That is why it is absolutely essential that we get to the bottom of the events of the morning of—of the April morning in question." He licked his finger and lifted a few pages, setting them down carefully outside the folder. He stopped on a page that seemed to catch his eye. "Now, Andrew, as opposed to popular belief among fraternity brothers, the administration is—as am I—very aware of what, shall we say, *transpires* in the frat houses."

Really? I was thinking. Really? Because that's probably not the case. "Yes, oh, I'm sure. Absolutely—"

"But I, in my many years here at the college, have never heard of any of our students . . . chugging a cup of, well, *bodily fluids*." He paused and laid his hand flat on the paper.

I could see specific sections of text highlighted in yellow—a bit too phosphorescent of a hue to suggest urine, but inauspicious nonetheless. "Hm, yes. Quite interesting . . ."

"In the statement submitted by one of the Kappa Omegas, he mentions a drinking game—doming, was it called?—

that was to begin by both competing students drinking cups of urine."

"Ah, I see."

"Your urine."

I paused. I stared directly into his eyes and hopelessly tried to buy time to think of a suitable explanation. Nothing I could say wasn't probably already contradicted in his manila folder. Except, maybe, that Pulaski drank the pee, not me, and certainly not the Kappa Omega, who'd seemed quite averse to the idea. I gave up staring. Faltering, I closed my eyes and prayed to a wrathful God I hadn't spoken to in at least a decade.

Then the Administrator threw me a curveball. "If you're wondering, Andrew, there are no disciplinary charges pending against you regarding this incident, if that helps sharpen your recollection of events." He closed the folder decisively and slid it into a drawer. I opened my eyes. He smiled and set his elbows down on the desk, on top of a fresh calendar page for the coming month—if this was April, what would May be like?—and leaned toward me expectantly. It must after all have been the Kappa Omega's permanent record, not mine.

I just continued staring. "Are you . . . sure?" I ventured cautiously.

He frowned at me and said something like "If someone wants to do . . . unusual and gross things . . . sadly that's their choice, right? In a voluntary setting, of course." He'd accidentally hit the nail on the head: pledge term, hazing, it's like, yeah, technically, strangely, wasn't it in some way . . . voluntary? Where do you draw the line between voluntary degradation and coerced degradation?

"Hm. I guess you're right."

"Level with me, Andrew. What is doming? Can you describe this game to me? Why are brothers willing to play it?" His elbows didn't move an inch. I was shocked that he didn't know what doming was—it was a rote aspect of Greek life, a vocabulary word even nonchalantly thrown around in the school's newspaper. Everyone knew about doming. It wasn't a big deal.

"Well, it's not much of a game, per se," I said. "And it doesn't usually involve urine. That was a slight modification, um, made that, um, morning. So, you're not aware at all of what really goes on in the frat houses?"

"If you tell me more, I guess I'd be aware of more, correct?" he shot back. "Completely off the record of course. But first, I'd like to talk about the fight as it pertains to pending charges against the Kappa Omega. Did he punch you? In the face, in the chest?"

I'd already been coached by the frat not to pursue any action against the guy. It was a fool's errand, as one of my brothers had pointed out; even though the guy's father was only a small-time donor, probably nothing could be done; and pointing a finger at the guy would inevitably point more than a few back at me, and then, by association, the house. Too much was at stake. I'd been instructed to just let it go. Plus, one of the guy's lawyers had already met me in person briefly once; on a sunny afternoon, he was sitting on a bench in front of the Hop waiting for me like something out of a movie.

"Andrew Lohse?" he'd asked, flagging me down. Somehow he knew what I looked like. He suggested that it would not be *prudent* to say too much about the *incident* given so much *doubt* over what went on, due to everyone's *intoxication,* especially since I was *underage,* they said, his tone simultaneously ominous and friendly.

"Andrew . . . ?" The Administrator cleared his throat. I'd lost my focus.

"Well, no," I found myself saying.

"So this Kappa Omega did not punch you? That's not what the report in my folder suggests." The Administrator nodded toward his bottom desk drawer. "In that report, I must say, the prepositional phrase reads, very specifically, 'in the face.'" That was how I'd explained the event to the officer filing the report. Before I was coached.

"Oh, hm, well, there might have been some kind of contact, but . . ."

"But it wasn't a punch?" He didn't seem suspicious. I got the sense that he, too, realized that nothing could be done about the son of someone who'd been generous to the college and might be more generous in the foreseeable future. It seemed he was more interested in the sociology or anthropology of fraternity life in general.

"It was more of, um, a . . . graze."

"His fist happened to graze your cheek. All right." He scribbled something down on a legal pad and underlined it. I figured he knew that I was obfuscating the truth, knew that the guy had most likely socked me in the jaw, but I didn't want to admit that I probably deserved it, and that I'd been all sorts of fucked-up.

"Back to my original question. Urine?"

I noticed that the legs had stopped passing by the window

over his head. Class must have started again. I'd be late for Postcolonial Lit, but this meeting was too important to attempt to excuse myself from it.

"It was stupid, I know. But stupid things like that are part of the frat culture. We were trained to do that stuff from day one of pledge term," I blurted out, hardly able to stop myself.

Pausing to breathe, I realized that I'd just blown it—I'd in some part betrayed the secrecy of the house. I should've just denied that anything ever happened, denied that any brother urinated anyway; that's what any craftier liar would have done. But somehow, part of my repression, and part of that deeply internalized mantra *What Happens in the House Stays in the House,* had cracked. Out spilled the truth. It occurred to me that I had a desperate need to *tell* someone what really happened, though I also realized how reckless—or sensible, depending on how you looked at it—it was to be spilling out my trauma to the school's disciplinarian.

We talked about vomit. He didn't say much. He might have been holding his breath.

When the conversation returned to pee, he seemed to have more to add: "I understand that, developmentally, and psychologically, urine is an animalistic way of marking one's territory."

I wanted to elucidate for him that, in Kappa Omega—a house very similar to the Animal House, after all—brothers peed in grates that lined the basement whenever they felt like it. *Abandon all hope, ye who urinate here.* Behind his eyes I suspected that he was thinking, like an outdated computer performing some calculation; I'd said far too much, yet somehow I didn't feel guilty. In fact, when I walked out of Parkhurst and back into the spring afternoon, I felt a great sense of relief.

THE AIN DIET

Caroline and I met up with Price at Chi Heorot's Highlighter Party. He was wearing a white T-shirt. Scrawled over the back and front of it in glowing lines of pink and orange were such gems as ΣAE SUCKS, I'M A HOMO, and NO ONE HANGS OUT ANYMORE. Poor guy was standing by himself against the wall in the main basement room while the dance party pulsed, just chain-smoking and sniffling, drenched in sweat, dark crescents under his eyes that almost resembled bruises. He looked awful. I walked over to him as Caroline forced her way through the crowd to the bar to try to get two full beers for us—instead of just the one cup of foam that any nonbrother would, presumably, be given at a party of this magnitude.

"You look awful, dude," I said to Price.

"Yeah, don't worry about it." He watched me blankly, the whites of his eyes glowing under the black lights. Then he looked away, squinting at a pair of freshman girls in white V-necks and glowing headbands grinding on each other. I looked, too. When I turned back to him, I noticed his eyes twitch, but in the basement's glow I couldn't make out if his pupils were dilated. I wasn't sure why he was so apathetic all the time. He was a wealthy kid, smart, well dressed, athletic.

He didn't seem to have a reason to be so disengaged. Then again, most of us were ungrateful assholes.

"Do I look worried?" I asked. "I'm not worried. Are you actually here alone, dude?"

"I was with Beaufort, but I don't know where he went. Do I actually look awful?"

"Kind of, dude. Can I bum a cig?"

He turned his squint toward me suspiciously. The fresh pack of menthols stuffed in my pink shorts bulged suggestively.

"Cig?" I asked again. Since I wasn't a trust-fund kid, I tried to save money whenever I could, mostly by conserving one cigarette at a time. You gotta start somewhere. He handed me a Lucky Strike. Opting for an abrupt change of tone, I smiled and told him that, no, he actually didn't look so horrendous tonight. He probably knew that I was saying it just to placate him. I lit his cigarette, then mine, then he inhaled deeply and exhaled through his nose. He always did that—through the nose, like a cartoon of a charging bull.

"I'm on the ain diet," he goes, shrugging.

I jogged my memory. Was that one of those things for rugby? Like protein supplements or shit like that? Or maybe it was something from TV, some fad diet. Maybe it was from some rap song? I wasn't sure. I went for the safe guess. "So that, like, must be some kind of rugby thing, huh? Cool, bro," I offered intrepidly, also trying to remember why I felt as if we were such good friends. When did this undying bond begin? What could justify it? All that came to mind was pulling his trigger once at pledge meetings the fall before and feeling his dinner—sashimi, of all things—

slide viscously over my fingers into a trash can that reeked of piss. No one else in the room had even noticed. Those experiences were just, like, part of the scenery.

"Are you kidding me? The ain diet. We're both ΣAEs. You should know this, Lohse." He was actually annoyed. He was strung out, I suspected. The whole conversation seemed to sway between the tragicomic and the simply sad—snorting drugs and partying while trying to survive at an Ivy League school, what a balancing act. Everything became emotionally trying, even after we'd given up trying to be real people.

My mind raced through its limited knowledge of fad diets and the weird and usually pointless things athletes did with food and supplements. The ain diet. All I could think of was "ain't nothin' but a party," but that, I figured, was probably incorrect. I kept thinking.

"Chow mein?"

"Chow mein is B-side." He frowned. "I don't eat chow mein. Chow mein is for plebeians. That shit isn't even authentic."

"Lo mein?"

"Champagne," he goes, not even looking at me, exhaling through his nose again.

"Plantains?"

"Cocaine," he added with finality.

I guess it should have been obvious. Champagne and cocaine, the two major food groups. To Price's annoyance I continued trying to guess the other elements of his diet. "Complain? Pain, maybe?"

"No, asshole. Do I look like I ever complain? What is

this, the fucking rhyme game? That's it. Champagne and cocaine. No lo mein, that shit is grim."

"I'd guess that you're in some kind of pain right now, though."

We watched the freshman girls. They were still grinding away on each other obliviously.

"You have any more of those ain dietary supplements?" I asked. Out of the corner of my eye I watched Caroline finally heading back over toward us through the humid, overcrowded basement. She held two half-empty cups of Keystone, guarding them like holy wine from erratically dancing bystanders. Half-full or half-empty? I wondered. Dealing with Price had made the entire universe seem half-, if not at least three-quarters, empty. Since the known universe included the Chi Heorot Highlighter Party, the cups must be half-empty, I deduced. It's easy to find disappointing answers to every philosophical question when you're in a frat basement.

"Do I have any more plantains? No, fuck you," Price grumbled.

I coughed on the smoke spiraling toward me from his nose. "I meant blowcaine. Brocaine. You know."

Caroline handed me a beer. She sipped hers and scanned the dance floor.

Price hung his head and reached for another Lucky Strike. "Lohse, no more fucking rhyming. If anything, I should be asking you two about brocaine. Look at Caroline, rubbing her nose like that, like it's Allegra season or something. Come on. Don't blame me for asking, guys."

"Hi, Price," she goes, "great to see you, too."

"Can you go get me a beer? I don't have tits."

"No. My allergies are acting up."

"Can you help my allergies worsen, too, then? They are starting to, like, heal, and I'm not really very, um, content at the moment." He ran a nervous hand through his hair, eyes listless.

The ain diet—I thought to myself, was that really a *thing,* to call it that? Was that a *thing* I should remember to do? Did people actually say that?

"What's it worth to you?" she goes.

"I'll give you a little smooch." He puckered up and exhaled smoke in her face. He always said that. It never got less grating. And this time it was like, yeah, typical, the dude doesn't even bother trying to be charming even when hard drugs are on the line.

"Price . . ." She shook her head. "Why are you so immature?"

There was no need to WebMD it; Price was showing classic symptoms of ain deficiency. He just stared at me, gave me the, like, Jack Nicholson look that he imitates when he's drunk, that look that Nicholson gives Shelley Duvall in *The Shining* as he follows her up the hotel's grand staircase. After he goes crazy.

Neither Caroline nor I had the energy to resist. Anyway, it would have made us feel guilty. The kid needed the blow, so she conceded, sighed, pointed to one of the pockets of her J.Crew skirt, the skirt that she wore like, maybe almost every other going-out night that spring—I have all these gorgeous images of her like that in my memory—that was our world one spring, the daffodils and blue shadows and grass stains and smells of fresh, clean air when the nights were through and we'd climb up out of the basements motormouthed and messed up.

Caroline motioned for us to follow her up the stairs. We removed ourselves from the party and that was fine because I didn't want to dance, I'd never liked dancing, and neither did Price or even Caroline, and our friends weren't even there and after all it was just a bunch of freshmen getting too heavy on each other and a bunch of blacked-out bros in blaze orange vests and I was choking on our own smoke. Thank God for the coke, I thought. Everything about the scene depressed me. We found the frat's bathroom.

6
THE PERFECTION OF WISDOM

Suddenly it was May, and Green Key Weekend—the spring's equivalent of homecoming—loomed before us. For the sake of definition, Green Key is one of the school's old traditions, one of its "big weekends," a time when alumni return to the alma mater. There must once have been some kind of ritual on which the traditional weekend was founded, but I never knew what it was, and no one cared. I think it had to do with seniors passing on the key to the Green. That would seem logical. But everyone knew it was only about parties now.

Before any partying was to be done, though, I first had to pull an all-nighter to write a paper for Mahayana Buddhism. I found myself shuttered in Wheeler's study room, poring over all of the banal sutras and monastic manuscripts I hadn't read all term, trying to craft some vague postmodern argument about mantras or the lesser vehicle or the greater vehicle or something like that. Incomprehensible Sanskrit translations were burning more of a hole in my cerebellum than any stimulants ever did, and the more I tried to understand *The Perfection of Wisdom Sutra,* the more I wanted to sprint across the street and play pong until I passed out. Sleep-deprived and nowhere near enlightenment, I teetered on the brink of giving up.

From time to time Pulaski would saunter over to distract me by talking house politics, but every conversation made me feel shitty. He sat down on the table, picking up my barren Buddhism notebook.

"Looks like someone hasn't been going to class," he smirked.

"It's interesting stuff in general, just not when you have to write a paper about it." I sighed, pushing back in the uncomfortable wooden chair.

"I know, Lohse. You just want to pretend to be some monogrammed polo-wearing Jack Kerouac and find your enlightenment in a frat basement. A little bit phony, don't you think?"

He thumbed through my untouched copy of *The Diamond Sutra.* "Isn't Beaufort in this course, too? I bet he makes it to every class. I bet his *Diamond Sutra* is full of highlighter, interesting side notes, and all other various and sundry ways of earning a good grade in a non-econ course."

———

The sun rose. Birds chirped outside the dorm, that same shrill and somehow comforting song. It was time to start actually writing—about six hours until D-day and I didn't have a single word on the screen.

I finished the paper midmorning, a mortifyingly insubstantial piece of work, clearly written overnight, more like around breakfast, I guess, without the aid of amphetamines. A lot of other potent shit was on my mind—my vision of how Dartmouth was supposed to go for me hadn't been coming to fruition, and it seemed the more I tried to make it go the way I'd imagined, the more I tried to do what everyone else was doing, the more dissatisfied I became. Written under neither intellectual nor chemical stimulation, the Buddhism paper displayed perfectly my failure to understand, even on a basic level, anything about wisdom.

I left Wheeler, stepping into an idyllic spring day—sun dripping like lacquer over the campus, sky perfectly clear. Heading toward the religion department in Thornton Hall, I realized that I'd forgotten how beautiful it all was, those peerlessly gorgeous spring mornings I was usually too comatose or hungover to experience, the smell of cut grass, the girls floating across campus in short dresses. Despite this realization, I was excited to be spending the better part of the coming days underground partying in frat basements. I walked by Rollins Chapel. Its doors were wide open as if inviting in all wayward undergraduates to preemptively repent for the sins they'd probably commit over the remainder of the week. Sex, drugs, vomit, not observing the Sabbath— the usual suspects.

"Not yet," I mumbled, shielding my bloodshot eyes from the sun's glare. I'd forgotten my Wayfarers. I passed Beaufort as he exited Thornton.

"Happy Green Key," he said, reaching out to give me the grip. I demurred and nodded in his direction, left his handshake hanging, went inside the building, dropped my paper in the plastic bin marked RELIGION 69, went home to Wheeler, slept until dinner.

MISBEHAVING PARTY OF FOUR

Almost midnight—meetings consisted of a drunken recap of the sophomore summer election results, wherein I tried to make light of my defeat for social chair by doming Tim over which of us was the bigger failed ladder climber. We'd both lost the positions we'd run for, but he won the dome after I, twelve cups deep, projectile-vomited a magenta slime into the trash can we were huddled around. I was prepared to let him boot on my head, but he didn't want to boot on my head, but then Randall said he wanted to boot on my head, and for some reason I was like, "Fine, sure," but then immediately afterward, his vomit dripping down my neck, I kind of regretted it, since I think we might have had Alpha Phi coming over for some kind of tails event that night.

A ton of alum bros had shown up, too, appearing from Boston and New York and D.C. and San Francisco like overexcited, vaguely unwanted relatives. After the close of meetings in JV, after Schultz recited the Greek secret text, everyone jockeyed for the pong tables.

Edwards, Price, and I walked up from the basement to open the front door, which was always locked during meetings, for Caroline. Then we climbed the stairs to 9, bolted the door, turned on Clapton. *If you wanna hang out, you've got to take her out . . .*

"Cocaine!" we yelled together. That's probably why we woke up Davis. He stepped out of the inner room in his Brooks Brothers boxers looking feverish.

"Fellas," he said, ". . . and lady. I'm really sorry to disrupt the party, but I'm not feeling well."

"We have something that might make you feel better," Price suggested, nodding down toward the blow, which Edwards was about to dump out on the Old Man of the Mountain.

Davis shook his head. "Sorry." He rubbed his forehead. It glowed red. "I'm trying to sleep. Edwards, I told you. No one hanging out in Nine tonight."

"Our bad, brah," Price monotoned as soon as Davis had retreated back into the inner room. He rolled his eyes. Sweat had stained through his polo. He offered me a cigarette as we left 9, but I pointed up at the smoke detectors in the hallway, and Caroline laughed and said something like, "You know better, Price," and Edwards was too drunk to notice.

We tried to set up shop down the hall in the Libes, but Sean, who was turning on the basement music from one of the computers, intercepted us. "Not in here," he said, drunk eyes vacantly searching for some fixed point on which to steady himself. He chose Caroline's chest. Price gingerly reached toward the wall to remove the framed parchment of "The True Gentleman," but Sean leapt up and grabbed it first. The two briefly wrestled over the sacred artifact. Sean pulled away, clutching it to his T-shirt. "You kidding?" he slurred.

"No one hangs out anymore." Price rolled his eyes melodramatically and again tried to light a cigarette. Clutching the frame with one hand, Sean knocked Price's white lighter to the carpeting—an act of war—and as I grabbed Price's shoulder to pull him back from pouncing on Sean, I noticed that Edwards had already drifted downstairs. He was nonconfrontational and only bad-mouthed other brothers privately, a key ingredient of his popularity.

"You guys are fucking bad news," Sean said.

"No worse than you are. No worse than anyone else in this house," Price spat as Caroline and I dragged him back to the third-floor landing.

Sean's eyes still hung on Caroline's chest. She hadn't said anything—she was kind of like our mom, usually a calm observer, or maybe like your friend's cool mom who does drugs with you. The door arced to a close; we let go of Price's polo, but as soon as we were out of reach, he thrust his arm into the Libes and hit the lights in retaliation, and the room went dark and all we could hear was Sean screaming, "What the fuck!" as Price kicked the door shut, cackling. We caught up with Edwards on the second-floor landing.

I don't remember who suggested the pool room. It was

never anyone's first choice, especially not for a conspicuous and already-misbehaving party of four. Sure, the ambience was elitist enough, and it had a surplus of glass-top-framed composites to use, but it wasn't a private space. Six could be bolted, and visitors weren't allowed in the Libes, but too many people came and went in the pool room. Especially on the first night of Green Key. But we commandeered the room anyway. What was anyone going to do about it?

SOME WILL WIN, SOME WILL LOSE

"Who has the highest max on their credit card?" Price asked.

The coke glistened on a composite laid flat on the pool table's purple felt, powder like a crumbled tusk, collected neatly between the smiling pictures of the EMINENT ARCHON and the EMINENT DEPUTY ARCHON. We each fumbled with our wallets and tossed our cards down on the felt next to the composite's frame.

There's nothing more pretentious, even at Dartmouth, than a rousing game of "Who has the highest max on their credit card?" I burped, got a taste of Keystone and boot, instinctively wiped my mouth, and then wiped my hand on my critter pants. American Express, Chase Manhattan Signature—my student Visa was trifling in comparison. In that moment my outsider status was laid bare: Lohse, you are literally not a card-carrying member of this crowd.

"$X0,000," Caroline said, completely serious.

Price slid his card on top of hers. Clearly, this was why he wanted to play the game. "$X0,000," he goes, and I believed him because no one was joking around, because credit-card limits were a rather serious deal to some people.

"Clearly, Price takes the prize," I said, deferring the question. Price won the honor of chopping the blow into eight rails. I pulled the curtains shut. No one gave much thought to the door, since it had a bros-only punch code.

"Can we snort them off my face?" Edwards asked.

"Of course we can."

Price displayed his dexterity with the razor blade by shifting the lines from the EMINENT DEPUTY ARCHON to the picture of Edwards's face staring up at us from the composite, that same smirking smile with piercing brown eyes.

A few snorts into the proceedings someone knocked on the door. Price lifted his head from the composite and slid the rolled-up hundred into his pocket—he was the kind of guy who'd keep it if things went bad.

Edwards flipped the latch and we all watched intently as his head swiveled back and forth outside the crack. Then he ushered in Tracy, some girl with whom he may or may not have been hooking up.

"I'm sorry. I didn't know the punch code," she said.

"Only brothers are supposed to," Price sneered. That would be the problem. "Care to partake?"

Tracy sat down on the couch and crossed her arms. She was quiet. It was beginning to worry me.

"Are you sure you're not interested?" I asked her as Caroline snorted a line.

"Not interested. I should probably go now, too."

"Stay with us," Edwards said.

"I feel a little uncomfortable."

In the basement beneath us we could hear "Don't Stop Believin' " blasting as if nothing else were happening in the entire world. The foundation shook. A group of brothers screamed the words—*Some will win, some will lose*—as they banged their pong paddles to the beat on the tables.

I didn't notice when Tracy left the room.

A minute or two later we heard someone punch in the door code. Probably just Tracy, I thought, not all that nervous.

Then I thought, wait, no, the whole point was that Tracy didn't *know* the code.

BAD NEWS BEARS

Rector's head appeared in the door's crack. In between sniffles I was thinking, yeah, this is definitely an unpleasant development in our situation. He just stared at us, looking dangerously sober and calculating. That was one of the things that had consistently scared me about him since pledge term—he was always so calculating. His glasses were kind of fogged over this time. Edwards blew his line and lifted his head back and snorted loudly, gratingly, wiping some white dust off his nose, then saw Rector and yelled, *"Get the fuck out!"* Rector pulled his head back into the foyer as Edwards forced the door shut with his shoulder, almost crushing the edge of the former's glasses in the crack.

"Bad news bears," Price smirked. "Rector doesn't like to hang out." Then he paused thoughtfully, looking down at the composite. He cocked his head to one side. "In fact, *no one* hangs out anymore."

"We should probably close this out," Caroline said, compulsively rubbing her palms on the front of her shorts, leaving vectors of sweat over the red fabric. Her pupils had become two massive black holes that threatened to swallow up the entire room if we didn't move quickly. Gorgeous black holes, but still. Someone punched in the door code again and we all tensed up, even Price, until Gibbons walked in and forced the door shut behind him, running a hand through his hair. I don't know why we weren't moving faster—I guess we were more annoyed than scared. At least until Gibbons opened his mouth.

"Guys, Rector just called Safety and Security. They're probably going to call the cops. I don't know what you're doing in here, but you better get the fuck out before the police arrive."

Silence.

Then it hit us: we had to get rid of the coke.

We snorted the rest as quickly as possible, then Price used the bottom of his Lacoste Polo to wipe the residue off the glass. Someone hung the composite back up over the fireplace.

THE VIEW FROM THE BEACH

I can't claim to know with exact clarity what happened after that. My body was swallowed up in adrenaline. Gaps of time went missing. Like an out-of-body experience, it was almost as if I were seeing this all happen in the third person, watching myself from above, watching us all scramble out of the pool room.

But I do remember this: I watched Edwards push Rector against a wall in the foyer as a crowd gathered, gawking. He laid two hands on Rector's chest, maybe grabbed his shirt with balled fists. He roared, *"What the fuck is wrong with you? Does the house mean nothing to you?"* But Rector didn't touch him back or say anything, just gazed through his glasses until Edwards let loose his grip and ran upstairs.

The foyer emptied out quickly after that. The party was clearly over. Schultz appeared, exhorting nonbrothers up the basement stairs and out the back door. My legs were weak beneath me but my head was spinning over endless possibilities—the unthinkable was happening. Full law enforcement access with probable cause. Brothers yelled about hiding kegs, hiding punch, locking doors. I don't know where Price and Caroline went; I turned and they were gone. Then I found myself up on Pebble Beach, somehow, by accident.

From Pebble I watched as both Safety and Security and Hanover Police descended on the house. An SNS officer biked up to the back door, radio crackling on his belt. Seeing me standing alone, he shone his flashlight up toward the balcony, but the beams trailed off in the fog and for a brief moment his face was illuminated beneath me, mouth pursed in a frown. This was probably the last thing he'd like to be doing this early on a Thursday morning.

Then it actually started to rain and I stared up at Baker Tower, overcome with the feeling that my Dartmouth dream was probably over. It seemed appropriate to smoke a cigarette while I waited to be encircled by cops, but when I fished around in my pocket, all I found was a crushed, empty box. No luck—only strikes.

IT SEEMED LIKE A MORBID GESTURE

The rain fell in cold streaks; fog rolled over the campus. Standing there, I felt as if I were caught in one of those rare déjà vu moments when you imagine that everything that's ever happened in your entire life has brought you specifically to where you are, the kind of realization where you accept that you are just a part of everything that's happening—I guess some people try to live life like that, as if it were a movie, as if they were characters in an inevitable plot.

But nothing happened.

No one came to arrest me.

When the SNS officer had biked away from playing point to choke off any back-door escapes, and I'd watched a duo of cop cars extinguish their spinning blue lights and drive away from the house down North College Street, I climbed down the balcony's fire-escape ladder, slipping on its wet metal rungs, slunk across the yard, and jogged back across the street to Wheeler.

I sprinted up all four flights of stairs in the dorm to find Pulaski and Caroline sitting around the coffee table with some freshman girl I barely knew. I bolted the door and collapsed on the futon—the cinematic moment was over. I was sweaty. My fingertips pulsed; I mean, I was tweaking so hard that you could have described my fingers, maybe, as even oscillating. It had been an intense close call.

"Dude, you would not believe what just happened—" I started, darting my eyes at Pulaski, then the TV, then Pulaski, then the TV again. *Super Smash Bros.* was stuck paused on the screen, buzzing dimly but still too full of color for my weak eyes to handle.

"Actually, *dude,* I can believe what happened."

"I'm glad it's over."

"Yeah, I see that you've gotten away." He laughed.

"I climbed down the ladder and peaced." I tried to make a gesture to accompany the word *peaced,* but my hands shook too hard and it seemed like a clumsy gesture to make anyway. Meanwhile, Caroline and the girl said nothing. The former's eyes welled with tears. She sat down on the futon.

"Where did you and Price go?" I asked.

"Price disappeared. I just came back here, thinking you were here, but you weren't." She faltered, the tears shimmering in her eyes.

"We should probably smoke a bowl and reflect on what just went down," Pulaski offered. We did need something to chill the adrenaline flowing through the room. He slid open his top desk drawer and pulled out the piece we shared, placed a sparkling nugget of weed within it, and handed it to me as I fumbled in my pocket for my lighter. I lit the bowl, passed it to Caroline. It seemed like a morbid gesture, but it was the only one we had left to make. I closed my eyes.

SWEET PANTS. WERE THEY FOR THE PARTY?

We heard a banging on the door, inconveniently at the exact moment that a massive cloud of smoke floated toward it. The sound brought me back to that first night of pledge term, ducking into Edwards's car with Peterson, affixing my blindfold. Like Pavlov's dog I reflexively stood up and opened the door—relaxed at that point—and was greeted by a duo of SNS officers.

"Are you Andrew Lohse?" one asked, sniffing the air suggestively.

"You're going to have to come with us," the other said.

Thing was, they didn't seem to care that we'd sparked up a bowl in our dorm room—they clearly had bigger crimes to prosecute. Without a backward glance I followed them downstairs, out the same door I'd exited on bid night. They drove me to Dick's House, the campus health center, where they led me to a room I can barely picture in my mind. I realized that the night hadn't been a close call after all.

I sat by myself in the room for a while. I counted seconds pass. I contemplated jumping out the window, escaping, seeing how far I could get out of town and down the interstate, but didn't.

If you think that good-cop, bad-cop routines are only for the movies or lame TV dramas, I'm here to tell you that they are, in fact, real, though not exactly terrifying when you are so heavily intoxicated and cross-faded that you barely comprehend that you're participating in—or the victim of— one.

A cop sauntered in and I wondered if I should stand and shake his hand, but that might have been awkward, the kind of thing you'd do at a job interview. He was a pretty self-consciously intimidating-looking guy: square jaw, muscles, beady eyes like cell-phone camera lenses.

"Ah, Mr. Lohse. I'm Detective McDermott from Hanover PD."

"What's up?"

"I'd like to have a word with you if you don't mind."

"I guess I don't." It didn't seem as if I had any other choice. What was I going to do, say I was busy? Since I have a habit of talking too much, feeling too guilty, and giving it all away—as I basically did to the Administrator that one time—I'm shocked that I didn't immediately confess our crimes and cry like a little girl begging for forgiveness. All I could process through my tunnel vision was a few walls plastered with horrendous wallpaper, a repeating motif of key Dartmouth buildings. Maybe a filing cabinet or two.

First came the litany of bad-cop questions. Detective McDermott set his unflinching eyes on me, and I did my best to seem unflinching, too, which is actually pretty easy when you're so egregiously fucked-up that your facial muscles are perpetually stuck in a neutral expression.

"Did you do cocaine tonight?"

"No."

"Did anyone do cocaine tonight?"

"In the world? I don't know, probably."

"You know what I meant."

"Detective, could you be frank?" My drunkenness had left me slightly uncooperative.

"Did anyone in Sigma Alpha Epsilon use cocaine tonight?"

"Which chapter? There are hundreds of chapters across the country—it's one of the most prestigious fraternal organizations in America," I mumbled, face frozen expressionlessly.

"I'm going to ask you again. Did anyone in Sigma Alpha Epsilon—your chapter here at Dartmouth—use cocaine tonight."

"Of course not."

"Have you ever purchased cocaine?"

"Of course not."

I was steadfast, ironclad. This must've been the bad-cop part of the routine—all that was missing was a two-way mirror, and sadly, it was a lot scarier than Buzzby's interrogation. Then McDermott left the room. I stared at the wall-paper, swam in sweat.

When he came back, he was all smiles and bonho-mie. Just another good old boy. He strutted around the room, sized me up, smiled too much. I was wearing some stupid preppy outfit—Rugby Ralph Lauren skull-and-crossbones critter pants, an ΣAE BEACH PARTY 2010 T-shirt, loafers caked in sod from my hasty escape across the lawn.

So then he goes, "Nice pants, dude. Were they for the party tonight?"

"What?" This surprising reversal was enough to make me uncomfortable, enough to make me wonder if I'd dreamed the first part.

"Sweet pants. Were they for the party?"

And I was thinking, like, um, yeah, exactly, what?

"Um . . . no. These are just my pants. These are just regular pants. That people enjoy. That people enjoy wear-ing," I mumbled, willing my eyes to focus on his face.

"Where'd you get them? They're cool."

"What?"

"Your pants are cool."

"Um, thanks."

"Cool pants."

". . . Yeah." I was trying not to let him get anywhere, so he probably reasoned that his best chance was an abrupt change of strategy. He probably hoped to catch me in a Freudian slip. So he pulled an abrupt play fake.

"How many people were using cocaine in your frat to-night?"

"'Fraternity,'" I found the pledge robot inside of me repeating. "'You wouldn't call your country a cu—'"

"Answer the question."

"'What happens in the house stays in the house,'" I blathered.

"Do you mind if I just test your eyes by having you look at my finger for a second?"

"What?"

"Look at my finger. Follow my finger."

"Um, sure."

"Your pupils are somewhat dilated." He jotted something down in a little notebook. "Why might that be?"

"It's Allegra season."

"It's what?" He stopped writing and looked up.

"It's Allegra season. You know, the time of year when people take Allegra."

"And your allergies . . . ?" He seemed confused. "Your eyes . . . ?"

"Clearly proof that I didn't ingest cocaine, because my pupils wouldn't just be somewhat dilated in that, um, hypothetical circumstance."

It seemed that my hitting that bowl with Pulaski had helped to jam McDermott's radar. Red eyes, dilated pupils, unfocused drunk eyes, allergy season—all the above.

"I'm going to go ahead and ask you to blow into this Breathalyzer for me." He passed it to me. Whenever someone says "I'm going to go ahead and have you ____," it's a pretty good sign that you shouldn't be doing it. It's like in those low-budget pornos, *Back Room Casting Couch* or whatever, where the guy claims to be casting for glamour models and then says, "I'm going to go ahead and have you get on your knees and . . . ," and at first the woman is taken aback, insulted even, but the lie about being cast as a model is too compelling and the scenario always plays out the same. I'd seen enough episodes of *Back Room Casting Couch* not to fall for McDermott's cheap ploy.

"I'm sorry, Officer. I cannot consent to that at this time," I mumbled robotically.

"I see." He set the device down next to his chair and wrote more in his little book. Once this routine had run its course, some nurse gave me a bed. Apparently, Caroline came by later to try to spring me, but no one let her get past the front desk.

MY LEFT TESTICLE DANGLED THROUGH THE FRAYED APERTURE

Waking up with no pants on in a hospital bed—and not being exactly sure as to how I got there—was not amusing. It was like waking up in some dorm room next to some unfortunate-looking girl you didn't remember meeting the night before, trying to piece together what vague details and mechanisms of the hookup culture had deposited you there. Tequila shots? Was it that ninth game of pong at Tri-Kap? Had you taken ecstasy? Were you that last-call fratstar trolling around the Chi Gam basement for an eligible female as the sun rose over the college? I tried to barter with the nurse to discharge me, but her negotiation skills far surpassed mine.

"This is just a regular Thursday-morning hangover," I explained. "I'm not sick. I don't belong in Dick's House. This place is practically a hospital."

"You're still drunk, Andrew."

"No, I'm not. It's morning."

"That's not what the Breathalyzer says." She sighed.

"The Breathalyzer says it's not morning?"

"The Breathalyzer says you're still intoxicated." She rolled her eyes. "Don't make this harder for yourself."

"I can't be drunk. It's morning," I tried again, but she walked out of the room, her clogs sticking to the floor tiles. It seemed like just another technicality—I wasn't allowed to leave medical custody until three in the afternoon. There I was, with no pants on, in a hospital bed, for God's sake, and I had to find out what the fuck had happened the night before, not to mention what the consensus was among the brothers on how to proceed.

First I had to locate my *totally sweet* pants, which was a challenge since someone had stuck a needle in me and hooked me up to an IV so I wouldn't, apparently, die of dehydration. I swung my feet over the bed's guardrail, grabbed the rolling IV tower, and shuffled around the room in my boxers.

The nurse returned. She thought I was attempting to escape. "Andrew . . ." she sighed. "Really, you're not going anywhere until you blow into this Breathalyzer."

"I'm not doing this in my underwear," I muttered. I realized that the pair of boxers I was wearing had an unfortunate and less than inconspicuous rip underneath the crotch. I looked down and identified my left testicle dangling through the boxers' frayed aperture. I hadn't planned for this type of exchange when I'd been digging through my pile of laundry under the coffee table the day before. "Could you excuse me for a second?"

Having probably seen my left testicle something like nine times already, the nurse wasn't shocked, but I tried to be modest anyway. She walked out the open door again. I found my pants on the other side of the room and put them on, realizing that the skulls were splattered with mud—probably why I'd drunkenly taken them off. A few hours later I was sober enough to be discharged.

LORD OF THE FLIES VIBE

Stumbling across campus, I gravitated, like a drone summoned back to the hive, straight to ΣAE.

That afternoon the house looked more imposing than usual as I approached it from the back, walking slowly up the hill toward the back door, but the air was fresh and it was really spring, finally, a time of year that I always looked forward to but now found kind of depressing since I assumed I'd soon be going to jail. Spring seemed like an awful time to go to jail.

I passed the Dumpster at the bottom of the hill and, like Hansel, followed a trail of garbage strewn haphazardly through puddles of beer. The back door was propped open with a rotting log from Bradford's woodpile.

For some reason I went first to the basement. Maybe it

was just instinct. Two alums were already playing a one-on-one game of pong in JV, their Ralph Lauren shirts draped from a ceiling pipe. They were both chain-smoking, pale, and slick with beady sweat.

"It's Lohse!" one yelled.

"He's alive!"

"Hey, Mike," I said, not in a particularly good mood.

"We're looking for two more for pong. Yeah? Can you be one?" Mike seemed to be staring past me. I looked behind me and no one was there—just a heaping pile of empty plastic cups and cardboard boxes near the coffin.

"No thanks, man. I'm just here to find out what happened last night."

Mike looked at the other alum. They laughed slowly, then kind of trailed off, and Mike picked up his paddle and turned his eyes back to the pong table. "You should see what happened in Varsity," he said, not looking at me. Then the other guy served the ball.

I walked into the other room. The alums—a clean-cut crew of mostly junior Wall Street analysts and corporate consultants—had apparently drunkenly ripped the basement apart with sledgehammers and crowbars. Wading through a literally shin-high sea of empty beer cans and cracked plastic cups in Varsity, I found that the wall paneling that Rector had renovated in the room was gutted, smashed violently; shards of wood hung by splinters from bent nails. I walked back into JV.

"Hey, Mike?" I called out.

"Yeah?" They didn't stop the game this time.

"Who did all this damage?"

"I don't know, man. It's a good time." Mike sank a cup and smiled deviously as the other alum chugged the beer and pulled his polo off the pipe and wiped his mouth with it as I unsteadily climbed the stairs. More details became apparent as I continued my investigation; it seemed that every project that Rector had ever done as a pledge or as house manager had been mauled. Even the rock used as a doorstop for the pool room, the one that had DOUGLAS C. NIEDERMAYER carefully painted across it, had been smashed. How the fuck was that even possible? The thing was like a boulder.

This was just the beginning of the carnage, as the brotherhood continued to literally tear the house apart. It was a fantastically strange thing to witness that weekend. Police documents later revealed that Rector had even been threatened by an alum, an otherwise mild-mannered guy, who'd wielded a sledgehammer while asking him suggestively, "How's it going, Rector?"

Surprisingly, no brothers seemed particularly angry at Edwards, Price, Caroline, or me—at least not publicly. Most seemed angriest at Rector, or at least excited that the house's civil war could offer an outlet for their repressed destructive tendencies. Though I felt guilty, the brotherhood, judging by its rage, made it clear that what Rector had done was worse—he'd broken the most important rule: What happens in the house stays in the house. By contrast we imagined ourselves to be absolved of any wrongdoing.

As I walked around the house trying to piece together what was going on, I was more unsettled by the *Lord of the*

Flies vibe in the air than anything else. I turned to leave and ran into Schultz on the portico; Rector was sitting on the step next to him. He seemed deep in thought. I didn't want to know what he was thinking.

A MODEST GUESS

I returned to 9 later that night to talk with a then finally sober Edwards about what the next play would be. He said that he, too, had been interrogated the night before, but in the Libes—most likely a first for the fraternity. He said that he was so drunk and coked out that he could barely focus on the detective's face, but was steadfast in his denial of any illicit events, claiming to be so intoxicated he couldn't remember what had transpired, putting his drink count for the night somewhere between twenty-five and thirty.

"A modest guess," he said, smirking.

Edwards also said that Schultz had told him that the police had tested composites in the pool room. Considering that practically all of the composites in the room were laced with cocaine residue from brothers huddling over them at one time or another in the last few years, we figured it was only a matter of time before warrants were out for us—even if the residue was someone else's.

After the evacuation debacle the night before, Schultz was worried about the events lined up for Green Key. Mostly the Glow in the Dark party the next night. A whole weekend of partying stood before us; the paranoia in the house was palpable. The execs were afraid of warrants being delivered during massive party scenes of hundreds of wasted, underage kids, cops not just hauling out the accused cokeheads but raiding everyone else's fun, too, because I guess little goes on in fraternity houses that's above the scope of the law. Gathering together to discuss this, Edwards and I, we calculated we could probably do nothing about our impending doom; our only choices were either to hide or enjoy our last days.

Just when everything had seemed to die down, Davis waded into the fray. In typically eloquent language he denounced Rector in a housewide e-mail and then privately encouraged a few brothers—who were a part of what was called the Smash Brothers lineage, so named for their propensity to get drunk and break things—to "send a message" to Rector. Over those next few days the brotherhood so harassed Rector that he was forced to move out of the house.

FLUORESCENT ADOLESCENTS

No cops crashed the Glow in the Dark party. It was actually pretty boring. I was assigned bar duty—handing out glowing drinks in one corner of JV. The basement was so packed with bodies that a cloud of condensation had formed under the black lights substituted for the usual bulbs; girls waited for drinks with their hands outstretched as their teeth glowed brilliantly white. Bright orange shirts floated through the darkness.

Edwards and Price and I had split up on the chance that the police would deliver warrants that night—at the time it seemed like a good idea, though looking back, it seems our impetus for doing this is unclear. Would splitting ourselves up somehow foil Detective McDermott? Our demise was nonnegotiable, something to be accepted. Our tenure as normal members of the college community was a terminal illness.

I stood behind the bar filling cups with cheap vodka and tonic water under the purple lights. Caroline came down the stairs and I watched blankly as she forced her way through a crowd of freshmen to the bar. "Any sign of the cops?" she asked, brushing her hair behind her ear.

I stopped pouring the vodka. Impatient girls glared at me under their Day-Glo headbands. "None."

"Could this be a trap somehow?" She looked paranoid.

"I doubt it."

"Um, are you going to, like, pour those drinks?" one of the girls interrupted, posting one elbow on the bar and forcing her upturned palm at my face.

Caroline turned to her icily, then asked me, "Where's Edwards?"

"At AΔ, I think."

BLACK SMOKE

Late that night after the party had died down and the basement population had been reduced to a few brothers in pinnies silently playing pong under the black lights and some drunk chick dancing by herself next to the coffin in JV, Caroline and I witnessed a curious series of events.

We were walking through the foyer. Caroline was in the middle of saying something like "I'm so tired, let's just go to bed" when I turned to look in the living room and saw a group of shirtless brothers, including the estimable Goodrich of all people, dragging this table Rector had made in the wood shop—fitted with a self-aggrandizing plaque with his own name and then "donated" to the house in the name of brotherhood—out the side doors. We froze on the foyer's floor tiles, mouths agape.

"What the fuck are you doing?" I asked the brothers. Someone had dimmed the lights. The wood floor sheened dully, creaking under their boat shoes.

"It's a good time," Price hissed through teeth bitten down on an unlit cigarette. Douglas, shirtless, stood next to him waving a sledgehammer.

"You guys probably shouldn't be here," Goodrich said. A little unsteady on his feet, he smiled like a commodities trader who knew the fix was in. Caroline and I kept a safe distance—I guess to maintain the patina of *plausible deniability,* a phrase we'd all been throwing around since the Administrator's hazing investigation. The front pair of brothers pulled the cumbersome table through the French doors, its hind legs dragging and leaving deep scratches in the floorboards, as the rear brothers kept trying to lift the thing up.

Bros in the rear assaulted it with saws and power tools

that weren't even plugged in, and in a flashback to Dartmouth founder Wheelock's myth of the untamed savage, the kind of savage the school had supposedly been founded to educate, one brother even wore an Indian headdress. Some of the others were smeared with war paint, their sweaty chests rising and falling as they chopped the table into chunks and dragged them across the porch, down the grassy hill, and hauled them onto the patio's grill.

Caroline and I followed from a safe distance. I was afraid that if I got too close, even I might be infected with the Smash Brothers' urge to deface every material piece of Rector's existence as a brother—and for once I didn't want to be implicated in the house's madness.

"In four years of hanging out I've never seen anything like this before," Caroline whispered, gripping my arm as we stood on the porch watching the group of brothers pose for pictures, the one dude's Indian headdress fluttering in the spring breeze. They sang as they squirted lighter fluid onto the pile of smashed table shards: *"Caauuse, I'mmmm, Phi Alpha born and I'm Phi Alpha bred, and when I die, I'll be Phi Alpha dead! So, rah rah, Phi Alpha Alpha, rah rah Phi Alpha Alpha, rah rah Phi Alpha Alpha Σ-A-E!"*

The table burned slowly.

A cloud of black smoke overtook the house as the sun rose in the distance—just past the pines, past cautious, gauzy rays—and Caroline seemed a little bit disturbed so we turned back to Wheeler.

ZERO-SUM GAMES, TRYING TO COVER ALL THE BASES

Next night was a sober night. More rumination as a group—running over all possible scenarios, pacing around 9, debating, theorizing. Posts on the anonymous campus gossip website Bored@Baker had christened us "the ΣAE 3." I can't say we weren't amused by the title, and "Free the ΣAE 3!" became a sardonic rallying cry.

Sunday morning I woke up in my bed, the bottom bunk, next to Caroline. Pulaski was already awake, sitting at his desk. He was nursing an Odwalla; a mild stench of vomit lingered somewhere in the room. I rolled the comforter off my torso as Pulaski gazed up from his computer.

"How's the hangover, pal?" I asked.

"Shitty. I guess not as bad as getting busted by the cops, though."

I'd just had a pretty good dream and had forgotten about that whole police situation. Bummer. It was also the first Sunday morning in at least an entire year for which I was not so hungover I felt physically handicapped. I considered the meaning of this little coincidence.

"I'm not hungover at all, can you imagine it?" I bragged as Pulaski closed his laptop, face puffy and droopy, and turned toward me in his chair as I threw myself down on the futon. "And it's the Sabbath."

"What are you suggesting?"

"Maybe now's the time to go to the Lord and repent. Yeah?" I yawned. I looked over the edge of futon and found the source of the vile smell: someone had booted in my trash can.

"The question is, what are you repenting for? Does one have to repent for frattiness?"

I contemplated going along with the script—clearly the bro routine would be to brush the question off, act as if being fratty were carte blanche for sinfulness. I yawned again. I didn't care about either frattiness or Jesus. I just wanted answers about who had soiled my trash can. Then I wanted to not be arrested.

"So are you going to own up to booting in my trash can?"

"Okay, Lohse, just because you didn't happen to pee in *my* trash can last night does not mean that I happened to boot in *yours*. Grossness is not a zero-sum game."

"What's a zero-sum game?"

"It's a game when one player wins by another player losing."

"Makes sense."

Too much sense, actually.

I grabbed the trash can and dumped its contents into the bigger trash can in the hallway. The viscous chunks didn't bother me so much. The brotherhood had taught us to glorify vomit, and I guess it'd become sacramental for us, like the spirit becoming flesh or vice versa or whatever. At least Pulaski wasn't trying to eat it this time.

When I returned to the room, Caroline was awake and

sitting on the edge of the bottom bunk, hair in her eyes, gorgeously confused.

"I just had the weirdest dream," she said, rubbing her neck.

"Me, too," I said sarcastically as I tossed the plastic trash can over toward my desk. "I dreamt that Goodrich, Douglas, Price, and a bunch of other bros lit Rector's table on fire and posed for pictures while they were doing it."

"That was probably not the best idea," Pulaski said. He took a massive sip from his Odwalla and, looking queasy, shook his head at the other brothers' stupidity.

"Wow," Caroline goes, "yeah, that wasn't a dream after all. This weekend has been surreal." She sighed. Then I watched her face morph into a querulous lip curl, as if she was about to cry.

"Do you guys—do you guys think you should, like . . . flush out your systems? In case someone tries to . . . um, drug-test you?" Pulaski asked, causing a few more tears to cascade from Caroline's eyes. "Someone being . . . Detective McDermott?"

"That'd only be relevant if we get arrested." I was stumbling between denial and acceptance.

"We will get arrested," Caroline said. "It's only a matter of time." Then she started sobbing. We'd pretended that everything was fine, that everything was funny, that it didn't matter. We'd pretended so much that I didn't know how to react when I watched this girl—this girl with whom I was kind of falling in love—sob in front of me in a dorm room vaguely redolent of vomit and Pulaski's dirty socks.

Though I guess we could've picked a more romantic setting, we clearly weren't masters of circumstance at that
point.

"You guys better go to CVS."

"Let me look up what kind of shit will do the trick." I
said, trying to take charge. Just so Caroline would dry her
eyes. I flipped open my laptop and grabbed a photocopy
of *The Perfection of Wisdom Sutra* from Religion 69 and
scribbled down a detoxifying shopping list on the back; it
would probably amount to nothing, but it was a way to
jump the gun. I always wondered what that phrase meant.
I guess it means that if someone, say Detective McDermott,
pulls a gun on you, your best chance would be to jump
him instead of waiting to lose everything. But I'd always
imagined a little man jumping over the barrel of a gun, as
if he were jumping rope, something futile and absurd like
that.

At CVS we filled our basket with an exotic mix of supplements—as exotic as a chain pharmacy in New Hampshire
can offer—vitamins, cranberry extracts, and sundry other
products used to game drug tests. On seeing the breadth of
our purchases, how they all interrelated into one pathetic
and most likely ineffectual narrative, the aged lady at the
cashier, with her frizzy hair and sagging, leathery jowls,
fixed us with a suspicious look. There was no use denying
the obvious. Better to jump the gun.

"We're trying to flush myriad controlled substances out
of our systems in case we get arrested this week," I said,

trying to look as apathetic as possible as the woman tossed our black-pepper extract and St. John's wort into a plastic bag, next to a month's supply of cranberry juice and three bottles of saw palmetto.

Basically, we had not a single fuck of a clue of how to *actually* game a drug test, but shopping for supplements gave us something to do to pass the time.

"We've never really done this before so we're trying to cover all the bases." I raised my hand to high-five Caroline, but she just smiled incredulously and shook her head.

The checkout lady awkwardly adjusted the name tag on her vest—TIFFANY—and didn't speak a word besides reading our total, lips pursed in a scowl. Caroline tried to suppress laughter. That made me feel a little better. I hated seeing her sad.

SAMSARA IS ENDLESS

Monday after Green Key. Stages of grieving began. Surprisingly, I went to class. Beaufort tried to talk to me as if nothing had happened. Only notes from Religion 69, scrawled over the top of a blank Moleskine page: *Samsara is endless.*

DIAN HUA, CHINESE FOR "TELEPHONE"

Wednesday we learned by blitz that warrants had been issued for our arrest.

Seriously—apparently these days the authorities advise you over e-mail that your arrest is imminent. We all gathered in 9 sans Price, whom Rector apparently hadn't named in his testimony, and for whom there was no warrant. I imagined Price hiding out in his room in Wheeler, saying, as he always was, "Sucks to suck," or Price staring into his mirror mouthing to himself, "Gimme a little smooch." Even Davis had been charged for witness tampering because of the e-mail he'd sent to the Smash Brothers suggesting that they destroy Rector's shit.

Despite the hot, bright day the air-conditioning in 9 was oppressively cold, and I shivered as I leaned back in Edwards's desk chair. Caroline read the e-mail aloud. I stared up at the mural of the Ralph Lauren logo.

"We have twenty-four hours to turn ourselves in," she concluded, looking around the room.

"What if we wait for the cops to come get us? It would be more dramatic to be pulled out of class in handcuffs," Edwards suggested. He tried to laugh but faltered.

God, I thought, I can't watch him cry. Like, please don't. Davis just stared at his computer screen. He showed no signs of life. Just sat there like a J.Crew mannequin with real-life glass eyeballs.

"Edwards, that's a terrible idea." Caroline squeezed his hand.

I stood up and paced a lap around the coffee table where all this mayhem had begun in November, watching our dim reflections move across the television's blank screen. It was just another way to pretend that we hadn't just discovered that our lives were probably wasted.

"You're right," Edwards conceded.

"What are we going to do? I thought Price scrubbed the composite as we were leaving?" I turned from the television. "And why is there no warrant out for him, by the way?"

"Rector, apparently, left him out of his statements to the police. His final parting gift of playing favorites, like he always did with cleanup fines," Edwards said.

Caroline looked around the room. "What are we going to do? We are going to go to the police station tomorrow morning and turn ourselves in."

"But—"

"How can we do that?" Edwards said. "There's no way we can do that." It wasn't just Edwards about to cry, but Davis, too, who'd been so silent—he was still lifeless—I saw his blue eyes fog over. He just stared at the computer. I guess if he looked closely enough, he could see his dreams unravel in front of his eyes, too.

"How do we—how do we—tell our parents?" Edwards ran a hand through his hair.

"I guess we just have to call them," Caroline responded. We all took turns pretending to be composed. It must've been her turn. As long as one person was composed at any given time, we wouldn't go insane. That was what I realized. That was the theory.

"I'm just going to do it now and get it over with," I said. "I'm just going to make the call."

Caroline and I went into Davis and Edwards's bedroom. Family pictures on their dressers, bow ties and blazers hanging in their closet. An empty wine bottle on the windowsill. Artifacts of an expired way of life. Hands shaking, I slid my phone out of the pocket of my critter shorts, scrolled to *Mom,* and pressed the green button. Seconds rolled by like revolutions of the earth.

YOU JUST LOST THE GAME FOR US

We went out to dinner that night. Last Supper kind of thing. We promised not to talk about the next day, but walking through Hanover toward the restaurant, we couldn't help but occupy ourselves with paranoid, idle talk.

"So what if Price gets nabbed, too?"

"How much do you think lawyers will cost?"

"Do you think they'll try to pit us against each other like some police drama?"

"Yeah, that might get kind of crazy."

"You think? We're all friends and brothers, and you guys are dating, so no one is turning on anyone, okay?"

"Yeah, agreed—"

"What if—"

"Okay, guys, seriously," Davis said, finally joining the conversation. I hadn't heard his voice in hours. I associated his voice with strength, authority, frattiness—and it scared me to have it silenced. Stockholm syndrome dies hard. You never expect your pledge trainer to be at a loss for words.

He tried to muster his best trainer voice; something about it was always both psychotic and effective. "Let's play a little game. Let's play a game where we try to pretend this is all not happening. We can win the game by not mentioning this, or anything related to it, or anything related to cocaine, for ten whole minutes."

"Sure."

"Yeah, sounds good," I said. "Okay."

"All right."

A booth by the window. I touched the glass and it was cold, as if a film of ice were caught within it. When the waitress came to our table, I ordered a Coke and we all looked at each other, Edwards choked up, Davis somber under the lip of his baseball cap. It wasn't possible to avoid what was waiting for us.

"You just lost the game for us, Lohse," Davis said.

After dinner we rented a movie. The video store smelled like plastic, like a funeral parlor for something you couldn't remember, and the bearded burnout behind the counter frowned like a mortician when Edwards made a stupid joke about *American Psycho*, about returning videotapes.

We went to Caroline's place and tried to zone out. Some vapid teen movie.

I'M HERE TO, LIKE, TURN MYSELF IN?

Our times to turn ourselves in at the police station the next day were scattered throughout the morning; we no longer had the luxury of working as a group. We steeled ourselves for interrogations by promising that no one would utter a word without attorneys present—attorneys we didn't have yet. Despite our dramatic preconceptions about what was going to happen, the day's events were pretty mundane.

I put on khakis and an oxford and my navy blazer and a red-striped tie that had belonged to my grandfather and got in Edwards's car, the same car that had brought me to ΣAE on bid night, and drove myself past the golf course where I'd run with the pledges in almost that same outfit.

Edwards and Caroline were supposed to turn themselves in later. I'm pretty sure Davis was already at the police station by the time I got there. I drove all the way there without breathing or blinking. I opened the front door, its glass mirroring the morning's hot light, and I walked up to the desk. "Hi, I'm here to, like, turn myself in? There's a warrant out for me, I believe." Does that sound ridiculous or what? Like, that's actually exactly what happened.

The dude at the desk just looked up at me. He'd seen it all before. His face was incapable of surprise. He had a thick brown mustache. "Name?"

"Andrew Lohse."

He looked at his computer. "Go sit on the bench next to the water fountain," he grunted, motioning down the hall.

Then a guy with a massive handgun holstered in his belt, like a Cougar Magnum or something, came to get me, took me into some sterile back room with thick metal doors and too many security cameras. I straightened my tie, tried to stay cool. I tried to smile for my mug shot but couldn't force my face to follow orders. After being fingerprinted—my hands gruffly slammed down on the ink pad and directed to the appropriate spots on my fresh file's paper—I looked up at the cop. He fluttered my file closed.

"Anything else?" I asked.

"You are free to go."

I didn't expect to hear that.

FOR WHAT IT'S WORTH

I was walking across the Green when my phone rang. It was Schultz.

"Lohse?"

Who did he think would pick up, a corrections officer? I stopped walking and paced a circle in the grass while kicking one boat shoe off my foot; feeling the breeze. I stared across the lawn at Sanborn, Baker, and Rauner Library, arrayed in front of me like mausoleums of some dead empire.

"Yeah?" I was impatient but don't remember why. I guess I was in the middle of going somewhere.

"Can you come to Pebble? Douglas and Wallace want to talk to you. I think it's really important."

"Why can't they call me themselves?"

A brunette senior in a sheer sundress, a girl I could vaguely identify as a Kappa who might have been in my Victorian Lit class, a girl with perfect dimples, walked past me toward Sanborn. I flipped down my Wayfarers.

Schultz was still talking about something in his gratingly nervous voice. ". . . said he doesn't have your number. . . . Can you please just come, like, at now . . . important . . ."

I lacked options. I slipped my Sperry back on and headed toward the house, sun setting over one side of campus, its core like a blood orange, rays the color of spilt beer.

As I approached the yard, I heard the Stones song "Under My Thumb" droning from the speakers on Pebble. I strongly associate that song with that spring, with a feeling of hopelessness so extreme it was almost funny—and I also associate it with meaningless things like day drinking, playing boccie, and throwing footballs with douche bags I didn't like, accidentally ashing cigarettes on myself, and this prank that Pulaski and I used to pull on each other of peeing into a Lay's bag and then offering the other guy a chip.

Instead of entering through the frat's front door and climbing the stairs, I decided to ascend to Pebble via the fire-escape ladder. Douglas and Wallace were already up there. When they saw my hands grip the top rung of the ladder, they stopped talking. I noticed that they'd situated a chair across from theirs—clearly, that was where I was meant to sit.

"Lohse, could you please use the stairs next time?" Douglas whined, readjusting his backward hat. "We could get fined by SNS for brothers using the fire escape in broad daylight."

"I guess there are worse things going on in people's lives right now," I said.

They stared at me, unamused. Wallace was packing a fat lip of dip and would from time to time spit tobacco juice into an empty beer can he clutched in his long, tan fingers. "We have to talk to you about something," he said, waving at the unoccupied chair I'd correctly assumed to be mine. My interrogations just never seemed to stop. Before anyone else said anything, I watched the sun finally go down, then watched the sprinklers behind Baker Library pop up out of the lawn and spray the grass with jets of water.

"Let's just cut to the point," Douglas said. "You're not going to be able to live in the house for sophomore summer. National says you are no longer a brother. We asked Schultz what to do about this, and he said it was up to us since we are the incoming execs."

"In our eyes, for what it's worth, you're still a brother," Wallace reassured me. I've also learned that whenever someone has to preface something with "for what it's worth," it probably isn't worth much.

"You're just going to have to find another place to live. Livermore"—one of the most B-side '12s—"will be taking over your spot in Two."

They probably said other things, too, but I wasn't paying attention. After they dismissed me, I didn't say anything and climbed through the window to 4 and walked down the stairs and silently kicked over an overfilled garbage can in the foyer, slammed the door violently on its hinges. Then I left.

ALL THE SHIT THAT'S FIT TO PRINT

Pacing outside Robinson Hall with Caroline, waiting for Davis to show up. Rumor had spread that *The Dartmouth* was going to run a story about our arrests. Everything was falling apart. Edwards was in class and couldn't confront the editor in chief with us.

"There he is now," Caroline said, pointing down Administration Row toward Baker Library. Davis was making his way toward us across the grass. He was easy to spot in a sky-blue polo, khakis, baseball cap pulled down over his eyes like a celebrity trying to evade the paparazzi.

"You doing okay?" Davis asked as he gave me the grip, then hugged Caroline.

"I'm fine," she said.

"I'm all right," I said.

"Let's give these vultures a piece of our mind." He appeared resolute for the first time in a while. We climbed the stone steps into Robinson, crossed the polished foyer floor, walked past the trophy cases, and scaled the grandiose stairs to the *D*'s office. I wondered how many times my grandfather had floated across those same tiles.

"We're here to see Gretchen Phillips," Caroline said to some random girl in the newsroom.

Writers and editors, all sitting at identical iMacs, stopped whatever meaningless tasks they were idling away at and simultaneously stared up at us. Davis looked across the sea of staffers and scowled.

"I'm sorry, she's in a meeting right now," the girl said.

"We have to speak with her this very moment," Davis told her.

"I'm sorry. You can come back at, like, nine, though."

"The issue will probably be closed by then," I said, "so we're going to have to talk to her now."

"I can go and see if maybe she—"

"We can do that ourselves." Davis waved the girl back into her overly ergonomic swivel chair. Caroline and I followed him through the newsroom to Gretchen's corner office; he knocked once, like a doctor, then opened the door without waiting for permission. No meeting was going on. Gretchen Phillips was just sitting at her desk—like a villain in a bad movie, as if she'd been waiting for us the whole time.

"Does this mean that you are granting us an interview?" She downplayed a smirk.

"This is all off the record," Caroline said.

Davis slumped down in one of the chairs. "You can't print our names," he blurted. "You can't do that."

"Guys . . ." Gretchen goes, a little irritated. "I understand your concerns. But the *Dartmouth* is merely reporting the news. It's not our fault that the news involves you and your fraternity. We have a journalistic obligation to name your names. That's simply what journalistic integrity is all about."

"Bullshit," Davis said.

"Plus, this is all public record, see?" She held up a stack of papers—the police reports. Our names were circled. "Do you see this?" She waved them around apathetically. Somehow, she had a way of making it seem as if she were more put upon than we were—I could've sworn I saw her roll her eyes at us.

"Where did you get those?" I demanded. "That was, like, yesterday."

"Anyone can get them, Lohse. That's what *public record* means," Gretchen sighed. "I'm very busy right now, guys."

I looked over at Davis. Underneath the brim of his cap he began to cry. I was sitting in the *D*'s office watching my pledge trainer, the guy who'd made me chug vinegar, the guy who'd made me drink until I puked, like, every other day, the guy who'd made my friends wear week-old-vomit-soaked clothes that had been buried in the backyard, the guy who'd become my friend despite all of that—I was watching him sob, then cry, then bawl his eyes out. Gretchen Phillips leaned back smugly, clutching a pen, waiting for him to stop. *Journalistic integrity.*

"This is going to ruin our lives," Davis managed. "Do you understand that? Can you empathize with that at all?"

"That's not my job," Gretchen said. "My job is to run the oldest college newspaper in America."

7
IT'S CREEPY

Summer dragged on and our criminal cases made their way through the justice system; I knew my days were numbered. Also looming over me like a death sentence for my youth was my eventual Committee on Standards disciplinary hearing. Edwards and I had hundreds of pages of paperwork, explanation, and defense to sketch out. Compelled by the same kind of recklessness that had gotten us into our bad situation, we resolved to fight our way through the college's charges and keep our promise to the secrecy of the house, though the thought of continuing to lie gave me a nauseous feeling. Especially since I was starting to see that the brotherhood was riddled with hypocrisy.

I tried to understand my conflicted feelings about the house. They appeared irresolvable, at least for someone whose legal well-being was tied up in the debauchery of frat life, and especially since I'd seen what had happened to Rector when he tried to say something about what went on. We punished people who didn't follow the script; ultimately, I felt as if I had no other choice but to defer a mea culpa about my life until I'd somehow, eventually, gotten far enough from ΣAE to get some perspective on—and a reprieve from—what happened there. Like coke, the frat was something that got you hooked. It exhilarated you at first, but would always crush you.

I went to class and did normal things, and for a while I tried to avoid the house even though I kept getting pulled back into meetings and blacking out and chain-smoking cigarettes all night and inhaling whippits on Pebble and talking about "us" and "them" and house politics and bullshit, even though I knew my whole life was stamped with a fast-approaching expiration date.

One night I borrowed Pulaski's VW just to drive around and clear my head. I'd found him in the Libes, stoned and studying for Astronomy 1, his computer lit up with calculations and pictures of Neptune, and asked if I could have his keys. I tried to talk to him, but nothing he was saying made any sense, and he just kept glancing up at me from his computer screen and muttering something about the star Alpha Centauri and smiling sincerely, so I gave up and went down to 2 and found his keys in his desk and drove away.

Then Blair texted me. For some reason we agreed to meet up, so I turned the car around and drove to frat row and picked her up in front of Tri-Delt. The VW's running lights framed the passenger seat in an ethereal glow when she got into the car, and all I could see was her face—she looked pale, though she said she'd been tanning all day, and I could see a bikini under her white dress. That Bon Iver song "Skinny Love" came on the stereo.

"This is strange," she said, her eyes floating in the dark, floating in the air that smelled like leather. I turned the car down toward Occom Pond and drove pretty slow.

"Why'd you agree to see me?" I asked. Maybe she wanted to say good-bye before I got kicked out. Maybe she wanted to reminisce, revisit all of our disappointing vignettes and stunted images of what could've been.

"I don't even really know. Recently I've been trying to run into you around campus. It hasn't worked though. Where've you been?" She pushed a piece of dark hair away from her eyes. "Is Caroline here? I thought I saw you with her at Theta Delt last night."

"She's in Boston. I wasn't at Theta Delt last night anyway. You know I don't hang out at Theta Delt."

"It must have been Price, then. You guys are starting to look alike for some reason. It's creepy."

"Yeah. It's creepy. I guess."

I didn't know where to drive so I headed away from campus, headed north on Route 10. The road wound through shadows ahead of us and we sped by white churches and post offices until I saw a sign: we were already far north of Lyme, which is, I guess, maybe ten or twelve miles north of Hanover. We were out in the still north and the sky was clear. Constellations hung over us—the Great Square, Great Bear, Orion, Andromeda, whatever.

She turned to look at me again and I thought she was going to say something, but she didn't and I wanted to say, *I'm sorry about everything,* but the words were lost in my throat even though I still felt something strong for her—the kind of thing I'll always feel but will never be able to explain to you.

The road opened up into a big valley. Some lights of houses or buildings or porches were lit up across the road on a large hill glimmering in the summer gloom. She half smiled and turned the music down; the words being sung were *I tell my love to wreck it all,* and she looked at me and muttered, "It's creepy," again, and I wasn't sure if she was talking about Price or not, and eventually I turned around and took her back to Tri-Delt, went home to my apartment, smoked a joint by myself, watched porn for at least an hour, eschewed my Shakespeare reading, felt sorry for myself, fell asleep.

PHI ALPHA

Ripley was on campus for the summer. We decided to get the ΦA tattoo together. I guess he wanted it to show his undying love for the brotherhood. I had other, more complicated reasons. As a way of trying to forget that I'd actually agreed to do it, I'd blacked out the night before and booted all over the corner of JV and then in the morning woke up on one of the green leather couches in the Libes. All I remembered was playing pong with this girl from my creative-writing course, this girl who had some boyfriend in Luxembourg or something, and possibly trying and failing to make out with her.

In the Libes the air-conditioning was set to sixty and I was shivering and in severe bodily pain—as if my stomach had turned itself inside out, a queasy feeling accompanied by a harsh burning in my nasal cavities that seemed to indicate that the night before I had snorted something along the lines of broken glass. No memory of that either.

I rolled over on the leather and saw Ripley sitting with his feet planted on one of the library tables. A shaft of light from a dormer window cut across his face. I blinked. He was just sitting there, watching me sleep, or maybe he'd been asleep himself in the chair. Behind his head the windowpanes glowed with clear blue sky.

"Wake up, whaleshit," he grunted.

I murmured, still half-asleep, "I'm not a whaleshit anymore."

"Some small part of us will always be whaleshit, bro." He said this with a falsely pensive affectation, a narrowing of his brow. Then he snorted his trademark high-pitched laugh. Something about Ripley never seemed quite right, as if something maddening was always on his mind that he could never talk about. I think it had something to do with the frat and how it had changed him, but maybe I'm projecting.

After all, he used to be pretty conservative. Never drank, never, God forbid, put anything up his nose. Not the kind of guy who displays his anus on videotape, you know?

Then he joined ΣAE. He, or more like the role he played within the house, had become the grim punch line for every joke about fratstardom and excess, failing classes and never showering. I think he hated it. Hated it like I hated it all, but he couldn't turn the game around. So a nagging existential doubt was lodged in his brain like a shotgun shell rattling around and leaving him deeply conflicted, and sometimes I would see it come out and it would worry me. He'd probably have said the same about me.

Like this one time that summer, a few nights before. We were drunk and wandering around campus and ended up near School Street, past Panarchy, a counterculture coed society that used to be a frat, and we just walked up onto someone's porch, some guys I vaguely knew—I think they were Bones Gate brothers—who were smoking hookah and drinking beer.

Walking up, I sat myself on the porch's ledge and the BG handed me a duo of warm Stellas. I turned to hand one to Ripley, but he was MIA; for some reason he'd felt the need to perform. That's the only way I can understand why he did what I'm about to describe, because he then walked across the street and into a random house. Just let himself in the front door.

As I was saying something to the effect of "Yeah, my friend Ripley, he's a little drunk, maybe a little crazy, too," we watched, rapt, as a screen was kicked out of a second-story window and Ripley lumbered onto the roof of that house's front porch in his pajama pants and bright yellow ΣAE jersey with his pledge name written on the back.

He stood unsteadily on the little pitched roof.

"Ripley . . . you probably want to get down from there," I yelled up from across the road.

"Don't worry, bro, I got this," he yelled back.

"Hey, man, come on, that's stupid. Don't do that," one of the Bones Gate dudes yelled.

"Does he live there?" another asked.

"No," I said.

Ripley just stood there, up on the little pitched roof, staring at the ground beneath him. I took a picture with my phone. I figured it'd be a good story if Ripley ever ran for Senate back home or something, or at least a good story to have him dome over at meetings the following Wednesday. Then again, a Senate bid probably wasn't in the cards for him—opposition research would eventually get their hands on the anus tape, the shaky moving image of his wrinkled, hairy asshole.

He leapt off the roof into a bush. I jogged over to him as he was dusting himself off. He smiled wide, no sprained ankle or bones jutting from his kneecaps. I was both impressed and terrified by his absurdity.

"Wasn't that high, man," he said. I guess we've all had that moment—the moment when we want to jump off something tall just to see if we'll be fine, and that night he got lucky.

But I opened my eyes, and, as I said, we were in the Libes and Ripley was just sitting there staring at me from across the empty room. Staring at me over a pile of empty Chinese takeout containers and a ziggurat of snus tins and Keystone cans.

"Someone had a rough night," he deadpanned. "Don't worry, though, I passed out in here, too. Just woke up, man."

Rubbing my eyes, I asked, "What time is it?"

"Almost time to go to the tattoo place. Mike and Eric should be here soon." Ripley got up from his chair and paced the room, making sure not to step on the giant gold ΣAE letters in the purple carpeting. You know the rule—don't step on the fucking letters.

Mike and Eric, two alums, were coming up from Boston to get the ink with us. I guess they wanted to relive their glory days, which weren't that far behind them. For me, the idea of closing the ΦA circuit—Davis, Edwards, and Rector all had the tattoo, accuser and the accused—seemed compelling.

But that early in the morning, with the kind of hangover that left me feeling like a crinkled, useless rind of a human being? I was getting cold feet. The thought of a possibly HIV-riddled needle piercing the soft flesh around my rib cage left me nauseous.

"Is there time to go get some food? Are you hungry?" I mumbled from the couch. Silence. I felt anemic. I tried again. "I could really use a burrito, dude."

Still pacing, Ripley shook his head. There wasn't enough time, he explained. We would have to do it on an empty stomach. "This'll be an adventure in collective self-laceration, bro." Vintage Ripley. You could never tell if he was serious or not, earnest or ironic. I winced, about ready to back out—what would my grandfather have thought? I didn't think frats or secret societies were into tattoos back in the day, considering that body ink was then probably reserved for hoodlums, mystics, and drunken sailors—and when the Libes door swung open and the alums walked in with the air of smug cynicism popular among recent Ivy League graduates, I considered just rolling over and freezing to death on the couch.

"Wake up, Lohse." Eric rustled me. I didn't even know him all that well, but he was getting in my face.

"I'm up, dude, I'm up. Chill."

"You need the ΦA to protect you from the evil whims of the judge," Mike added. "It's like a magical protection."

Ripley and I didn't say much on the way to the tattoo place. The alums did most of the talking.

"We've wanted to get the ΦA since senior spring," Mike ranted, one hand on the wheel, driving like a maniac, looking up at me in the rearview to make sure Ripley and I were paying attention. I tried not to.

"But other circumstances intervened," Eric offered, "namely, like, binge drinking and the casual ingestion of mind-altering substances." He cackled, then started telling us some story about how he and Mike had watched *Requiem for a Dream* while rolling on E once, as if that were going to somehow cure my obviously frail mental state. He was saying something about Mike's crying for hours and reaching out for the TV's glow in Room 2.

I nodded along and tried to suppress my rising bile, which was derivative in equal parts of my hangover, Mike's wild jittering of the wheel, and my repressed fear of having my painful experiences committed indelibly to my dermis. Mike and Eric kept bantering to each other in the front. They told stories, reliving the lifestyle Ripley and I were currently trapped in. *Samsara is endless*. They were jealous of me, I was jealous of them.

How'd I find myself in situations like that, always just outside of my comfort zone? Most of the other brothers probably felt that way, too, sometimes, because being in a frat to begin with was a kind of collective self-abuse. But I didn't want to get the ΦΑ for any cheap reason—I didn't want it because I loved my brothers, and certainly not because I wanted to signify my honoring the supposedly hallowed secrets of the house. Everything was inverted. I didn't love them. I was getting the tattoo because of the trauma of the spring. It was a way of dealing with life, marking how things could never be the same again.

The tattoo parlor sat above a dirty Chinese restaurant in a dismal, down-on-its-luck New Hampshire town, the kind of place only good for junk shops and dive bars. As soon as we arrived, I made vague promises to myself that I'd never return, even if Ripley tapped me for the secret society Edwards had tapped him for, the one I wanted to be in.

Ripley and I paced around the room while Eric took off his pants and lay down on the vinyl table. He was getting the mark on his hip. The tattoo artist was swarthy and covered in ink himself. As the guy fumbled with the needles and tubes and glistening tools, he asked the rest of us, baring his yellowed teeth in a smile, if we were drunk.

"Booze dulls the pain," he said.

When it was my turn, my face got too close to the guy's metallic rolling cart of mechanized needles and little plastic things that looked like dental dams. Too late for doubts. The first prick. Flowing ink.

A MIDSUMMER NIGHT'S DREAM

Some Monday, sitting in English 24: Shakespeare. The prof was reading a line from *A Midsummer Night's Dream*.

" 'When they next wake, all this derision shall seem a dream and fruitless vision.' " He read the line, like, three times, but no one seemed to notice, and from my seat in the last row of the lecture hall—Carson L01, windowless, freezing-cold air-conditioning—I could see a group of Kappas checking their BlitzMail, an AΔ on ESPN.com, a Bones Gate bro who was, for all intents and purposes, so stoned he had fallen asleep.

Blair invited me over that night. She opened Tri-Delt's front door for me. Some sisters were mopping the front hall, and the whole house smelled like antiseptic. One gave me a dirty look. I didn't know why. I followed Blair to the back of the house and then found myself in her bedroom.

"Show me your tattoo," she said, closing the door behind her and clicking the lock. I lifted up my polo, showed her one side of my rib cage, under my forearm. The tattoo was still fresh, skin inflamed, and the black lines of the phi and the alpha and the laurel leaf showed as raised black ridges.

"Very nice." She ran a finger over it, making me wince.

"Chill, the wound is still fresh."

"You think?" She smirked. I assumed that she was trying for some double entendre. She was always angling for some ice-cold play on words, but whether she was referring to the disaster of our erstwhile relationship or the disaster of my life, I couldn't tell.

We sat on her bed as the sound of banal hip-hop washed up through the floor from the basement, and I frowned for a second as I identified the song, this Flo Rida song "Right Round," and I could hear a bunch of girls beneath us yelling, " '. . . right round, right round!' "

Blair pouted, lips magenta. We'd run out of things to say. Her phone pinged. A text. Her douche Kappa Omega boyfriend.

I looked up at one of her walls—unframed pictures taped in rows, mostly pictures of Blair in black dresses at sorority parties and formals with her new boyfriend, leaning to one side in what, I assumed, was some kind of humorously carefree pose. Eventually she said I had to leave. I said, "I'll see you later," but didn't see her again for years.

SUPER WEIRD

I ran into Ripley in the Chi Gam basement later that night, and I don't think there was even a party happening, just the house drink, Sleepyfeet, being served from recycling bins, and we were drunk and showing off our tattoos to each other even though they were both exactly the same and he was telling me about how later on the day we'd gotten them done he'd rolled on ecstasy with some townie and then went skinny-dipping with her in Mink Brook and then passed out on her couch and how weird it was that she lived in a *house* with her *parents* and *worked* in the *town*. Wasn't that *super weird*? he wanted to know. I pointed out that the tattoo guy had said not to go swimming for a few weeks, least of all in a grimy creek full of stagnant water and protozoa, something about how the spot might get infected and need to be redone, but I realized that Ripley wasn't listening to me, because he had next on the pong table we were standing next to and a few Chi Gams were watching us from across the table, whispering.

AN EDUCATIVE EXPERIENCE

In July, Caroline, Edwards, and I settled in court for minor offenses, misdemeanors. A few thousand dollars and a few plea bargains later, our lives weren't ruined. Then came the more terrifying hurdle: the Committee on Standards. That, the Administrator promised us, would be an educative experience.

The hearing. It couldn't have been more sanctimonious. Suits and ties. After hours of monotonous questions about cocaine and alcoholism and composites, threats of expulsion, methodically timed bathroom breaks, and lengthy conference calls to interrogate witnesses with such complicated legalese as "Did you see Lohse and Edwards insufflating a white powder?"—"Yes," the formal proceeding culminated in what we'd imagined to be our "If the glove don't fit, you must acquit" closing statement, an expertly crafted defense we'd practiced for hours.

I slid my chair back and rose from the conference table. Buttoning my blazer and straightening my tie the way I'd seen lawyers in movies do, I stepped over to the room's whiteboard and drew an elaborate blueprint of the fraternity's first floor, making sure to offer a compass rose as a reference point. Then I delivered our proof, *ladies and gentlemen of the college,* that, because of the placement of the room's door and the dimness of the overhead lighting fixtures, Rector couldn't possibly have seen if we were snorting something or not. And, we pointed out, as one final smoking gun, *he hated us;* we'd just been looking at a composite, leaning over it, quizzing each other on fraternal history. The coke residue? Truthfully, it could have been from any one of the composites, we pointed out. *But it definitely wasn't ours.*

The committee members stared at me.

One professor squinted. Another let out a lengthy sigh.

Immediately after the hearing I met with Dean Applegate in the next conference room over. Applegate had been appointed my "adviser" to lead me through the *educative experience* of getting kicked out of Dartmouth; she'd sat through the entirety of the nearly six-hour-long hearing without uttering a single word, glaring at me the whole time. An icy woman, she'd just hours before seemed incapable of human emotion, robotically warning me that I'd probably be expelled, then advising me that I belonged in rehab, not the Ivy League.

Applegate now laced her fingers together and looked me in the eyes and actually smiled. She said she was proud of me for telling the committee the whole truth. I nearly fell out of my seat. Even now I'll probably never be sure if Dean Applegate was straight-up fucking with me, because a few hours later I found out that I was suspended for a year.

A SOLID ENDING POINT

After that, ΣAE dominated M@st3rs, the ultracompetitive sophomore-summer pong tournament, earning what appeared to be a crucial spike in social capital. We all got drunk and descended to the "pit" at ΓΔX, their subbasement level, which at various times had apparently been a squash court, a swimming pool, and a basketball court, where the tournament was to be played. Price and I blew smoke in the opposing teams' eyes—it was for me, I imagined, my going-away party, my last night as a fratstar.

Cruising to victory on one-half of the bracket, Wallace and Gibbons knocked out Sig Ep, then beat Theta Delt's A team, the heavy favorite, until losing to ΣAE B, Livermore and Sullivan, in the final. No other houses stuck around for the championship. Most other frats hated us. We marched back to the house with a victory plaque.

I left campus the next morning. At least I knew I wasn't going to jail. That's always a solid starting point, a point from which you can't lose, from which your life sits before you like an empty page. It was also a solid ending point. Feeling completely emotionally bankrupt, I assumed that I might transfer elsewhere, to another school, or at least never return to ΣAE if I came back to Dartmouth. I couldn't imagine relapsing down the same path.

8

YOU'RE JUST A KID WITH CHUBBY CHEEKS

I took a job at a restaurant busing tables at home in Brattle-boro. Though I guess I don't mind picking up people's waste, it was the kind of job I didn't want to publicize to fellow frat brothers or wealthy school friends.

One of the cooks asked me about Dartmouth once. "How'd you end up here, busing?" he asked through the line window, nodding toward the restaurant's back door, back to where you could walk outside and see rusted train tracks and the Connecticut River and a row of worn-door warehouses that used to hold the town's industry. I figured the nod was his way of saying, *This place sucks.* Then, wiping down the line with a damp rag, he stared at me under his baseball cap. I could smell a piece of meat burning in a pan behind him.

Inexplicably, I felt that I owed him answers, owed him some kind of explanation as to how all of my Algerism had backfired, but "Long story, man" was all I could manage. All I told him was that I'd been in a frat.

"Like, a frat frat?"

As opposed to . . . ?

"Isn't that, like, groupthink? Everyone making each other do stupid shit?" He sniffed over his shoulder. "You can't do that groupthink thing, man. You don't seem like that kind of guy."

"I'm not."

After closing once, I was sitting at the bar counting my minuscule take for the night while the bartender, Jimmy, a raging douche bag with a perpetual five o'clock shadow who'd consistently try to instigate conversations with me about Thai hookers after I told him that my brother and I were going backpacking in Asia, polished glasses.

"So what's the story, Andy?" he kept asking. "What happened with you and *Dahtmouth*?" He stacked the dry glasses beneath the bar. Then he collected dirty coasters and cocktail napkins off the bar and slid them into the trash, not once taking his beady eyes off me.

"I had to take a year off. That's all."

"Come on, Andy, no one just 'takes a year off.'"

One of the servers turned the lights all the way up, stacked chairs.

"People definitely do. Dude, when were you in college, like, the nineties? Things are different."

"What was it, you smoked too much weed? I bet that was it, I guarantee it. Little Andy smoked too much weed." He didn't even look up from adjusting his credit card tips. I could see his well-tanned, eminently punchable face reflected in the mirror behind the bar, suspended between shelves of overpriced wine.

"You really wanna know?" I put on my backpack. "The truth?"

He turned from the credit card machine.

"Coke, in my frat, cops, witness-tampering charges, all sorts of shit." I walked away before he could say anything—or before I felt embarrassed.

"Wow," he said, caught off-balance, fumbling with a stack of receipts. Then he regained his dry, douchey demeanor. "You're just a fucking kid. You're just a kid with chubby cheeks. Kids with chubby cheeks don't sniff coke. What kind of fucked-up frat were you in? I can't even picture that."

"Me neither," I said.

YOU'D BE THE PERFECT PERSON

My brother, Jon, and his boyfriend, Harry, hung around our mom's house the end of that summer and the beginning of the fall. Harry was into radical politics and had written some scathingly anti-frat op-eds. His Women and Gender Studies major was mostly crafted around queer theory, and he liked to look at frat life through that lens—I talked with him and Jon a lot, spent late nights drinking wine and debating the frats. Harry and Jon took turns psychoanalyzing the frats' systems of power, referencing Deleuze and Chomsky and Lacan and Foucault and Spivak and who cares.

Inevitably, we talked about hazing. Harry was fascinated, though not surprised, by the depravity of my pledge term, the truth behind ΣAE's polished facade. Jon already knew almost everything about my hazing.

"This is fascinating," Harry said, leaning against the refrigerator as I talked about the vomelette and all the chugging and the booting.

"I don't think pledge term is *that* fascinating, though," I said. "It's just what happened. Isn't everyone's Dartmouth experience like that?"

They stared at me, eyebrows raised.

"Um, I don't necessarily think so." Harry laughed. "Few people in the world can say they were coerced to chug vinegar or vomit all the time to get into some club."

"Isn't this all beneath the name of Dartmouth College? And beneath the name of any school, anyway?" Jon pointed out. "And just beneath general humanity?"

"You're right," I agreed. But what could be done about it?

"Sig Ep hazed—even though we said we didn't—but it was all optional, not to mention PG compared to your experiences," Jon added.

Then Harry asked, "Have you ever thought, maybe, that the hazing and psychological abuse you suffered were done so you would just accept them as commonplace?"

He was right—at some point during pledge term I'd just accepted my experiences as the new normal, a trauma compounded by other radical shifts in my life. Now I had to accept that the trauma itself had changed me, had affected my behavior and attitudes.

We continued our late nights in the kitchen hashing out the flaws of Greek life, how it could be redeemed, and even I could agree, having left the Dartmouth bubble and having methodically come to these conclusions myself—after all, I had plenty of free time for introspection—that what went on there was fucked-up. I wondered if somehow the system could be changed from the inside, reformed, made safer, or whether the whole thing had to be stopped. Caught between these ideas, I agreed that someone ought to do something about it so that no nice, naive, ambitious kids found themselves in the position in which I'd found myself.

I just didn't think it would have to be me.

I'd decided to try to go back to Dartmouth.

"No," my brother and Harry argued back some other night, "you'd be the perfect person to do something about it." At first I was nonplussed, but they gradually forced me to weigh the good my admission would do against what I might lose. They forced me to question my experiences, articulate my views—as I tried to reconcile the way I thought I loved Dartmouth with the terrible things that happened there.

Knowing what I knew, having experienced what I experienced, did I have some kind of moral imperative to make sure that other people weren't hazed the way I was? My biggest fear was becoming like Rector. But, I wondered, was the imperative different when people were hurting each other instead of themselves?

These were tough ethical questions for a twenty-year-old whose identity was so thoroughly enmeshed in a depraved fraternity life, so I reasoned that maybe I could just tune out Jon and Harry's arguments. But wasn't that the easy way out?

"It's perfect that President Kim is a public health expert," Harry argued. "We need to get this information to him. What if he doesn't know about all the hazing? If he did, I'm *sure* he'd do something about it."

"And if the administration doesn't do anything—" Jon said.

Harry cut him off. "We shame them."

GO TO SLEEP

We went to Martha's Vineyard at the end of the summer. Caroline came. Jon and Harry kept the heat on me, kept up their arguments that the fraternities were wrong and needed to change; I changed my mind about all of it daily.

Some days, I wanted to call up the Administrator and say, "This is what *really* happens to people in the frats. Please help us change it"; some days, I wanted to pop my collar to deflect Harry and Jon's anti-frat rhetoric; some days I felt as if everything we talked about was an attack on a college that I still worshipped with a conflicted love.

Walking along Katama Beach one afternoon, the sand almost white, I tried to talk to Caroline about being a frat whistle-blower.

She cautioned me against the whole thing. "It's just not you, not something you would do," she said, stepping over shells. Out in the water I watched a sailboat cut the waves.

"But what if it is? What if I do it out of affection for the school?"

"Is there a way to do that?" She let go of my hand.

"There must be."

"You're not some social revolutionary. You're just a guy. You're just a guy who has to move on with his life."

"But what if there's something *I* can do to change the frat life and make it less fucked-up for people like me in the future?" The tide slid up under us. I realized that I was partially annoyed that I seemed to have fared worst out of everyone from that spring—everyone else was moving on with his or her life, and it was easy for Caroline to say that I should just stay quiet, do nothing. I asked her the question that burned most ferociously in my mind.

"Would doing this make me no better than Rector?"

She didn't respond.

A few yards later, down the beach, I looked at her, pale in her blue-and-white-striped rugby, eyes hidden by Wayfarers, and asked, "Well?"

"Look, I agree that's it fucked-up. We both know that. I just doubt that there's anything you can do. Don't trust Harry and Jon's scheming. They're trying to rope you into something you most likely don't want to be roped into. You're better off just going back to school and not making a big deal of anything. Go back to ΣAE. You have to give them some credit after all. Your brothers protected you."

"Are you kidding? We were the ones who protected Price."

We drove away from Katama with Harry and Jon and stopped at a roadside stand and got lobster rolls, smoked cigarettes, bought beer. The sun went down; dusk settled over the road as we turned back to Oak Bluffs.

I sat up in bed all night as Caroline slept next to me, her breaths rolling in waves over the comforter bunched around our torsos. I stared at the nautical prints hung on the wall, the scraped wooden oar, the dark tops of trees out the window. Given the space to reflect on how I'd ended up where I was, I finally let myself feel my complete disappointment with both Dartmouth and myself. I wondered why I'd even wanted to go there so badly in the first place.

Had my grandfather whitewashed it? Had he been too misty-eyed, too nostalgic? Had he chugged vinegar, too? Had he blown lines off pictures of his frat brothers? Did they, like, even have hard drugs back then? Had he blacked out and fallen on his face as much as I had? Had he ever swum in filth?

Something had changed. I'd been caught in the middle of a culture that had literally been destroying itself and destroying the kids trapped in it, the kids who believed it would remake them, slip them the American Dream under the table when no one was looking.

I nudged Caroline. She mumbled inaudibly through her retainer.

"Are you awake?"

"What?" She yawned. "I'm trying to sleep."

"This is important."

"You always say that." She pushed her face into the pillow.

"I'm serious," I whispered. "Do you think it was weird, all the things we did? That I put myself in a weaker position by trying to deny the charges to COS?"

"We're on *vacation,* and I'm trying to sleep," she lisped, and rolled over the other way. "Give this a break."

"I'm an honest guy," I whispered. "You know that, right? Right?"

"Of course."

"You know I love Dartmouth, right?"

"Go to sleep."

PROJECT HOT FRIES

Once free of Caroline's caution, I continued my discussion with Harry and Jon. They clued me in on something they'd been working on with another '12, this girl Elle, this thing they called Project Hot Fries. It was their top-secret plan to change Dartmouth's Greek culture. It was definitely top secret, but there wasn't much of a plan.

Working together we made some modifications.

The idea of the revised version was to bring public scrutiny to bear on the frats and ultimately force the administration to address the hazing issue by abolishing the Greek system or forcing it to become coeducational. That was the idea we landed on—leveraging viral media. I was still doubtful, still conflicted about ΣAE, but I followed along with their plan as long as I could. I still wanted to give President Kim a chance to make a change internally before we went public.

Another notion was to offer the administration a prime opportunity to address the school's hazing culture, then blow the lid in a fireworks-laden media display if they didn't act.

I sketched out a column I'd write detailing my experience of being hazed as a pledge. We planned how we could synergize my revelations with a broader media strategy. Elle contacted reporters from large newspapers about the potentially breaking story. I scheduled a meeting with top administrators to discuss the hazing issue. Hedging my bet on the efficacy of Project Hot Fries, I planned to remain anonymous; not only was my goal never to cause the school embarrassment, but I figured they'd be happy to hear from me, happy to receive the information I'd relay.

I guess that's where things got fucked-up. Institutional power is not exactly activism's most passionate bedfellow—maybe the two occasionally hook up, but it's always clear who's doing the fucking.

TAKING IT TO THE TOP

I'll be specific.

On Tuesday, November 16, 2010, at one P.M., I met with

David Spalding—President Kim's chief of staff and a for-mer vice president of alumni relations—and the Adminis-trator in a conference room in Collis. The unseasonably warm day was bare and self-pitying. I wore jeans, loafers, a navy-blue shawl sweater, and a white polo that I'd already soaked through with nervous sweat before the meeting even began. I recall Spalding wearing khaki pants and a striped oxford shirt and an ugly tie—I swear to God the thing had little Santa Clauses on it even though it wasn't Christmas—choked in a Windsor knot.

I'd set up the meeting via e-mail with the Administra-tor, with whom I'd remained in contact following my COS hearing. I'd told him that I felt the need to share with high-level administrators of the school the details of what I called "my Dartmouth experience" so that they could be aware of the troubling behaviors common in the fraternities, if they weren't already.

We began our meeting in a conference room next to the Administrator's new office—he'd since been promoted out of Parkhurst's basement—until he pointed out that peo-ple in the hallway on the other side of one of the room's walls, presumably students, might be able to hear our con-versation, causing us to move to a more isolated conference room on the other side of the building.

I brought with me a dossier on fraternity hazing, in-cluding at least one picture of ΣAE pledges obviously about to be hazed—that picture from the night our Wheel of Misfortune tasks were assigned.

"See this?" I slid the picture across the conference table. "That's me in the heinous red women's peacoat."

"How many cups of beer is that, Andrew?" the Administrator asked.

"Five hundred and fifty," I said. *Take a beer and make it disappear.*

"That's a lot," he said. I registered Spalding's aghast expression. He said that he'd never seen or heard anything like that before. Then I showed them a picture of myself leaning over a fellow pledge vomiting in a trash can after pledge meetings—a picture that would ultimately be published in *Rolling Stone*.

Later, in January 2012, Spalding would comment to *The Dartmouth* that he "[did] not recall seeing pictures" during our meeting.

"So basically, this is the story of pledge term . . ." I began, speaking from an outline I'd prepared about my experiences, observations, and research about hazing at Dartmouth. I described the vast majority of Sigma Alpha Epsilon's pledge-term hazing, from bid night to sink night to vinegar meetings to the vomelette to "The True Gentleman" challenges—the whole deal. The Administrator noted that the administration was already aware of milk meetings from their earlier investigation, so I didn't go into too much detail about that except the game of Revolutionary War and the burial of our clothes in the backyard, which were rather novel details. It took me almost an hour to explain as many hazing events as I could. Still, they didn't seem able to grasp what exactly we'd done, and why. I guess I couldn't either.

The meeting concluded with the Administrator and Spalding promising that the administration would take serious action in regard to the systemic hazing I related, as that fall's pledge term was well under way. I hoped that they'd start an investigation and then be able to use it as a first step for serious reform of Greek life.

I reiterated that I wanted to remain anonymous to protect myself from what would most likely have been bitter retaliation, as I'd seen firsthand. They agreed that protecting my anonymity was a priority, a fact I appreciated. No one said that my anonymity would handicap reform efforts in any way. Later, a top administrator would claim that the administration couldn't do much, since I had asked to remain anonymous.

IT WAS PROBABLY POINTLESS

I went home.

On Tuesday, November 30, 2010, at 1:42 A.M., I e-mailed the Administrator to follow up regarding our meeting and regarding the Hell Night hazing to be held on December 1, 2010. I hadn't heard from him at all since our meeting. He responded that there was going to be a forthcoming Hanover Police "sting." I wrote a lengthy e-mail back suggesting that a sting might not be, like, the best way of addressing the issue, as it might only produce a small change in the system—one fraternity's derecognition— and not across-the-board change, as ΣAE wasn't the only house to employ abusive hazing practices.

At the time of that discussion I wasn't aware that, as *The Dartmouth* reported on January 25, 2012, "administrators also discussed plans for 'Hell Night,' the culminating event of pledge term, with the then-president of ΣAE to ensure that the event would not violate the College's hazing policy, Spalding said."

A few months later I followed up with the Administrator again, further referencing the pictures I'd displayed in the meeting: "With the wealth of details, facts, images, and e-mails I gave to you and Vice President Spalding, I'm sure that you—especially with Dr. Kim and his public health focus at the helm—have put together some really great projects to start addressing the issue at Dartmouth over the last few months." The Administrator didn't respond to my message. No such plan was outlined.

I followed up with him again two months later, asking him what updates he could relate to me about President Kim and Spalding's assumed action to address hazing. He didn't respond to that message either. Then it was summer. The clock ran down on my suspension.

I realized that it was probably pointless to try to take on Greek life, realized that no one wanted to touch it, realized that I should just do what everyone else was doing, pack up my shit, go back to Dartmouth, try to remember why I'd once felt as if I'd fit into the college's culture, couldn't remember, couldn't deal with anything. Returning from the real world, Dartmouth life seemed even more absurd and toxic than usual, somehow scraped clean of the allure I'd once seen in it, and my body was starting to reject it like a black-market kidney transplant.

THEY KNOW EVERY LITTLE DETAIL

Some afternoon in Alumni Gym. The grandiose semicircular windows cut into the building's brick facade cast columns of light so bright over the treadmills and rowing machines and free weights that I could see constellations of dust swirl through the air, could watch drops of sweat fall from girls' foreheads onto the digital screens mounted on the elliptical machines. Everyone was sweating out the Keystone.

In between sets of whatever nominal lift I was performing—I only went to the gym for face time—I walked over to the water fountain to get a drink. I was sweating the Keystone out, too, working to expunge my usual hangover and knock the fog from my stupefied skull. As I approached the water fountain, I noticed a boy's nervous form shuffling in a vaguely oval path on the rubber floor, checking his BlackBerry and then dropping his arm to his side, then checking it again. He seemed to be waiting for breaking news. He saw me coming toward him. It was Gene, one of my best friends of the ΣAE '13s. He observed me grimly and dragged me toward one of the walls in the gym's corner. We lingered near a stack of foam yoga mats as he bled anxiety, nearly tripping on a wayward medicine ball while shuffling in front of me.

"What's up, Gene?" Since he habitually overreacted to minor life events, I expected his nervousness to be a function of some convoluted story about some Tri-Delt he had a crush on, some girl who wouldn't sleep with him, but his parents knew her parents from Palm Springs, and how some Phi Delt he'd gone to Israel with had fucked her sister, and what had *we* all done with our lives? But he seemed genuinely distressed. He wasn't looking for girl advice.

"Have you heard the news?" he whispered, gazing over my shoulder. I instinctively looked behind me, too. Nothing there—just a Chi Gam doing pull-ups a few yards away across the floor tiles, studying himself apathetically in the spotless mirrored wall. The gym smelled like cheap disinfectant. It smelled like ΣAE's foyer after cleanups.

"Nope."

"About the guys at the national conference?" Some of our brothers were in Connecticut or Massachusetts or New York at some annual fraternity meeting; I was only vaguely aware of this since I'd slowly been disconnecting myself from the life of the frat and wasn't up-to-date on house politics or the recent gossip. My one trip to a national conference during my pledge term—a purely political move just to showcase my dedication to the house as I prepared to run for rush chair—had been a dismal, morbidly banal experience.

"Get to the point." I shook some sweat from my T-shirt.

"Well . . ." He measured each word in a hissed whisper, suspiciously eyeing two AΞDs in yoga pants who walked past us toward the ellipticals. "A couple of brothers are at the conference right now. They said that our province archon keeps catching them in private and grilling them about our hazing."

"So?" I tried to seem nonchalant but, as they too often did, warning bells echoed in my head. Though I barely went to the house anymore, I felt guilty that I hadn't formally depledged after trying to speak to the administration about stopping hazing.

"So? What do you mean *so*?" His mouth was agape. "Dude, they apparently know everything. We're going to hold execs tonight and talk about how to deal with this. They know every little detail."

"How could they know so much?" I knew the question was rhetorical, but Gene didn't know that I'd told the Administrator so much months before, that the Administrator must have filed a report with national. I ruminated over that.

To most of the sophomores I'd be above suspicion as the source of the leak. They'd probably conclude, I reasoned, that no one who'd been snitched on by someone in the house would snitch on the entire house itself.

"I gotta get back to my reps," I muttered. "But keep me posted."

"This isn't good, man."

"Of course. I mean—of course not, dude."

I gave him the grip. Mostly to make him feel better. I'd known Gene since I was rush chair, and bringing him into the house had been a personal project of mine from sophomore winter on. Now that he was a brother, now that he cared so much about it just as I once had, how could I tell him that it meant nothing to me, that I was unconvinced that it should continue at all, that it struck me as being kind of, well, twisted?

I did another set, made sure Gene was out of sight, then hustled myself out of the gym and back to my room and stared at a blank e-mail addressed to the Administrator. What would I write? It looked as if this occasion might spark some reform in the house—the '13s seemed incredibly anxious about these hazing revelations—maybe it would bring about some institutional changes. I reasoned that was one benefit of remaining in the house. I lined up excuses like clay pigeons.

But not having been around for the previous pledge-term hazing, having only visited once, how could I be a whistle-blower if I wasn't an actual witness? Then again, if I was a witness, or even a participant, I'd be guilty, too.

9
RESET

Suddenly it was as if someone had hit reset on the entire school. It was fall again. Senior fall. Or whatever it was supposed to be. I was nervously thrust back into a world that no longer seemed familiar to me.

The days got shorter, the leaves turned, and something was wrong. I'd been out of sync with my peers since being Parkhursted—suspended—but I didn't feel the contrast so acutely until they all returned to campus and I noticed that they were all subtly different, somehow simultaneously more aggressive and more apathetic. Finance internships had matured them. They seemed even more secretive; it seemed as if they only talked about money and status. They got their shirts dry-cleaned.

While I'd been backpacking through Southeast Asia, they'd been working in private equity, finance, banking, and consulting; while I'd been living in Kathmandu on a few dollars a day—and was smuggled across the India-Nepal

border in the back of a Suzuki, long story—they were exist-
ing exactly as we all once had in Hanover: going to frat
meetings, tweaking each other's résumés, drafting cover letters, completing econ problem sets, getting tapped for secret
societies, doing drugs whenever they felt like it, blacking
out multiple nights a week, chasing girls, gossiping about
house politics, doing whippits on Pebble and throwing the
empty canisters into the yard for someone else to clean up.
The usual. They knew that they'd soon be launched into
the world in search of the good life—if they didn't already
have it. I was finding it hard to take it all seriously.

I HAD TO TELL SOMEONE

I lived alone in Lord, one of the Gold Coast dorms—brick
walls and arched porticos and Dartmouth-green shutters
and vaguely Gothic lamps and all that. My room had a
fireplace, a huge closet, and a bay window. It was a nice
place to live, though I no longer felt as if I belonged in
places like that, buildings that projected a superficial class-
iness and conflated aged appearance with higher learning.

The bay window looked out over the college's grave-
yard, a depressing sight for a guy who too often contemplated his own mortality, not to mention an unpleasant
view to wake up to hungover, stomach eddying like a fish-
bowl of bleach—sometimes I imagined that one of the graves
was open for me and I could just roll myself out of bed and
into the wet earth and call it a day.

In trying to get out from underneath the culture's gravity, I'd made it out to the frat's fringe, to the Oort cloud of brothers who barely showed up for meetings, rarely answered housewide blitzes, didn't do their cleanups, and probably wanted to depledge but lacked the courage to do so. Social anxiety overtook me; more terrifyingly, I wondered if anyone knew that I'd tried to be a whistle-blower. My mind ran over the possibilities of what the brothers might do to me if they found out. I'd be ostracized, attacked, yet there didn't seem like a way out while remaining at the school.

What sustained me was my weekly meeting with Richard Crocker, the college chaplain—I desperately needed someone to talk to. He'd reached out to me over the summer after this anti-corporate-recruiting column I'd written had gone viral, and after that, during our meetings, I ended up spilling all of my turmoil and doubts to him. He was the finest man and finest mentor I knew at Dartmouth.

We'd talk about moral issues, Dartmouth's culture, growing up, politics, literature, and then, sporadically, religion. When I explained to him my conflicted feelings about Dartmouth, about ΣAE and the lifestyle I was struggling to leave behind, Crocker said something that struck me as unusual.

That afternoon I sat in my armchair soaked with a brine of perspiration. For some reason I was wearing a sweater, one with an itchy shawl collar, though the weather hadn't turned yet. I was feeling a little frantic. Maybe I was feeling a conflicted sense of guilt and morality, and I had to tell someone, anyone, preferably someone I could trust, about how I'd tried and failed to be a whistle-blower.

"There's something I want to talk about today."

"You can count on me." He was always saying that. Normally, I don't believe anyone who says that—my frat brothers had said that to each other daily, ranted about trust and fidelity and secrecy. You can tell when people are lying when they have to repeat the same things over and over, almost as if they're trying to convince themselves most of all. Funny thing was, I believed Crocker when he said it.

"It's a long story. Last fall I came forward to the administration with information about all the hazing that goes on in ΣAE. I wanted the information to reach President Kim. Somehow I thought he would do something about it. I was surprised when nothing seemed to happen."

"Hm."

I paused.

"Please continue." He closed his eyes, his mien uncannily similar to Robin Williams's in *Dead Poets Society*.

"I wanted to see if I could help make a real change for the school, make it better, stop these things from happening, and I've been grappling with my own failure since. And I'm worried that it's made me a hypocrite because here I am still, well, kind of a brother of the frat."

"What do you mean?" He opened his eyes.

"Am I hypocrite? I tried to out the hazing and am still a brother. I don't know what to do, and I don't know how to handle this. It seems like staying here and trying to continue the exposé would be social suicide—making myself a pariah. And I still have friends I care about in ΣAE, friends I don't want to hurt."

"What kind of hazing are we talking about?"

I told him about pledge term.

"You appear to be in a very delicate situation." He removed his glasses and polished them with his tie, then placed them back on the bridge of his nose.

I'd exhausted myself from talking. I had nothing else to say—I felt too sick to my stomach to create any more language.

"Andrew . . ." He leaned back in his wing chair and flattened his tie down on his crisp white dress shirt. "Andrew, it seems that your life is entangled with the life of the college. A time for choosing will come in your life. Maybe that time isn't yet. But eventually, perhaps sooner than you think, you will have to decide who you are. I have faith that you will make the correct choice."

Our meeting expired.

I'd wanted answers from Dean Crocker, but I had to accept that no one could help me. No one could tell me what to do. I'd have to decide. I pored over Crocker's final quote for weeks, that thing about my life's being entangled with Dartmouth's. It seemed like a grandiose notion. Maybe he said it to everyone, like, I figured, what could one person mean against such an overpowering tradition? Pledge term was about to start.

MALE FRIENDSHIP. I'LL NEVER UNDERSTAND IT.

Things were falling apart.

One night Pulaski and I got into a vicious argument in Room 2. In years of friendship, through an arrest and hazing and being roommates and cleaning up each other's vomit and multiple incidents of urine drinking, we'd never gotten in each other's face. So it was weird. We found ourselves screaming two sides of an impossible argument—whether it was better to be right or be happy. Pulaski said I always wanted to be right but never ended up happy. I said Pulaski's happiness was ignorance because he never cared about being right. I guess it made no sense. I don't even remember what ignited the fight.

I think we'd planned on getting high and hanging out with his girlfriend and watching a movie, but shit got too weird and then we both started violently sobbing, me in the inner room with the bunk beds, he in the outer room, sprawled out on one of the couches as bad hip-hop bubbled out of his computer speakers. This is all impossible to explain, I guess—not very fratty—hidden grievances and unanswered traumas bursting to the surface.

When I left the room to go downstairs to the basement and get drunk and try to forget about the inexplicable exchange, I nearly tripped over Pulaski's girlfriend. She was sitting on the floor between his door and a recycling bin overflowing with empty bottles of vodka, her knees surrounded by a constellation of stale pizza crusts.

"Lohse. Lohse, what the *fuck* is going on in there?"

"Don't worry about it." I tried to push past her. "I'm heading down to the basement."

She exhaled a melancholic sigh as she fixed the shoulder of her pink-and-green dress. "Male friendship," she muttered. "I'll never understand it."

"Me neither," I yelled over my shoulder. Then I got drunk with people I didn't like.

Later, Pulaski and I made a shaky peace—mostly because we were both embarrassed at how we'd broken an important bro code and revealed our hidden sensitivities. Our truce revolved around how we'd agree to run the same car for bid night kidnappings for the '14 pledge class. Kind of like a bad idea.

A few days later I couldn't get the feeling of that bawling out of my mind, though, and everything around me had become a symbol of my inability to be happy with the life that seemed to content everyone else. ΣAE became for me the ultimate token of emptiness, decay, and disappointment, a simulacrum of my Ivy League disillusionment, a reminder of my parents' divorce during pledge term, a reminder of my arrest, a reminder of Blair and Caroline—who'd broken up with me over the summer. I couldn't be happy. I couldn't seem to be right either—even my whistle-blowing attempt was a failure.

Paradoxically, the more I understood what I'd lost in the house, the deeper in I went, relapsing, like a reckless gambler, to try to win back the past. I promised to ride shotgun with Pulaski on bid night to prove I was a team player. I buried my doubts and told myself to be a yes-man.

YOU KNOW WHAT TONIGHT IS

Pulaski and I had some shopping to do before rush.

Our first stop was Stinson's, Hanover's booze and packaged-goods store, the place where every frat bought their beer—urban legend was that the tiny shop was one of the largest Keystone Light retailers in the continental United States. It was the kind of place where you knew every employee if you were enough of an alcoholic. Sadly, we discovered that they'd already sold out of Mad Dogs and Boone's.

"Every single bottle?" Pulaski asked the cashier while I spun a swiveling rack of porno mags.

"Well, you know what tonight is." She smiled. All the other fratstars must have done their shopping early. It seemed perverse, funny almost, that even the Stinson's cashier—a kindly, middle-aged woman with frizzy blond hair and glasses—seemed to know about bid night and its correlation to a spike in the sales of bum wine.

So we sped to West Leb to hit up the state liquor store. Using a complicated financial algorithm Pulaski had devised while interning for a private equity firm the year before, we calculated that the optimal purchase was a disgusting-looking bottle of eggnog with simultaneously the highest alcohol content and lowest price of all the beverages in the Disgusting Beverages section of the store; it'd have to take the place of the sacramental Kiwi Lemon or Orange Jubilee Mad Dog. Then I grabbed a bottle of Riesling for myself to help drown my searing doubts about the rest of the evening.

Swiping my credit card at the checkout, I yawned and turned to my side to see Pulaski staring straight at me with a vaguely satanic grin plastered across his face.

"Dude," he goes.

"Um, yeah, did you want to split paying for this egg-nog? You know I'm broke." I turned back to the cashier.

"Dude," he goes again, arching his eyebrows. The cashier was getting impatient with us. Nothing new. Then Pulaski arched his eyebrows again and casually nodded down in the direction of the floor. I was terrified that he might have whipped out his dick—an altogether-not-unreasonable fear since the only other time I'd witnessed that kind of casual nod paired with Pulaski's eyebrow-arch tic was this time when he'd nonchalantly dangled his penis out of his suit pants while we were playing pong with our dates after sophomore-year spring formal.

This time I was relieved to see a dozen tiny bottles of peppermint schnapps stacked on the conveyor belt instead of Pulaski's uncircumcised penis, which vaguely approximated an aardvark fetus. The little bottles glistened in the store's dull fluorescent light. The alcoholic's ultimate impulse buy, like toddlers grabbing M&Ms at the supermarket checkout lane.

"Are you sure that's . . ."

"A good idea?"

"I swear to God, Pulaski, comatose pledges is a bad idea."

Before I could argue further our purchases were collected in brown-paper bags and we were walking back to the VW. I hid my Riesling under the passenger seat for later.

RUSH

Two years after we'd rushed, our synapses surging with anxiety, I'd somehow evolved to the point where I found the entire thing boring. Maybe it was a coping mechanism, a way of trying to insulate myself against the night. But I didn't bother wearing a pocket square—or even a tie. My shirt was unironed and untucked, my boat shoes unlaced.

As I moved through the living room, pool room, and foyer, through the crowd of smug brothers and anxiously chattering sophomores, Pulaski kept winking at me, from time to time randomly muttering to the rushees, "I hope you guys like peppermint schnapps and *eggnog.*" He'd deadpan it, hands thrust in the pockets of his blazer, arms swaying nonchalantly at his sides.

"What? Excuse me?" they'd ask. Maybe they were a little bit disturbed, or so disturbed they were excited, or so excited they were disturbed.

"Oh, nothing," Pulaski would smirk. I got the impression that he considered the night *his,* that he wasn't going to let it slip away from him, that he was going to mug it at knifepoint and empty the contents of its wallet. My flying wingman for the night's hazing was, sadly, part of our reconciliation after our fight—mending the fences of our boozy, drug-addled friendship by expanding its circle to bring in fresh dudes who'd promise that our legacy might be passed down or perhaps canonized. For Pulaski, who had the benefit of stability and continuity in his collegiate experience, that night was the culmination of two years of climbing the frat totem pole. In his own way he probably imagined himself a big chief in a small fiefdom, and by the criminally deviant twinkle in his eye I could tell that he saw himself the way Davis had once seen himself, before everything had gone wrong.

For me, though, it was the same scene I'd tried to run from—all the meaningless small talk, the formal attire, the specific instructions and private knowledge and appeals to undying traditions. The booze and yelling. Yet there I was in my only suit. Part of me wanted to feel connected to Pulaski and the other guys again, or maybe part of me just didn't know what else to do; that was the part that had given up trying to resist.

GOOD GUY OR FUN GUY?

Rush was such an important, mystical night in Dartmouth's ritual calendar that to forgo it, to beg out of it, would seem, even for someone in as delicate a position as I was, like missing out on the birth of your nephew or something.

After shake-out we sang the sophomores out from the frat's portico, two choruses of "Rigsby's," then sprinted up to the Libes. Pulaski got there first and saved me a good seat; the bonhomie of bringing in the new class quickly fizzled as delibs dragged on without an end in sight. Impassioned debates played out over which rushees were good at pong, which were B-side, which were B+-side, which had girlfriends in A-side houses, and one of the age-old philosophical quandaries: Was it more desirable to fuck a B-side girl in an A-side house, or an A-side girl in a B-side house?

I tried to summon Pulaski's intense enthusiasm for these matters of fraternal inquiry, but between my guilty knowledge of my involvement with the administration's failed investigation of the prior year's hazing, and my own *Hamlet* routine over defection, the bickering of the induction voting seemed foreign.

Though I'd backed away from the first hazing exposé, I knew, sitting there in delibs, that my arguments from a year before were still valid. Yet there I was, taking part in the exposition of the house's hazing plots, an accessory to what were, I guess, impending crimes.

We were barely halfway down the list of the rushees when I got so bored that I opened my computer and started scrolling through my Facebook newsfeed. It seemed populated solely by pictures of sorority pledges wearing flair, lithe girls in tutus throwing their house's respective gang sign. There was no escape. Images of Greek life were everywhere I looked.

I slumped back in the chair next to Pulaski, who was constantly whispering to me about which pledges we should kidnap: "What about Phipps? He's a cocky little fucker. I'm sure we can knock him down a peg. Or Hanson? Hanson used to date Jackie Campbell. We both know *you* knew Jackie pretty well."

"Hanson is a definite," I whispered back, trying to appear committed to the idea.

On the other side of the Libes the rush chairmen alternated between reading from the list of sophomore boys and calling for a vote on each one as his name came up.

"Phipps?" Ferguson yelled over the chattering in the room. Behind him, in the window framed by two built-in bookshelves on the far side of the Libes, stood the frat's Indian statue: Straight Arrow, this dude with a headdress. Kind of like when the bros lit up Rector's table, how one guy had miraculously pulled out a straight-up feathered headdress and propped it on his head.

Straight Arrow had once been the frat's mascot, back before political correctness—as if anything was politically correct about sitting around a frat library with silk ties cinched up to our necks debating the superficial merits of fifty nineteen-year-old boys. Or later forcing them to vomit on each other, chug vinegar, swim in filth. I wondered how many times Straight Arrow had peered down from his perch and passed judgment on the asinine things that happened in the Libes, like if he ever looked down on sniffling pairs of brothers snorting blow off "The True Gentleman."

I refocused my eyes on Ferguson.

"Speaker's list on Phipps?" the chairman next to Ferguson called out again. The kid leaned back in his Windsor chair, brass buttons of his blazer glinting under the fluorescent lights like freshly minted coins. Brothers raised their hands as Ferguson cycled through the speakers, giving each a minute to express his feelings on Phipps. No one had anything substantial to add, so Ferguson walked us all through the metrics: B+-side pong player with sketchy tendencies who somehow fucks A-side girls though still a questionably B-side guy. Hung jury.

"Is Phipps a *good guy* or a *fun guy*?" Tim asked, gazing out across the Libes and lifting his hands like the sides of a scale. That was usually the most in-depth question ever ventured—it was asked of every rushee and had become a meme in the house—was the dude too nice, or did he like to rage? Did he drink a lot? Did he play an A-side sport? Did he have any position of influence in any extracurricular group? Would he be able to handle pledge term and not whine like an asshole? Could he talk to girls and help everyone get laid?

Having never been in bid-night delibs before, I was kind of surprised that little time was given to any aspirant's major, hometown, hobbies, or moral fiber. In this light the house just seemed to be a self-perpetuating psychological pyramid scheme. It was never about the brothers or who they were or why they were that way; it was only ever about continuing the organization itself. Its members' wellness seemed pretty irrelevant, and that reality is symptomatic of institutional pathology.

"Look, Phipps isn't a bad kid but I think he's kind of an asshole," Gibbons said when it was his turn to speak.

"So you don't think he's a *good guy*?" someone yelled from another corner of the room.

"He's a fun guy! Not a good guy!" someone from one of the couches called out.

Wallace hissed at the interjectors. "Guys, let the speakers speak so we can get out of here and deliver these bids." He was exasperated. "This is the future of the house we're talking about here. There'll be no pledge class if other houses grab the guys we want first."

"I just don't know if Phipps is ΣAE material," Gibbons continued. "Like, he's really full of himself and not very preppy, and I just don't think he'd make a good brother. I suggest we give him a callback for tomorrow night."

Pulaski started to argue back but was cut off by one of the rush chairs.

"Vote on Phipps?" Phipps got a bid. Gibbons threw his hands up in frustration; Tim's *good guy–fun guy* scale had been thrown out of balance.

"Next we have Robert Hanson," the chair called out.

"Motion for a vote," Beaufort yelled.

"Seconded!"

"Seconded!"

"Raise of hands for Hanson?"

"That's more than two-thirds for Hanson. Write up his card."

Pulaski turned to me and whispered, "Go grab his bid card before anyone else can."

Then, for the next hour, the brotherhood debated, cat-called, and voted on the remainder of the rushees.

"Vote on Bayard?"

"Good guy or fun guy?"

"Speaker's list on Carlisle?"

"Vote on that Asian dude we had to kick out last week for booting on the stairs?"

"Motion to vote on William Cardinal—"

"Seconded!"

I grabbed Cardinal's bid card, too.

"Cardinal and Hanson. Not bad," Pulaski goes, looking at the cards as I closed up my computer and slid it into my backpack. "Let's go kidnap some pledges." He rubbed his hands together.

I walked past Wallace and muttered, "We're outta here," and Wallace looked at his watch and then at the Excel spreadsheet that he, Tim, and Gibbons had printed out about who was manning which car. The same organizational skills the brothers had developed to market themselves to potential employers were the skills they applied to the fraternity's hazing:

High-risk portfolio analysis.

Mergers and acquisitions.

Management skills.

Trend forecasting.

Risk leveraging.

Risk management.

"Take them wherever you want, but be back by one, all right?" Wallace said.

"We're taking them to the ledges," Pulaski smirked.

"Brilliant." The mnemonic device rolled of Wallace's tongue: *"Pledges to the ledges."*

Pulaski and I sprinted downstairs and he fired up his VW and gunned it to Lord, where we ditched the car on the grass behind the dorm and ran in and changed clothes, trading out our formal attire for ΣAE hoodies and plastic scream masks. Then we walked down the hall and pounded on Cardinal's door, which he opened slowly, cautiously. He was wearing pajamas and peered nervously at us out of one eye.

"Hello?"

"Find a blindfold. Give me your phone. Now."

We jogged him out of the building. Next was Richardson Hall. Hanson seemed super-stoned and not at all surprised to find us there kidnapping him.

"Get in the car, whaleshit," Pulaski grunted.

PLEDGES TO THE LEDGES

The idea to take the pledges to the ledges had been easy enough to conjure.

This is how it came to us—Pulaski was sitting on the edge of one of the couches in 2 hitting the bong; I was half asleep on the other, staring into the TV. This was a few nights before rush. *The Roast of Charlie Sheen* was on but muted, and the remote was lost somewhere behind the couches.

Coughing and sputtering erupted on the other side of the room. I was so high that I'd forgotten that someone else was there until Pulaski's face appeared through a parting cloud of smoke, his eyes feral, and I stared into them for a few seconds, a little bit puzzled, actually, kind of afraid, as if I were staring into the eyes of insanity for the first time even though I knew it certainly couldn't have been only the first time.

"Let's take the pledges to the ledges!" he roared, gripping the bong underneath the tattered American flag. That was the beginning and the end of the discussion, the alpha and the omega. The pledges would have to go to the ledges—a nature area where undergrads swam in the summer, a stream

with big waterfalls and wooded trails. The kind of place where someone might accidentally fall off a cliff and crack his skull.

THE LIMIT DOES NOT EXIST

We sped over the bridge into Vermont—I guess you could say we were kidnapping across state lines. I fished the Riesling out from under my seat, chugged what was left, and threw the bottle out the window. I heard it shatter against the concrete. On the other side of the bridge Pulaski pulled a mad turn, slammed the brakes, and stopped the car in a dark parking lot. He switched off the headlights. We both swiveled to face the rushees.

"Do you know why you're here?" Pulaski growled.

"Because—" One looked at the other.

"Because we rushed ΣAE tonight?"

"We're aware of that," Pulaski answered. "Do you think we're fucking idiots?"

They shook their heads.

"Do fucking idiots get into Ivy League schools?"

They shook their heads again.

"Do fucking idiots become fraternity execs?"

I considered casting some doubt on this particular rhetorical question, but decided not to.

Anyway, Pulaski cut me off. "You're *here*"—he nodded at the back of his car, the blindfolds they had in their hands, then the unlit parking lot—"because we are giving you a *chance* to become pledges." He paused for a second. "A *chance* is not a fucking *privilege*."

This time they didn't nod. They just stared. Somehow, I realized, Pulaski had gone from goofy to intimidating in a few short years. Though I knew he was completely full of shit, I was almost catching the pledges' fright second-hand. He performed the role of hazer elegantly.

"One chance. But you are going to have to follow our instructions *very, very* carefully." He picked one pledge and stared at him for longer than was comfortable. We could see the bridge from where we'd parked. Lamplight shimmered off the black river below. Cars rolled over it listlessly. I hoped none were cops.

When my mom was my age, she used to babysit a girl; the girl became a woman and went to Dartmouth. The woman said once that she gets choked up every time she crosses the bridge into Hanover, every time she drives up the hill to the college. Staring at the river, I realized that I was already feeling circumscribed by a preemptive, fresh sense of loss. And some fear. It was weird—crossing the river out of the college's safe bubble, passing some natural boundary, thinking about how the unknown is dangerous and wild, about how something was electrifying about how dangerous and wild we'd all become at Dartmouth in pursuit of it, Pulaski and I, the brothers. Whatever it was, we were simultaneously fascinated and repulsed by it, inexorably pulled into it by some morbid gravity. I realized then why I'd relapsed back into the frat so many times: all the ways we hurt each other and hurt ourselves had an intoxicating grandeur.

I turned back to face the sophomores. "Put your blindfolds on," I heard myself saying.

"Which one of you whaleshit likes drugs?" Pulaski smiled at me.

"Because we like drugs." I pulled a vitamin out of my pocket. "We have a pill for you."

"We heard that *you* like drugs, Hanson," Pulaski said. "Give Hanson the pill. He'll take one for the team."

The pledged reached out blindly with one hand. "What is—"

"Do you have any heart conditions?" I asked.

I put the vitamin in his palm, closing his fingers over it. Then we got on the interstate. As Pulaski drove, I passed the bottles of peppermint schnapps, one by one, to the backseat. Beethoven's Fifth blasted through the car's speakers. We wanted to keep things traditional.

THE LEDGES

We fumbled at the end of a trail, both of us leading a pledge into the woods with his hand on our shoulder, just as had been done for us.

"Where's the flashlight?" Pulaski asked me.

"What?"

"Where's the flashlight, bro? It's dark."

"I don't know," I muttered. "I think we left it in my room."

Pulaski glared at me, then yelled, "Whaleshit, hold hands, keep your blindfolds on, and don't run off anywhere."

We left them at the end of the trail and walked back to the car. Pulaski rifled through the trunk as I kept my eyes on the road, becoming progressively more nervous with each passing set of headlights.

"Yeah, we definitely don't have it," he said.

"Bummer."

"Without it there's no way we can walk to the edge of the waterfall. God forbid one of those little whaleshits slips—we'd be dead, too."

"Well, I've got the hair gel," I offered. Another of our stupid ideas.

"And I've got the eggnog."

"Let's just get them deeper down the trail, dude—I'm starting to get worried about passing cars," I said, guilty conscience speaking. If I was going to give up resisting the culture, I didn't want anyone to know about it.

"No shit. Let's split them up. We haven't played the whole 'Who wants the bid more?' conceit."

"I'll take Cardinal. You take Hanson."

We walked back down the trail. Pulaski stashed the eggnog in his hoodie so the pledges wouldn't see it.

"Cardinal. Take your blindfold off. Come with me." I took him down a fork in the trail.

"Yes, sir?" he asked.

What a nice kid, I thought, taking this bullshit as

seriously as I had, indiscriminately throwing out the s-word.

"Look, you know that I want you to get the bid. But the way these things work is complicated."

"What do you mean?"

"What I mean is that Wallace—you know, a revered brother—sent us here with each of you to decide which one of you was getting the bid. Pulaski is backing Hanson. I'm backing you." That was all false, a script replayed every year for the pledges.

"What should I do?" he asked, literally breathless.

Over my shoulder I could hear Pulaski similarly coaching Hanson. I heard him articulate, like a used-car salesman trying to convince some dementia-addled grandmother that her Buick trade-in was worth half its book value, "Look, dude. Of course Lohse isn't going to back you. I need you to step up and beat Cardinal, okay?"

I thought over what to say. I turned back to Cardinal. "Let me clue you in."

"Yeah?"

"Pulaski has a bottle of eggnog in his hoodie. Hanson doesn't know about it, but you guys are going to have to drink the whole thing. So I'm giving you that advance knowledge. The more you drink that Hanson doesn't drink, the more you can help me win over Pulaski and Wallace and get you that bid."

"Yes, sir." He nodded. He was a really nice kid. It felt wrong to be fucking with him like that. Then Pulaski led us down the trail as far as we could go with no light. We could hear the waterfall but couldn't see it.

A WHOPPER, SIR. A WHOPPER WITH CHEESE.

"Cardinal, get on your knees." Pulaski handed the hair gel to Hanson. "Hanson, give him a cool hairstyle that you think is worthy of ΣAE. You know, we're a house that very much cares about our appearance."

Hanson molded Cardinal's brown hair into a Mohawk as the latter chugged the eggnog. We'd also come up with the hair-gel idea while stoned. The woods were dry and cold. We couldn't see the road. Then they switched spots. Pulaski called my phone.

"Yo? What's up, Wallace?" I let a few seconds pass to make it seem as if he were actually on the other end. "Yeah, we'll be back soon. It looks like Cardinal's getting the bid and not Hanson." I watched Hanson's face drop. "Why not? I don't know, man. Well, Hanson told us he'd taken some drug, some pill or something, before we kidnapped him. He's all fucked-up. Not cool."

We led them back up to the VW, stepping over pinecones and dead leaves. Pulaski pulled onto the main road and headed back for campus as I handed the pledges the rest of the bottles of schnapps. They looked ridiculous with their hair gelled and their blindfolds on.

No other cars were on the road. The backseat was littered with empty bottles of booze, and Hanson seemed particularly quiet. Then, looking back to check on the pledges, I noticed two rectangular headlights coming around the bend toward us.

"Slow down," I hissed at Pulaski, who was trying to drive while wearing his *Scream* mask. "Those headlights behind us look like cop headlights."

He ripped off the mask and darted his eyes up to the rearview. Yeah, it was definitely a cop—as it got closer, I saw the outline of its bumper guard, the shape of the soon-to-be-blaring sirens on its roof—the only other car on the road this late on a Saturday night.

"Fuck," Pulaski muttered.

I pivoted toward the backseat and vainly tried to scoop up all the small, empty bottles of schnapps and eggnog, hands shaking. *"Take your fucking blindfolds off!"* I screamed at the pledges. They did, eyes dazed, thinking they were still being hazed. "Pass me every single fucking bottle, *now*."

"This is not a drill, guys," Pulaski muttered. "Remember, you are not pledges of a frat. You are not being hazed. We just went to McDonald's in West Leb, okay? 'It's a good time,' okay?"

"They haven't learned the whole 'it's a good time' thing yet, dude."

"Well, they better fucking learn it right now! McDonald's, whaleshit, okay? *McDonald's.*"

Hanson: "Sure, McDonald's."

Cardinal: "Yeah, I love that place."

Hanson: "What about the hair gel?"

Pulaski: "Shut the fuck up."

Me: "Pretend I'm the cop. What did you get at McDonald's this evening, young man?"

Cardinal: "Um, I got a Whopper, sir. A Whopper with cheese."

Looked like we were totally fucked.

"Motherfucker, they don't fucking have Whoppers at McDonald's!" Pulaski screamed, pounding his fists on the steering wheel. *"Fuck!"*

"I meant—a Big Mac. It was really good." Cardinal chuckled. The cop car pulled up close behind us, probably running our plates. Pulaski slowed to just under the speed limit. I wondered if I should tell him to pull over, but that might have been suspicious and there was nowhere to get off the road anyway.

I crumpled up the bag of empty bottles and frantically tried to stuff it under my seat where the wine bottle had been, but it wouldn't fit so I clicked open the glove compartment as manuals and CDs and all the shit that Pulaski kept stuffed in there rained down on my knees. There was no way to fit the bag in there either.

"You make one mistake driving and we're doomed, man," I said to him. "Totally doomed."

NOTHING HAPPENED, THOUGH

A few miles later the cop turned off our tail, and Pulaski whistled a sigh of relief. Seeing the cop car was enough to remind me of the tenuousness of my position and how I was violating my own ethical convictions, whatever they were. Back on campus we deposited the pledges in the living room.

ANOTHER RECURRING DREAM

For a few months after Caroline and I broke up, I'd have this recurring dream every time I or the girl I was sleeping with would pee the bed because we were too drunk. In the dream I was swimming in warm, clear water in a cave, swimming in this sort of amniotic fluid. I could see rocks and fracture lines above me indented like the lines on the roof of your mouth. Caroline was there, treading water just on the other side of the cave. Too far away for me to touch her or whisper, "Why are we here?" But for some reason I knew what she would say anyway. That we were stuck there because of me. Because of some shitty thing I'd done but couldn't remember.

Each time, when I'd realize this, I'd fall backward into the warm water as if I were drowning. And then each time I'd wake up in a pool of urine next to some girl who wasn't Caroline.

The first time it was Miranda Morgan, this Kappa. Dazed from the dream, I threw the comforter off my torso and slowly rose from the bed, which was just a mattress on the floor, and watched the pee roll back to Miranda in the form of a tiny wave. I wasn't sure if it was mine or hers. Bad news, I thought to myself, real bad news.

Then, in a glorious moment of absolution, I realized that I had to pee. That meant that the pee soaking the mattress couldn't have been mine. This basic syllogism, a childish fact of life, made me feel better. Miranda woke up and squinted at me through one eye, the other obscured behind a lock of wavy black hair. I just stared at her. Then I tilted my gaze down at the pee. Then she looked at the pee. I mean, like, what was I supposed to say?

"I have to go now," she mumbled almost theatrically, as if she'd practiced the line. Maybe she did. Rising unsteadily, she pulled her sundress on over her pale body.

"Um—"

"But it was charming to hang out with you last night." She kissed me on the cheek. Then she gracefully walked out.

The second time I had this dream I woke up next to this other girl in my room in Lord. Senior fall. The urine was mine that time and it wasn't funny. I was sick the whole next day. So hungover I could barely move. The dream had been exactly the same, though. That was around the time that things got worse.

RIPE, FULL-BODIED, WITH A DELICATE NOTE OF FECAL MATTER

Because of the hazing revelation during the summer, ΣAE's execs, mostly Wallace, had made a new rule that all of sink night was to occur inside the house that fall. No gathering on the golf course, no running down Route 10 in formal attire. The changes the execs and pledge trainers had put into place didn't mean that that night of hazing would be easier. They just meant that the events would be more tightly controlled.

I'd been on campus once in the days leading up to the prior year's sink night; I guess I was getting information for the whistle-blowing attempt. A few different bros had shown me the garbage can full of piss, shit, and boot hidden in the basement's boiler room that was to be the kiddie-pool mixture for the pledges. The can was covered in plastic wrap, too, to seal in the smell, since it was heartbreakingly disgusting, and heartbreakingly disgusting scents are a nice flourish for any hazing event.

One of the '11 execs had been encouraging brothers to pee in the can whenever they hung out in the basement, he told me, instead of using the broken urinal and seatless toilet in the boot room. He was the same brother who'd boasted that he'd taken a shit in the receptacle. Though I never saw him do it, the specific notes of the stench— which I cataloged in my mind like a wine critic sniffing a glass of Château Latour—confirmed the presence of fecal matter. It smelled like diarrhea.

I witnessed the same behavior repeat itself my senior fall. I watched a top '12 exec call for more volunteers to pee and boot in the garbage can immediately before the pledges arrived at the house. I stood, spellbound, as Wilson leaned over the can and pulled his trigger and retched into the mixture. I watched multiple brothers whip out their dicks and hose into it as a part of last-minute preparations for the night—at that time, the pledges were upstairs being handed endless bottles of booze in the pool room. I also witnessed— from behind—the silhouette of one brother utilizing excessively jerky wrist and elbow motions while standing over the can for a prolonged time. The bro wasn't urinating, which he later confirmed to a group of brothers. The sad thing was, it wasn't out of character for him to ejaculate into the mixture. None of us seemed too surprised.

Then two or three bros hoisted the can together and dumped its contents into the plastic tub that would serve as the '14s' kiddie pool. As the pledges were being educated in Beer Die, brothers gathered in Varsity to prepare the baptismal scene. Someone plugged in the strobe light. The pool smelled absolutely rancid.

These visuals paired with the evidence I'd witnessed the prior year when visiting helped double the trauma of my own memory of swimming in the kiddie pool. Though I can't prove that such behavior had transpired when I was a pledge—that the mixture that year was full of bodily fluids possibly transmitting exotic bacteria—I can only imagine that the pool's annual mixture was, like most the things at Dartmouth, the work of *tradition*.

Given the pattern, it's illogical to think that the two following years were aberrations. If one of the highest-ranking members of the house was calling for more bodily fluids in the mixture the pledge term *after* our house's hazing had been revealed to national, in addition to being *after* the investigation from my pledge term, when we all knew we were skating on thin ice, why wouldn't it have happened when the brothers felt they could, and did, get away with anything—back in '09?

It's possible, too, that many brothers were unaware that bodily fluids were used in the pool's mixture. Many, if not most, brothers had been unaware that Edwards and Carver would, in an attempt at irony, routinely pee in the frat's punch, which was named Lemonade and served in recycling bins at parties.

Compartmentalization of knowledge is another symptom of institutional pathology, another way to keep secrets, another way to do fucked-up shit. I knew that this special Lemonade infusion took place because I was often invited throughout my sophomore year to hose in it myself—an invitation that Edwards and Carver assured me was a stamp of social approval.

It's strange to imagine how many hundreds of people drank our urine. Theoretically, it could even have been thousands. It's even stranger and more repulsive to remember that on many nights we were so drunk we forgot we'd peed in the punch and drank our own piss because we were that blacked out, that indifferent.

SINK NIGHT

As the pledges continued their obligatory chugging in Beer Die, I sat on a pong table in Varsity next to Tom, the rugger. He stared at the pool blankly. I wanted to say something to him, start a conversation, but didn't know how. I guess there wasn't anything to say. Once the strobe light was adjusted to the right setting, someone turned off the ceiling lights. The windows at the back of the basement were taped up with black plastic bags. Pulaski was standing near the door to the boot room. He looked positively gleeful. Everyone else looked stoic.

A majority of the brotherhood hadn't even shown up, probably because it was too gross—probably because they didn't want to remember what they'd experienced, didn't want to see it from the other side. I was morbidly curious to see what it looked like from a brother's point of view. I wasn't emotionally prepared for the spectacle.

The blue plastic kiddie pool had gone missing over the intervening year since the '13s had sunk their bids by swimming through the '11s' bodily fluids; the '12s couldn't find a store that sold kiddie pools in October, so they settled for an industrial-size plastic storage tub from Home Depot. The '14 pledges didn't have room to slosh around as we had. Tim and Gibbons just called their names one by one, and they climbed into the tub and sat there as if they were taking a bath.

One pledge initially refused, but, like all the others, he ultimately climbed in, probably because we'd deafeningly chanted, *"Whaleshit! Whaleshit! Whaleshit!"* until he realized that disobeying was most likely not an option. He kept his sneakers on, though, as if he were worried about getting hookworm or something. That must have been some sort of compromise with himself. After all, bargaining is one of the stages of grief.

SPELLBOUND

Looking around Varsity, searching brothers' faces through the strobe light's ghastly flash, I realized that no one was capable of making eye contact with anyone else. Spell-bound, everyone just stared at the tub and chanted.

The pledges climbed in and out, received their new names, dripped the pool's foul mixture across the concrete floor, slipped on it, and returned, baptized, to their spot in the circle. Some wore white briefs that were stained a new color. Most had no chest hair. Maybe some would stay lifelong friends; maybe in the coming decades from reunion to reunion they'd still refer to each other by those pledge names. They'd write them in parentheses on name tags they'd stick to Dartmouth-green blazers. If they were lucky, by then they'd have forgotten what they had to do to win them.

After all, they'd soon hit the showers, then we'd order them pizza. Nostalgia would cure the rest. Maybe someday, way off in the future, one of their pledge brothers might eulogize them. "Whaleshit Bukkake was my brother," one wizened old man might say, standing over Bukkake's open grave. "He was both a good guy and a fun guy."

CHAMPAGNE

Thursday of homecoming, ΣAE's traditional formal cham-pagne party—an hour couldn't even have elapsed and I'd already downed two bottles of brut while trying to hang out amiably with Peterson, who felt to me like someone I barely knew, a passing acquaintance, some random fresh-man I'd once tried to convince to rush. We were standing in the corner of the foyer near the pool room, chandelier glistening above us, talking to this girl, Juliet, together watching overdressed young bodies move through a crowd of other overdressed young bodies while the band fumbled through a version of "The Way You Look Tonight."

"So . . . how's that, like . . . poetry class?" Peterson asked, sipping from his champagne flute, spinning it between his fingers. "Sounds really, um, interesting."

He looked at Juliet, Juliet who was also in my senior poetry seminar, Juliet on whom I had a crush.

I didn't bother answering Peterson. It seemed like a huge waste to answer. Everything seemed like a huge waste. Time was wasted. I felt my education was wasted. I was wasted. The band played a sloppy Michael Jackson cover. Then they played the *Ghostbusters* theme song. Girls in black dresses orbited the bar; pledges circulated through the party, servant-like, refilling empty flutes.

Slowly, like someone applying the scientific method, I accepted that I was hopelessly depressed, thinking, between small talk, of kids sloshing in my friends' piss and vomit and worse as a strobe light pulsed in the background. Thinking about how I'd watched a bro jerk off in the mixture.

"It's a great course," Juliet said, and nodded a few times, and looked me in the eye. "It's a nice change from finance. You know, I believe in being well-balanced." She smiled, teeth perfectly white, eyes vivid and searching for something empathetic in my face as she lifted her champagne to her lips with one toned arm.

"Life is all about balance," Peterson said blankly, straightening his tie.

I was in the mood to disagree. "Balance is overrated." I don't know if I actually thought that, or if I said it because I felt physically unbalanced at the time. That's why I was leaning my shoulder into the foyer's wood paneling, pressing one loafer against the wall so the other wouldn't slide away over the tiles.

"You think so?" Juliet smiled at me again.

"Do you *really* think so." Peterson didn't even bother inflecting the words as a question. He was tired of me, I realized. I was beginning to feel narcoleptic, or hammered, and either he was bored or boring, or I was bored, or I couldn't tell.

I opened a third bottle of champagne. Peach flavored. Price had given it to me to pour for Juliet so she'd hook up with me, because, as he'd said, "Peach André is a fucking aphrodisiac," but I'd told him at the time, during my last bathroom break, before I'd returned to the futile conversation in the foyer, that Juliet was a nice girl who was in my poetry seminar and that I actually liked her, didn't just want to try to fuck her, but to Price, nothing I said made any sense and he laughed until I drifted away from the bar.

Juliet said she was tired and wanted to go home. Price, who was still clearly eavesdropping on our conversation, gave me a suggestive look. *Take her home,* he was trying to say. Instead I continued to lean against the wood paneling and briefly considered bashing my skull on it until blood dribbled out from my ears like thick cabernet sauvignon. I was so finished with everything and everyone. My life at Dartmouth had played itself out.

Peterson wandered away to find Zoe, the girl he'd lost his virginity to sophomore year, same girl whose house in Nantucket I'd gone to with Blair. He interpolated himself into the crowd, floated toward the girl. She was dancing near the guitar player with a half-empty champagne bottle in her hand. Above her head, over the mantel, our faces smiled down from the 2011 composite: ANDREW B. LOHSE, EMINENT RUSH CHAIRMAN.

I looked at her, I looked at her hand. I remembered that hand passing around tumblers of gin on her porch that summer. I remembered that hand clutching the side of her father's boat. The boat, buffeted by a rising tide, trapped in an inlet. The boat, too big to fit under the bridge. The recurring dream I'd had of Nantucket and my actual memory of Nantucket had become so hopelessly mixed that I couldn't remember which was which. As I studied Zoe from across the party, I concluded that the same thing had gone wrong with my Dartmouth dream. Peterson tapped her on the shoulder, said something to her. Then they danced awkwardly.

TIME WENT BLANK

I didn't make a play at walking Juliet home. She was probably too nice of a girl for me anyway. She left. I wondered if Blair would show up. I thought about drunkenly texting Caroline that I missed her. Decided not to. I took stock of my options. I stepped into the pool room to catch my breath. Instead, I bumped into a brother fondling some girl's ass and making out with her against the pool-cue rack.

Jesus Christ, nowhere for a man to fucking think around here.

Then Edwards texted me saying that he'd be at the house in five minutes. I didn't know he was planning to come up for homecoming. He said he was driving up from Manhattan with some of the '11s. They'd gotten stuck in traffic on I-95.

When he arrived, we posted up in 2 and drank most of a handle of Jim Beam and reminisced about the ΣAE 3, and he asked me how Caroline was doing even though he knew we'd broken up in June—he'd already heard at this party in Napa over the summer—and then we did two boxes of whippits and then wandered to Theta Delt in our suit jackets, and then I vaguely remember us getting kicked out of the frat for peeing somewhere we weren't supposed to pee. I blacked out. Time went blank.

10

YOU MUST TAKE THE PLEDGES TO BREAKFAST

I blacked in playing pong in Varsity with Edwards and some of the whaleshit.

Everything that had hours before seemed formal and proper was now disheveled beyond recognition. Wrinkled ties swayed flaccidly under collars as we volleyed; shirts, wet with champagne stains, would require rehab at the cleaner's; my blazer was dusted with a whole pack's worth of cigarette ash. I'd also somehow acquired a baby-blue DARTMOUTH GOP baseball cap—probably forced some pledge to hand it over to me or face punishment.

It was five A.M.

Again I briefly contemplated texting Caroline or Blair or even my high school ex-girlfriend Jane, wondering if she remembered all the "good times" or whatever, but decided against it. I'd been kind of disturbed since sink night. Nostalgic, I tried to pinpoint the exact moment when things had gone wrong, but couldn't.

Around six I started to feel hungry—something toxic churned in the empty space of my stomach where solid matter should have been. Then the remorse hit. It didn't have to be like this, I knew; I thought to myself, like, of course, Lohse, this is always where you find yourself, in the frat basement at dawn, underground, where you can't even see the gorgeous sunrise that will soon roll over the college and the town and bathe the yellow leaves falling from the trees with the kind of pale rays that landscape painters and amateur photographers spend their whole lives chasing. *What happens in the house stays in the house*—it had become too literal for me to deal with, and my life had happened so intensely in the house that I was beginning to suspect that I wouldn't like to stay in the disgusting basement beneath the busted mansion anymore, that maybe I would've liked to steal Pulaski's car and not stop driving until I got home and woke up my mother and just sobbed and apologized and said, *Well, Mom, I wish it didn't have to be this way.* That's what I was wishing for, my bloodshot eyes trailing the pong ball's bounce across the table to the other side. She'd say, *No, Andrew, it doesn't.* She'd say, *You're still a kid and there's still time.* She'd call me Andrew, not Lohse, because Andrew is my given name. Supposed to be biblical, Christ's first follower. I wouldn't know where to look for the dude anyway.

Then when I was done feeling sorry for myself I'd call up Wallace and depledge Sigma Alpha Epsilon and try to forget all the animalistic bastards who'd made me chug vinegar and vomit until the blood vessels around my eyes burst into little red dots that resembled some sort of rare tropical malady. I'd finally talk about how I'd come forward to the administration, and how, in my opinion, they hadn't done much to address hazing. I'd finally talk about how disturbed I was that I needed two hands to count all of my friends who'd been raped at Dartmouth. I'd purge myself for weeks, take a long trip, give up, maybe apologize to some people, find a way to atone.

It was six A.M. and I wasn't in a good spot.

I knew I should have ended the pong game and found a comfortable tile floor somewhere on which to sleep. In one of my last coherent thoughts, I told myself, Lohse, you epic douche bag, if you were halfway as decent as you think you ought to be, as you once were, you'd be cuddling in your bed right now with some moderately attractive blonde, some studio art major with a sizable trust fund and pearls on her neck the size of anal beads. The kind of girl who'd blush at her pearls' being compared to anal beads, but that's a conversation you'd never have with her, one that would only come up in meetings, and all the brothers would laugh about it and you would take a beer or twelve and vomit until everyone moved on to ripping some other guy. The kind of girl who'd confiscate your beers when your vision blurred because she's nice like that, total sweetheart, sympathetic, and she knew that your grandfather hammered impeccable manners into you, but that the frat tended to, well, downplay those manners.

I steadied myself against the pong table and focused my limited faculties on the gleaming cups of beer on the other side, the blurry, boyish faces of pledges, the fluorescent shadows of grime and spray-painted slang coating

the walls behind their heads: FLETCH HATES WOMEN; FREE
THE ΣAE 3!

My point of no return was quickly bearing down on
me—I knew the feeling with an impossible clarity but had
never actually gotten so close to the edge of life-or-death
alcohol poisoning before. The strange self-reflective vibe
had set in with that thirty-second or thirty-third drink of
the night, the one that began to subject my body to this
weird buzzing from my skull. The feeling isn't like a near-
death experience, not like any of the car crashes I've been
in, specifically, once skidding out on a torrentially wet
Vermont highway at ninety with a tractor trailer bearing
down on me, that summer I loved Blair—it was something different.

But now it seemed that self-destruction would end in
death without breakfast. I imagined that at some indefinite
point in the future—one out of the infinite and increasingly likely possible futures—for a bare instant, my coffin
was selected. Maybe it was even monogrammed, like all
the shirts I'd lost, the first letters of each name I was given.
Each stroke of the pong paddle became the colossus-like
gesture of a pallbearer. A voice from the future had reached
the present early and persuaded my inactive conscious
mind to surrender; there was no use delaying the inevitable, it said. You must take the pledges to breakfast. At least
there'd probably be no vomit in the omelettes.

FITS OF EXISTENTIAL REBELLION. WHATEVER.

The first blur of a damp New England morning glowed through the pines. Bands of thick white light and orange pastel crept over the east side of campus, giving the brick buildings an angelic afterglow. The world's a wildly beautiful place when you're awake to see it, even if you're so drunk you can only perceive fragments of it, still images sliced from the reel of your mind's eye. Stumbling through the dew, I congratulated myself on my self-control, my coming to the brink and pulling back quickly enough to realize that the grim reaper was swimming laps in that last beer.

We set off toward the Green. The fastest route to the diner was through a roped-off area around the bonfire kindling, a well-worn circle where generations of freshmen had run around the flames. It was always a powerful night—it was called Dartmouth Night after all, the freshmen's first dose of hazing, when they realize that there's something off-key about all of the "Welcome home! We love you!" shit. Something off-key about having to run around a giant funeral pyre while upperclassmen scream, *"Worst class ever!"* and push you toward the heat, exhorting you, *"Touch the fire!"* That would all start again in, like, twelve hours. Everyone would do what they were told to do. They all wanted to belong.

I ducked under the rope and instructed the pledges to follow. We sense like hunter-gatherers, charting the most efficient route to food. We didn't deserve to be castigated, but a raspy voice greeted us from around the structure; I had to squint to see its sneer. This woman's authority seemed to proceed not from the Safety and Security badge on her chest but from the tenor of the thousands of packs of Virginia Slims she'd smoked since adolescence. Couldn't she tell that we were practically starving to death, that breakfast is, you know, the most important meal of the day?

Whether the officer said not to walk under the rope I can't remember—according to an official reconstruction of events, I responded to the officer's injunction with the flat "I can walk wherever I want to walk," then picked up a folding chair and flung it with little finesse. That seemed to settle things. It was definitely not a violent act—in the woman's own admission, the chair landed, like, thirty yards from her. Sometimes I just have these, uh, fits of existential rebellion. Whatever. We continued to the diner without interruption. We ordered breakfast. Coffee, eggs, bacon. I made sure the pledges were on their absolute best behavior.

"Keep your fucking voices down, you fools," I hissed at them when they jabbered too loud. "This is a respectable establishment." Opened the year my grandfather gradu-ated, the place was practically a landmark.

EXCEPT, LIKE, NOT REALLY

Everything was going well until the silhouette of a burly cop appeared near the breakfast counter. I noticed an ex-tensive amount of finger-pointing in our direction. Then I watched, stupefied, as the hostess directed the cop toward us. The guy made long strides across the floor tiles as I stared into my whole-wheat toast and willed myself to disappear.

He stopped at our glossy linoleum-topped table. I smiled wanly. He said he was looking for a suspect in a pink oxford shirt, gray blazer, and blue baseball cap. I estimated the seconds it would take to remove these items from my person and wondered if, by some means of prestidigitation, I could complete the task before the officer realized that his question was rhetorical.

Instead I relented. After all, he was only asking for a word outside the restaurant, a word about that hypothetical chair-throwing suspect who was hypothetically wearing my exact same outfit. Disagreeable conversations with law enforcement are usually unpleasant for patrons trying to enjoy breakfast after a long night and morning of binge drinking, and I didn't want to put the pledges out, so I followed the cop outside. Wallace and the other guys were putting the pledges through too much hazing already, if you'd have asked me. But then again you shouldn't have asked me, because I was guilty, too.

We stepped outside. Morning had gone hazy and all the buildings on Main Street seemed to be blurred around the edges. The policeman was flanked by another Safety and Security officer, not the one from the Green. Neither of their faces seemed particularly memorable. I can only picture my own face, the innocently skeptical expression I'd practiced when dealing with law enforcement—which is strange; no one ever really knows how he appears, least of all after twelve hours of binge drinking. But the light caught my eye, that strange purgatory where neither night has ended nor morning has begun, the moment when the streetlamps seem to accidentally switch off early, the feeling of confusion caused by unanticipated lighting.

The cop informed me that I'd thrown a chair at a college official.

I continued my skeptical look while shaking my head respectfully. "You've got it all wrong. I didn't throw the chair *at* an officer. I'd never do that. But, yeah, certainly I can't deny that I *did* throw *a* chair, and if it was damaged in any way, I'd gladly pay to replace it if you'd only—"

There I go again, I thought, talking too much, slurring my words unconvincingly. Whenever I actually needed those manners my grandfather had hammered into me, they were usually caught somewhere south of my larynx.

Then came the inevitable flashlight in my eyes (which was wholly unnecessary and only an act of patronizing intimidation). "How much did you have to drink last night, Mr. Lohse?"

That recurring voice in my head from the future reminded me that I was, in the words of my older bros, *so fucked*. So I said, "Sure, I've had a few drinks, but—"

The Safety officer had no time to suffer though my shenanigans. He asked if I'd go with him to receive medical care for my level of intoxication. Whatever that meant.

"I have a very low tolerance for alcohol," I lied, climbing into his car.

The cop left then, so I figured everything must be cool. Except, like, not really.

...THE FOURTH AMENDMENT?

Next thing I knew I was in an examining room in Dick's House with two nurses and a new Safety and Security officer, and they were all acting as if I had some morbid terminal illness that was, like, contagious.

They wouldn't come near me. They were asking me to blow into a Breathalyzer. Before I blew, I coughed liberally to lay the groundwork for the suggestion that I was asthmatic from a childhood of all-American sports and excessive horseplay in my bucolic suburban backyard.

"Blow again," one of the nurses said condescendingly, while simultaneously maintaining a liberal distance and making sure to keep me in her peripheral vision as she turned to the computer to input my vitals. I faked a deep breath and blew a shallow one into the device and handed it back to her.

She looked at it and shook her head. "Again," she commanded, handing it back to me.

"I'm very asthmatic," I sighed. "All this blowing is really not good for me." I forced a cringe. Of course, no breath I offered was enough to sate these fiends, and they responded skeptically at any mention of the fragile state of my lungs.

"That must be why you smell like a carton of cheap menthol cigarettes," a nurse muttered. "If you continue to be uncooperative, I'm going to have write you up."

Whatever that meant.

I gave the machine another shallow breath and handed it back to the first nurse. Whatever red digital number the machine produced was enough for a round of concerned head-nodding from the assembled health-care profession-als. Our conversation then veered toward curtness.

"I think this BAL is enough to keep him here, don't you, Joanne?" the first nurse asked the second. "Even if he didn't even properly blow into the machine?"

"And I think we're going to have to give him an IV for fluids." Joanne scowled in my general direction. The offi-cer asked me if I'd promise to stay the morning, and po-tentially most of the afternoon, in a bed at Dick's House. I considered her offer judiciously but ultimately decided that, no, I couldn't make that promise.

"It'd be a violation of my constitutional rights," I blath-ered, still tasting the Jim Beam, leaning back on the raised examining bed—what are those called anyway? "As I'm of age, willingly seeking medical care, and if at some indefi-nite point in the future—like, in the next fifteen minutes—I no longer want to receive medical care, it's my right not to be entrapped in this sterile hellhole."

"Excuse me?" the officer managed. Her eyes bulged. She had a face like a baseball mitt. I assured her that my civil liberties argument was scrupulous. She was unimpressed.

". . . The Fourth Amendment?" I clasped my hands stoically in my lap.

"Okay, I've had enough. I've just had enough." The of-ficer waved to the nurses.

One shook her head in disgust. Presumably, she'd seen more disgusting things in her time as a nurse—people shitting themselves, kids with Ebola bleeding out of every orifice, stuff like that. I don't know. She acted as if I were the worst. "We can't take this one in. I'm sorry. We aren't prepared to handle this one."

HANDCUFFS

As I contemplated another constitutional argument about why they had to let me leave—considering possibly trying to leverage the full faith and credit clause, though I was too drunk to remember what that was—a dramatic revelation took place. A different police officer entered from out of hiding in the hallway. He'd been eavesdropping. I realized that the door had been open the whole time. I guess my Fourth Amendment argument had been vindicated—I wouldn't have to resort to my final plea, a desperate invocation of my freedom of assembly to, like, assemble in my bed in Lord instead of in a bed in Dick's House with a needle in me. The cop shook his head and smiled. He said I'd have to come spend some time with him at the lockup.

It was fully morning by the time he'd walked me out of Dick's House. I sat in the back of his cruiser with my feet angled to the curb. The cop handcuffed me and shackled my ankles, then fitted me with a metallic belt connecting all of my new hardware. He smirked the whole fucking time, as if he were lacing up his kid's ice skates or something.

YOU PROMISE YOURSELF YOU'LL NEVER FORGET

Green is the color of money, the color of envy, and the color of all the college shutters in Hanover. It's also the color I saw in a dry fever dream half-asleep in the back of that cop car driving me away from Dartmouth; in my shackles I leaned against the car's motion as it sped around Route 10's curves. I closed my eyes and all I saw were phosphenes, strange shapes sliding behind my eyelids.

And what was that feeling of being driven away from the college under the surprisingly cold sunbeams of a crisp autumn morning—the unlit homecoming bonfire dull and foreboding over the college Green, its wooden structure inscribed with names and organizations and strange oaths that from the disappearing point of the Crown Victoria's back window faded fast into unintelligible lines of crude paint waiting to be incinerated? I can't explain it to you except in the terms of a dream, the kind where you wake up unconvinced of what's real, and for a half second you're afraid, threatened by your own reality, before you accept the dream's end. If it's a good dream, you promise yourself you'll never forget, though despite your best efforts, you'll always forget.

The road bent around a line of pines, and finally the campus was out of sight, bonfire gone far in the distance, the last college building pulled out of view. Homecoming had started. I knew I'd be going home.

YOUR FRIEND THE CHAPLAIN

I was left handcuffed to a bench in the jail for a few hours. I kept trying to lie down and sleep, but a sergeant would, without fail, come by to rouse me and command me to sit upright.

"Pretend you're paying attention to the wall," he'd snicker. "Dartmouth, huh? Bet you paid attention in school. Now pay attention to the wall." Then he'd walk away and hassle someone else.

Eventually my mother appeared to pick me up. That was probably the nadir of the whole experience. It doesn't get worse than that. That was around maybe three in the afternoon, and my hangover had left me feeling like my skull had been fractured. I saw her face through the bars of the jail door; the warden gave me back my belt, which had been confiscated, apparently so that I wouldn't hang myself. They'd even confiscated my GOP hat, then given it back to me in a sealed plastic bag. It was probably considered evidence. But evidence of what?

My mom was crying. Her makeup ran over her face, thick like a melting watercolor, and it creeped me out. She drove without speaking until she cut the silence as we made our way back to campus.

"Do you have anything to say?"

"Yes."

"Well?"

"I'm sorry. I'm really, really sorry." I stared straight ahead. She sobbed. I was totally breaking her heart. It was like someone had died.

"Is there someone we should speak with? What about your friend the chaplain?"

I borrowed her phone. I'd lost mine the night, or morning, before. Typical. I called the desk at Parkhurst, and they connected me to Dean Crocker's office. I explained that I had to meet with him—as soon as possible. He promised to cancel a meeting. I suspected, maybe, that he'd seen this day coming; he had a prophetic glint about him whenever we spoke. I wondered what kind of dreams he'd had, if they'd ever terrified him, if he'd ever pursued an idea so fatalistic he couldn't help but be burned every time he reached for it. He was a chaplain after all, so probably not.

We met in his office, but all I remember was constant sobbing and me trying to explain to him what had happened, and him leaning back in his wing chair and nodding, rubbing the ring on his finger.

"Andrew." He looked me square in the eye. "Andrew. I believe that you are going to have to take a leave from the college."

Clearly.

"We all have different paths in life. Yours may be, in fact, long and challenging."

IT'S VERY, VERY HARD TO SAY

A week later I packed up my room while my mom waited in the car outside. When I was done, I walked upstairs to say good-bye to Peterson. I asked him if he'd talk to me alone in the hallway.

"What's going on, Lohse?" he asked.

I crossed my arms, uncrossed them, tried to lean against the wall, slid my boat shoes over the dirty carpeting. I couldn't find a comfortable way of saying what I wanted to say. I'm not sure why I felt obligated to explain my situation to Peterson; after all, we were barely friends anymore, and it would have been a huge understatement to say that we'd drifted apart since pledge term. More like fault lines had opened up between us, massive gaps in the tectonic plates of our experiences, and I'd stumbled down into the center of the earth that existed beneath and between us.

"I think I'm going to get Parkhursted again. So I'm leaving," I mumbled. I contemplated averting eye contact but instead experienced a sudden jolt of self-assuredness, or maybe defiance. For some reason I knew it was going to be the end, for all intents and purposes, of our fraternal relationship. So I just told the truth that I figured he already knew about me and braced for judgment.

"Peterson, I think I've got a problem with alcohol." Was I being melodramatic? I wondered. Histrionic? Narcissistic? All the words that Goldstein, and other bros like him, had flung at me from time to time. No—I guess I was just being honest.

Surprisingly, Peterson didn't blink. He didn't even say anything vaguely resembling "I told you so." Below his blond side part, above the collar of his perfectly crisp navy polo, his mouth moved, as if what he meant to do was spit out some kind of lozenge and the task of extruding it was delicate.

"You know, Lohse—well," he measured out. "It's very . . . hard. It's hard to know who has a drinking problem here and who doesn't. It's very, very hard to say."

Anyway, I left Dartmouth for good that day. On Halloween.

POSTSCRIPT
LIKE, KIND OF LATE TO ASK THAT QUESTION

I guess I never had one singular "come to Jesus moment." It took me a long time to get myself out of the frat, especially considering that I tried more than once, and especially considering the degrees to which I kept letting myself get pulled deeper and deeper into the substance abuse and hazing and shallowness.

Part of me wants to say that I suddenly changed in one solitary moment, like—"Well, then I saw the reverent face of the Virgin Mother in a pile of cocaine on my ex-girlfriend's vanity mirror, causing me to repent my sinful ways and cometh to the Lord"—but change never happens like that. For me, my growth was a steady beat, a few steps forward, a few steps back, interspersed with traumatic epiphanies. After I finally left school, I went home and put myself back together and then realized, as the weeks ground by, that I'd built up the courage to speak up about what happens at Dartmouth. I didn't want it all to keep happening to nice kids.

I finally wrote that whistle-blowing column about ΣAE's hazing, the column my brother and Harry had pushed me to write more than a year before. It was quick and painless—it felt good because I finally knew that I was doing the right thing. It was a 750-word weight off my conscience. I called it "Telling the Truth," and the last line was "It's a small college, but there are those of us who feel the need to tell the truth about it."

I blitzed Wallace, formally depledging Sigma Alpha Epsilon. Then I leaked an unedited first draft of the column to Joe Asch, a prominent alumnus and Dartmouth watchdog. He published it on his website, Dartblog. The *D* fact-checked the column, I understand, and published an updated version a few days later. They knew it was true; after all, an ΣAE was an editor. The Administrator called me. In hushed, nervous tones he asked if I was ready to go public. Obviously, I said. Like, kind of late to ask that question.

I GUESS THAT WAS THE TRAGIC THING ABOUT IT ALL

Before the column went to print, I thought it would be the right thing to do to call up my three closest bros to explain what I was doing and why. Give them the inside straight before everything blew up, I guess.

First I called Pulaski. "I'm driving to West Leb with my girlfriend," he said. "I'll call you back." He didn't.

Then I called Peterson. He said something like, "Lohse, you do realize what's going to happen to the brothers, what's going to happen to us?"

"I do," I said, even though I wasn't convinced that the college would actually drop the hammer too hard. And they never did; it seemed as if they spent more time questioning my integrity than they did trying to punish people and end hazing, that they were more interested in public relations than people.

"What should I do?" Peterson asked.

"About what?"

"What would your advice be?"

"My advice would be, protect yourself by telling the truth. You were on the fringes of the hazing, you were only a victim, so you have nothing to hide." Then I asked him something like "Are you worried about your parents reading this column?" What I heard through the phone was a long, pregnant pause that then erupted into a worried rant.

"Do I want my parents reading this? The idea horrifies me. I don't want anybody that I know reading this. I understand that I signed up for it and it was my choice not to depledge, but the point is, it's not something that I want to be published—despite the fact that I've had very little involvement. The institutions that you are a part of and the people you have around you do have a bearing on you. A perception of you anyway."

I guess that was the tragic thing about it all.

I never heard from him again. When the college ran their "investigation"—which was so incompetent as to make one wonder whether it was purposely self-defeating—he lied about everything, just like everyone else. In the end he was no different from anyone who had actually done something wrong. He said none of the hazing ever happened, even though he knew it did. Like a lot of guys, Peterson had changed.

My final phone call was to Ripley. All day he'd been sending me furious and confused text messages, the kind of texts I'd get from him when he knew I had coke, when he'd try to guilt-trip me into giving him some, tell me I owed him money for some pizza from weeks ago, tell me he'd helped get me a bid so I should give him a line as a tax or tribute or something, but who knows. I finally called him and explained that, gradually, over more than a year of turmoil and internal debate, I'd decided to speak up about the fucked-up experience we'd both had—some of which he'd done to me, even though he still ended up one of my best friends.

"Are you serious?" he asked, voice dry. The way he said it . . . it was almost as if he couldn't tell, as if he couldn't tell anymore what was serious and what wasn't.

"Ripley, do you really think things like—like, the vomelette—were good things to do? That they . . . um . . . built brotherhood?"

He lost his shit. In a bare display of anger, he screamed through the phone, *"I ate the vomelette as a pledge! I made your pledges eat the vomelette! It was a tradition!"*

There was nothing else for me to say. That was where I rested my case, where I buried my doubts about speaking up, and finally, permanently, turned myself away from the psychotic, destructive, nonsensical sickness of my fraternity experience. That was the moment where I become utterly convinced that I was doing the right thing by exposing it for what it was.

The column went viral, then *Rolling Stone* wrote their story about the college's hazing culture. They called it "Confessions of an Ivy League Frat Boy: Inside Dartmouth's Hazing Abuses." I went on TV and radio and stuff like that. I made some confessions. I bore witness to bad shit that my friends and I had let happen to ourselves, had done to each other, had done to kids we barely knew, in the name of some strange tradition that had seeped through us like a demonic possession.

Maybe sometimes I wish that none of it had ever happened. To anyone. I guess, though, that I'm not sorry, since my experience helped make me who I am—a better, more honest person. Maybe it was always supposed to be this way. Who am I to say? It just shouldn't have to be like this anymore, for anyone else. And that's why I'm telling you about it.

ACKNOWLEDGMENTS

Thank you to Nicole Sohl, my editor; Steve Ross, my agent; David Doerrer, Janet Reitman, Richard Crocker, Liz Canner, Alex Barnett, Joe and Elizabeth Asch, Ray Peachey, Cheryl Oram, Michael Bronski, Susy Struble, Bill Sjogren, Ernie Hebert, Zack Finch, Pulaski, Blair, Dennis Wygmans, Bill Haduch, the Bolinders, Aimee Le, Jordan Osserman, Michele Hernandez, Ellis Levine, Wei Wen Sng, and, especially, my family.

DATE DUE			